In the Footsteps of Gandhi

In the Footsteps of Gandhi

Conversations with
Spiritual Social Activists

Catherine Ingram

Parallax Press
Berkeley, California
An Institute of Noetic Sciences Book

Parallax Press
P.O. Box 7355
Berkeley, California 94707

Printed in the United States of America

Library of Congress Cataloging-in-Publication Data

Ingram, Catherine. 1952-
    In the footsteps of Gandhi: conversations with spiritual
social activists / by Catherine Ingram.
        p.   cm.
    "An Institute of Noetic Sciences book."
    Includes bibliographical references
    ISBN 0-938077-24-4
    1. Social reformers—Interviews. 2. Social Action. 3.
Church and social problems. 4. Nonviolence.   I. Title.
HN18.I54 1990
303.6—dc20   89-22855
                                        CIP

Contents

Acknowledgments

This project attracted help from both obvious and unexpected sources too numerous to name. The book exists in large part due to the efforts and kindness of friends, family, co-workers, assistants to the people in the book, and to the generosity of the twelve people who were interviewed. I am, in addition, deeply grateful to my publisher, Arnold Kotler, who encouraged me in this undertaking long after I'd given up on the idea, with whom it has been fantastic to work, and who has been my greatest support throughout the project. I also thank the Institute of Noetic Sciences, especially Tom Hurley, Dio Neff, and Winston Franklin, for sponsorship and editorial suggestions.

I thank Rick Fields and Ken Wilber for encouragement and tutorials in writing and editing all those years ago in Cambridge (and Ken for ongoing emotional, spiritual, and editorial advice); Wes Nisker for always being there and making me laugh (whew! it would have been *really* bleak); Charlene Spretnak for reminding me to keep the vision; Jerry Mander for suggesting a version of the title we used; Jack Kornfield, Idea Man, for years of brainstorming; Janice Girardi, Rebecca Nowakowski, Sharon Salzberg, Peggy Gillespie, Catherine Dean, Tara Goleman, Jill Carlino, Mary Chase, and Nina Wise, priestesses all, for sister love throughout (and Sharon, especially, for editorial brilliance); Richard Cohen, Bob Chartoff, Ron Stark, Ray Lipovsky, Joseph Goldstein, Joel Edelman, and Mitch Davidowitz for friendship, support, and kindness; Steve Klein at the King Center for Social Change for consultation on the civil rights movement; Michael van Walt and Michael Sautman for consultation on Tibet; Jack and Laurie Lawler and the

Chicago Zen Center for serving as hosts in Chicago; David Phillips of the Congressional Human Rights Foundation for heroic efforts on the Desmond Tutu interview and for hospitality in Washington, D.C.; Tenzin Geyche, Rinchen Kandala, and Tendzin Choegyal for hospitality in Dharamsala; Harish Budhraja, for many years of doing the impossible in travel arrangements within India; Ramchandra Gandhi, grandson of Mahatma Gandhi, for interest and encouragement in the project; Mushim Ikeda, Shoshana Tembeck, and Mark Burstein for editorial skills; Wende Elliot and Maureen Crist for research; Gay Reineck for cover design; Barbara Pope for design suggestions; Lisa McHugh for cover consultation; Alan Clements for twenty-three years of unbroken best-friendship; and Andrew Cohen for transformative dialogues on freedom.

It would be impossible to fully express my gratitude to my family for always tapping their feet and clapping their hands in the background to my decidedly different beat. I especially thank my father, Robert, who has been there whenever I needed anything, and who has continually believed in me.

Foreword

by Ramchandra Gandhi

I have no doubt that Mahatma Gandhi would have approved of the continuing work of the remarkable range of contemporary people interviewed by Catherine Ingram in this book. They, along with Catherine, give us ground for hope in the transformative power of spiritual illumination, and in the illuminating power of right action. Civil disobedience and spiritual endeavor are made for one another in the battleground of contemporary reality. However, ceaseless efforts on the part of vast numbers of people all over the world will be needed for the establishment of spiritual activism as an enduring ingredient of civilization.

The spirit of Gandhi summons us to *satyagraha*, truth's insistent call, in the service of the Earth *now*. For if the degradation of the resources of life and civilization continues at its present rate, a harried human species might throw in the towel in the near future. This book makes one believe that this need not happen.

October 1989
New Delhi, India

Introduction

The genesis of this book can be traced to one vivid night in India over seven years ago. I was on my way to Bodh Gaya, the village where it is believed Gautama Buddha attained enlightenment. Traveling by rail with friends Jack and Liana Kornfield, we had arrived in Gaya, the closest train stop to Bodh Gaya, located in one of the poorest states in India. Gaya is a medium-sized industrial city with no reason for any visits from tourists except those passing through on their way to Bodh Gaya. We emerged from the train in the middle of the night, exhausted from a long journey.

Thick, choking smoke from cooking fires filled the station and mixed with the smell of open sewage. Begging hands stretched out of the haze toward us, some of them missing fingers due to leprosy. Small, dirty children, many of them carrying naked babies in the midnight cold, pulled at our clothes. *"Baksheesh, memsahib,"* they pleaded. Give to me, white lady. It was a typical train station scene in India, but although I had spent over six months there on previous trips, I began to feel claustrophobic from the horror of it. I'm just tired, I told myself. This will all seem different once we're on our way to Bodh Gaya.

I was wrong. We pushed our way through the crowd and outside to the rickshaw stand, prepared to be assailed by several dozen drivers competing for our fare. However, when they heard our destination was Bodh Gaya, the rickshaw drivers refused to take us, despite our offers of great sums of money for the forty-five minute ride. Shaking their heads "no," they repeated one mysterious word: *"Dacoits."* We did not know at the time that in the six years since we had last been there, the road from Gaya to Bodh Gaya had become a dangerous night haunt of robbers and murderers, or *dacoits*, as they are known in India.

Suddenly out of the crowd an old man came forward and accepted our now ridiculously inflated offer. We piled aboard his dilapidated wooden rickshaw with our luggage, anxious to be on our way, not noticing that the horse which was to pull us this long distance was extremely sick. The old man took out a whip and clipped the horse several times. Slowly the horse took a few steps. Jack, Liana, and I exchanged apprehensive looks. This was going to be a long ride.

Every few steps required another lashing. As if in a dream, we watched as the beating went on. The horse grew more listless, the lashing more severe. We begged the driver to stop hitting him so much, but he waved his hand in dismissal as if to say there was no choice. By the time we were halfway there, watching the beating had become unbearable, and there was no point in turning back. We all fell into a stunned silence, each of us retracing the decisions that had led us into this situation where we were so directly the cause of a creature's agony, and one of us giving words to the unfortunate truth: "We should have stayed in Gaya overnight."

I suddenly had a flood of images. With each lash of the whip I saw pictures of suffering, faces of people in India, desperate with hunger and disease, animals even more so. Next came a kaleidoscopic montage, visions of worldwide suffering—torture, fear, loneliness, the degradation of the planet and what it portends for the future. On and on it went. I realized that my feelings of compassion had always occurred at a safe distance from the actual suffering. Now my heart was being ripped apart, and I was dead center in the pain. A rising panic set in as the very belief system by which I had lived began to dissolve.

I had been reading Eastern philosophies since I was in my teens and I had practiced Buddhist meditation since 1974. I therefore felt steeped in the belief in karma, confident that there was a lawful order to life, that cause-and-effect was a logical explanation for why some suffer more than others. This belief had always served me, particularly in India. How could it be that so few of us could have such incredible abundance while so many had so little? And elsewhere, why were innocent people, sometimes children, tortured? Why were babies born with terrible diseases? Why did tragedies occur seemingly at random? Why did some people have a genetic propensity for depression? The law of karma explained everything. But now, the conceptual framework which had made life logical and lawful was no longer accessible to me. The meditation practice I had done had only served to make me more sensitive, had removed the psychic callouses one needs to endure it all.

The horrible ride ended, but the crack in my consciousness remained. I had entered some new level of awareness, and I couldn't seem to get back to my old way of seeing, a view which was tolerable and made sense. A veil had lifted and blown away.

As it happened, the Dalai Lama was giving teachings in Bodh Gaya the following day at the spot where the Buddha is thought to have been enlightened. Although I had met him before, I now looked at the Dalai Lama in complete wonder. Here was an extremely intelligent man who was privy to extraordinary suffering, and who, as the leader of an entire nation of people enduring persecutions of the worst sort, worked constantly for their well-being. Yet there he sat, relaxed, alert, and happy, even jovial. How was this possible?

I decided to find out. I knew of "liberation theology" priests and nuns in Central and South America who worked nonviolently against human rights abuses; of Cambodians in Rhode Island working for a peaceful solution for Cambodia, led by a senior monk who happened to be out of the country when Pol Pot's genocide began; of "tree huggers" in India, the Chipco Movement, dedicating their lives to preserving what is left of Himalayan forests, often at great risk to themselves. Not only the Dalai Lama, but perhaps hundreds or thousands of people nonviolently opposed injustice, oppression, and ecological destruction, and yet maintained inner happiness.

Over the next years I sought out and interviewed spiritual teachers, activists, and practitioners who embodied both a state of wakefulness and a commitment to relieving suffering in the world. Thus began a career in journalism with spirituality and social activism as its focus.

The interviews and meetings, combined with my own growing awareness, have led me to see that averting our eyes from suffering will never lead to happiness. It is only through a courageous "sustaining the gaze," as Joanna Macy puts it, that we peer through to the other side, that we blend with others in a recognition of our interdependence. And this blending serves to give us a sense of belonging, which is a root cause for happiness. As writer Rick Fields said in a two-line poem:

> My heart is broken
> Open.

What I have discovered from the people I have spoken with is that doing for others heals the wounded heart and deepens joy amidst the pain. It has also become clear that the issues of spirituality and compassionate action are not separable. Wisdom cannot exist independently of compassion, and compassion requires extending oneself to others.

Throughout the years of my work, the name of Mohandas K. Gandhi has come up again and again. Gandhi blazed a trail of victory for truth, his lifework marking, for the first time in modern history, a nonviolent revolution as large as India's independence movement. This one man's clarity in motivation and vision has been a beacon to many who have followed, regardless of whether or not their efforts were "successful."

The power of truth and nonviolence is compelling. We are now witnessing rapid and remarkable changes on the world stage—superpowers, once enemies, now cooperating in peaceful solutions and weapons reductions;

conflicts in the Middle East and Africa being resolved; a growing world effort to save the rain forests; the opening of the Berlin Wall. Even the unsuccessful attempt for democracy in May 1989 of the Beijing students, who had secretly educated themselves in Gandhian strategy, and the Dalai Lama being awarded the 1989 Nobel Peace Prize have thrown a global spotlight on China's disregard for human rights and truth for the first time in several decades.

Despite these great changes, as we all know, we are living in perilous times. Our ignorance and greed, probably no worse than at any other time in history, has now been unfortunately combined with our technological capacity to destroy not only ourselves but the environmental support system for most of life on the planet. What will change our course? We need to wake up, and quickly. We can no longer afford decades of indulging in our affluence and development at the expense of the poor and of the Earth. We need a deepening of our hearts and spirits, an understanding of ourselves which will allow for greater love, generosity, and wisdom. We also need a global perspective which takes into account how our lives affect others. It is a tall order, but it is possible.

The dozen men and women in this book are a few of my personal heroes and heroines who embody the ideals which I feel are most needed in our world. Their words are a reminder that our steps here and now will condition what is to come. They also tell us that our hearts already know what is true, and that troubled times such as these are a call for us to listen deeply to that "still small voice" within, and to act on it. In the words of Martin Luther King, Jr., "I know somehow that only when it is dark enough, can you see the stars."

C.I.
San Francisco
November 1989

In the Footsteps of Gandhi

His Holiness the Dalai Lama

The interview was over. His Holiness the Dalai Lama sent his secretary, Tenzin Geyche, to get a Tibetan silver coin to present to me as a gift. As we waited alone in the receiving room of his private residence, His Holiness stood, slightly hunched over with hands clasped behind him. I stood near an open window which was framed outside by a bougainvillaea in full bloom, blazing pink in the late afternoon sun. Suddenly His Holiness said to me, "I think this lifetime as Dalai Lama is the most difficult of all the Dalai Lamas." As I let the power of that statement wash over me, feeling the poignancy of it, just as suddenly he looked at me there in front of the radiant window and burst out laughing, saying, "Life is so colorful."

* * *

Tibet occupies a vast plateau at one of Earth's highest altitudes, a country at "the roof of the world," ringed by the majestic peaks of the Himalayas. An exotic mountain kingdom for more than 2,000 years, it was known as "the land of snows." Wild yak, antelope, snow leopards, bears, and wild horses roamed this hidden plain. Aggressive, nomadic warriors, who practiced an animistic cult religion called Bon, ruled the land for thousands of years. At one time, the kingdom of Tibet, as one of the most powerful empires in Asia, ruled Nepal, Bhutan, Upper Burma, Turkestan, Tibet proper, and parts of Western China.

Under the auspices of the great Tibetan ruler, Songtsan Gampo in the sixth century, Buddhism became the religion of Tibetan royalty and even inched its way into nearby Mongolia. However, it was not until the great Indian master Padmasambhava came to Tibet a century later that Buddhism began to take hold among the Tibetan people.

The unbroken line of Dalai Lamas, heads of state and religious leaders of Tibet, began with the life of Gedun Truppa (1391-1475), although the title of Dalai Lama was not used until the third in succession.[1] The Dalai Lamas, each believed to be the reincarnation of his predecessor beginning with the second, have, over the centuries, guided the Tibetan people in Buddhist and state affairs.

In 1935, two years after the death of the thirteenth Dalai Lama, Tenzin Gyatso was born in a small farming village called Takster in a remote region of Tibet's Amdo Province.[2] When he was two years old, a delegation of lamas from the faraway capital of Lhasa visited his home, having been guided there by divine oracles and prophetic visions. Through a series of tests, the lamas determined that the young boy was the incarnation of the fourteenth Dalai Lama of Tibet, spiritual and temporal leader of the Tibetan people, and believed to be the embodiment of *Chenresi,* Bodhisattva[3] of Compassion.

At the age of four, Tenzin Gyatso was taken to Lhasa and installed on the Lion Throne in the Potala Palace, winter home to the last eight of the Dalai Lamas. He grew up in the cavernous Potala, and due to his rigorous studies in metaphysics and the philosophy of religion, he rarely left its chambers; fortunately there were a thousand of them. The Potala is "a city in itself," occupying the entire top of a large hill, almost a quarter mile in length.

---

[1] Dalai Lama is a Mongolian title meaning "ocean of wisdom," which was given to the third Dalai Lama in the sixteenth century by the Mongolian prince, Altan Khan.

[2] The Tibetan people celebrate the Dalai Lama's birthday on July 6, although this may not be the exact date of his birth.

[3] *Bodhisattva,* Sanskrit, literally "enlightenment being." A bodhisattva is a being who seeks enlightenment through the perfection of virtues, but who renounces complete liberation until all beings are free as well.

In summers, the Dalai Lama and several of his family members and escorts traveled to the Norbulingka Palace—a compound of temples built in a large walled garden—outside of Lhasa. The Norbulingka was the site of many happy memories for the young Dalai Lama.

Despite the demands of his training and the expectation placed upon him by an adoring 6 million Tibetan followers, the Dalai Lama grew up contentedly and felt that the Tibetan people were happy. He has since written, "In simplicity and poverty among our mountains, perhaps there was more peace of mind than there is in most of the cities of the world."

The young Dalai Lama was intensely interested in anything mechanical. He often took apart objects—his watch, an old movie projector—in order to study their workings and then put them back together. In the Norbulingka Palace, he delighted in tinkering with the palace generator which often broke down. More often than not, he was able to fix it. Years later the Norbulingka would be the site of the most difficult problem the Dalai Lama had known, one which would test all of his abilities to "fix" it.

In 1949, the Chinese army invaded Tibet from eight directions in order to "liberate" the country. Tibet had remained in deliberate political isolation with a kind of live-and-let-live policy that intentionally discouraged foreigners from settling there. As a result, the Tibetans had no friends abroad who would help them in their moment of need, and they were forced to watch as the fabric of their religion, their culture, and their freedom unraveled under Chinese occupation.

Once the invasion started, advisors to the Dalai Lama persuaded him to take over responsibility for the government when he was just sixteen, two years earlier than was customary. Throughout the early years of Chinese rule, the Dalai Lama attempted to maintain a moderate course of compliance in order to hold onto the few remaining vestiges of the Tibetan way of life. His experiences with statesmanship began in earnest when at age nineteen he visited China and met several times with Mao Tse Tung. He also traveled to India where he sought the advice of Pandit Nehru and other followers of Gandhi.

It was on this trip to India that the Dalai Lama first visited Rajghat, the site of Mahatma Gandhi's cremation. He stood on those grounds and wondered "what wise counsel the Mahatma would have given me." At that moment he felt that Gandhi's advice would be to follow the path of peace. The Dalai Lama determined at that time that he could never associate himself with acts of violence. He was twenty-one years old when he made this resolution, and he has never wavered from it.

Meanwhile, life in Tibet continued to disintegrate for the Tibetans. For the first time in their history, there were food shortages. In addition, they suffered religious persecution, forced labor (including children and the elderly), political imprisonment, torture, and, it is believed, forced sterilizations. Thousands of Tibetans were killed.[4] The Tibetan government became barely more than a symbol, with virtually no ability to exercise authority or protect the Tibetan people.

In these circumstances, the Dalai Lama, while staying in the Norbulingka Palace in March 1959, received a request to attend a theatrical performance at the Chinese military compound. The mysterious invitation immediately aroused suspicion. In four different places in the eastern provinces, high lamas had been invited by the Chinese to similar events and had disappeared, never to be seen again. The Chinese had also stated that the Dalai Lama's usual escort of twenty-five troops would not be allowed to accompany him past a certain point.

Despite these ominous signs, the Dalai Lama planned to attend the Chinese performance fearing that if he

---

[4] As of 1989, the Chinese occupation has taken the lives of 1.2 million Tibetans, approximately one sixth of the population.

were to refuse, reprisals would be taken against the Tibetan people, as had been the pattern when the Chinese felt he was not cooperating with them. On the day of the performance, he arose before dawn after a sleepless night filled with anxiety. Suddenly he heard shots, and, sending his advisors to investigate, discovered that approximately 30,000 Tibetans had surrounded the palace to protect him and to prevent him from attending the Chinese performance.

Over the next week tensions mounted as the Chinese brought fresh troops and heavy artillery into the area. At the same time, through a series of letters and meetings with the Chinese, Tibetan officials began to believe what the Tibetan people had suspected all along, that the Dalai Lama would be taken from them and the Palace destroyed. They realized they would have to get their "Precious Protector" out of the country to safety. The Dalai Lama, whose concern was not for his person but for his people, realized that his survival was what would keep the Tibetans' hopes alive. He later explained, "They were convinced that if my body perished at the hands of the Chinese, the life of Tibet would also come to an end."

Chinese artillery shells blasted into the Norbulingka. In the belief that there was no more which could be done within Tibet, the spiritual and temporal leader of the Tibetan people decided to leave his country. Under cover of darkness, disguised as a soldier, the Dalai Lama walked unrecognized past the thousands of devotees guarding the palace for his safekeeping.

Several weeks later, the Dalai Lama and his retinue, including his mother and sister, entered India. Although he was suffering from dysentery and exhaustion from the treacherous mountain journey, the Dalai Lama was warmed by the welcome which awaited him. Nearly 100 foreign journalists and hundreds of well-wishers celebrated his arrival, and Prime Minister Nehru sent a telegram offering hospitality. India has been his home ever since.

The Indian government provided an area for their new guests in the state of Himachal Pradesh in the Himalayan foothills. Dharamsala and Upper Dharamsala, known as Macleod Ganj, were once an outpost of the British, but had since become a ghost town. The revitalization of this beautiful hill station became the project of the Tibetan refugee community over the next years. About 100,000 Tibetans have since left their country for life in exile. They have walked over the snowy plateau at the top of the world, risking death from freezing or starvation, risking capture and torture by the Chinese. Many of them have settled in the Dharamsala area to be near His Holiness.

Sometimes called Little Lhasa, the area bustles with Tibetan activities. There is a Tibetan Children's Village, founded in 1960 to house and school orphans, a Dance and Drama Society, a Library, and the Tibetan Medical and Astrological Centers. The Tibetan government in exile, the Kashag, is located here. There is also the compound known as Thekchen Choling or "Place of Mahayana," which houses the Namgyal Temple, the School of Buddhist Dialectics, and the private residence of His Holiness the Dalai Lama.

Because of his outgoing nature, the Dalai Lama has enjoyed a life of friendships with foreigners that was not possible for his predecessors, and for this he is grateful. He feels that Tibet in the past was too isolated, and that this isolation played a role in the takeover by the Chinese. Now, he is charged with the task of preserving a country of refugees in exile and keeping hope alive within Tibet itself, a responsibility which requires appealing to the world community.

On September 21, 1987, the Dalai Lama presented a Five Point Peace Plan for Tibet during an address to members of the U.S. Congress. Several months later he elaborated on the plan in an address to members of the European Parliament in Strasbourg, France. The Five Point Peace Plan is perhaps one of the most elegant political documents ever written, calling for the establishment of Tibet as a sanctuary of peace in the troubled Himalayan region, insuring human and democratic rights for the Tibetan people, and protecting the whole of the Tibetan plateau as an ecological preserve. While the plan has been praised in the West, the Chinese have refused to discuss it. Beijing leaders did offer to hold talks with the Dalai Lama or his representatives at a time and place of his choosing, but when he suggested a January 1989 meeting in Geneva, they declined. As of this writing, the talks have not occurred.

I traveled to India in November 1988 to speak with His Holiness. After an all night train ride from New Delhi, I disembarked in the town of Pathankot in the Punjab, a state now riddled with terrorism. From there, I took a four-hour taxi ride to Macleod Ganj during which the driver told me frightening tales of kidnappings and disappearances. Although the state in which Dharamsala is located is relatively free from political strife, one must travel through the dangerous Punjab to get there. In fact, when it was time to leave the area, I was diverted from returning by train because the Pathankot rail station had been bombed the night before. I felt the insecurity that the Tibetans must experience even in India. Not only do they bear the burden of living near danger in a country which is not their own, but they are always mindful of the ongoing atrocities and daily hardships endured by those left behind in Tibet.

Despite these difficulties, the Tibetans are an unusually happy people. And the Dalai Lama himself is extraordinarily cheerful. Immediately upon awakening at 4:00 A.M. each day, he prays that everything he is about to do in speech, thoughts, and deeds will be of positive benefit to others. He lives simply and wears a maroon robe that has patches, explaining, "If it was of good material and in one piece, you could sell it and gain something; this way you can't." At daybreak, he spends time in the garden near his residence, where he enjoys dawn and the sounds of the birds. He then has breakfast while listening to the news on the BBC World Service. The rest of his day is typically spent in meditation, religious studies, discussions with his Cabinet in exile and other government officials, and receiving visitors. He retires by 9:00 P.M., but on nights with a moon he stays up a little later and reflects that the moon is also shining on his people in Tibet. "There is not one waking hour when I don't think of the plight of my people," he says.

I arrived early for my appointment with the Dalai Lama because I knew that I would have to go through a security check, a gentle frisking by Indian women behind a closed curtain. I was glad that these precautions are routine and that the Indian sentries I had noticed posted both outside and inside the compound seemed alert. Although many thousands of people pray daily for the Dalai Lama's long life, it is reassuring to know that the Indian government is doing its part to insure that actuality.

As I waited for my appointment, several people who had short time periods with His Holiness came and went from the receiving area. Watching them reminded me of the last time I had interviewed the Dalai Lama, six years previously in Bodh Gaya, India. Then, too, I witnessed the most remarkable transformations. Ordinary people—in this case, a group of European students followed by a Canadian professor—would enter the room and exit minutes later as though they had ingested a love potion. Faces glowing, laughing, and warmly waving to the lone visitor who waited her turn, they were almost unrecognizable from their formerly reserved and serious selves.

It was my turn next. At the doorway stood His Holiness, beaming at me, shaking my hand, and leading me to my seat next to his as though I were a long lost friend. Indeed, the Tibetans believe that we have been everything to each other—mother, father, sister, brother, wife, husband—countless times through beginningless life-times.

Throughout the one and a half hour interview His Holiness continued this sense of camaraderie, adjusting the microphone if I neglected to direct it to the translator,[5] breaking into deep laughter, which became utterly contagious for me, and earnestly considering my questions as though being interviewed was a novel experience for him.

The Dalai Lama has said, "Without inner peace, it is not possible to have world peace." Tenzin Gyatso, the fourteenth Dalai Lama, is a man of peace caught in a turmoil of struggle for his country. In addition, he is contemporary, informed, and playful. He often says, "My true religion is kindness." Those who meet him know that he lives those words.

It is nearly a year since my conversation with His Holiness in Dharamsala. I have just returned from a conference in southern California at which the Dalai Lama was in dialogue with Western psychologists and spiritual leaders. On the morning of my departure from the conference, October 5, 1989, we learned that the Norwegian Ambassador had just read a proclamation to the Dalai Lama informing him that he had won the 1989 Nobel Peace Prize.

Interview with the Dalai Lama
November 2, 1988 • Dharamsala, India

Catherine Ingram: Your Holiness, there are many people in the West who want to combine their spiritual practice with social and political responsibility. Do you feel that these two aspects are connected?

---

[5] Although the Dalai Lama spoke mostly in English throughout the interview, he periodically used the translator to clarify statements.

Dalai Lama: I feel that the essence of spiritual practice is your attitude toward others. When you have a pure, sincere motivation, then you have right attitude toward others based on kindness, compassion, love, and respect. Practice brings the clear realization of the oneness of all human beings and the importance of others benefiting by your actions.

CI: The Tibetan people here in India are refugees. They have lost so much, yet looking at them and talking with them, I sense a basic contentment and lack of bitterness. What accounts for this?

DL: I believe one factor is that it's a Tibetan tradition to realize the importance of human life. You see, Tibetan people usually regard life, any life, as something very sacred, something holy, something important. So therefore, even if a small insect is killed, we immediately react with some feeling of compassion. I can say that Tibetan people are usually good-hearted among the community. Of course, there are those who are fighting, even killing. But generally, there is harmony. It is mainly due to the teachings of Mahayana Buddhism; there is very much emphasis on kindness, tolerance, and love.[6]

CI: When you first visited Rajghat, the site of Gandhi's memorial in India, you spoke of feeling a commitment to nonviolence. But I've also read a story you tell of a bodhisattva on a boat who became aware that a man on the boat was planning a mutiny which the bodhisattva knew would cause the death of hundreds of people. In compassion for those people, the bodhisattva killed the

---

[6] *Mahayana*, Sanskrit, literally "Great Vehicle." One of the two major schools of Buddhism, it originated in the first century A.D. and emphasizes the bodhisattva vow to liberate all beings from suffering. See note 3 on page 4.

man who would have caused the death of hundreds, and thereby took on himself the karma of killing.

DL: Of course, yes.

CI: Do you think there are times when violence is the appropriate action?

DL: My commitment with the Tibetan problem is to nonviolence. In our case, it is almost certain that violence would not be helpful. I think it's out of the question. In that story, that man had developed *bodhicitta*, altruism. He had developed fully as a true bodhisattva. For a person such as that, the altruistic motivation is very, very genuine. With that motivation it is possible to follow some kind of seemingly violent method with confidence, in order to help others. In my case, I am not fully developed in that kind of altruism. Of course, I try. And as time goes by, it is increasing. Still I cannot say I am a bodhisattva. Maybe I am a candidate for being a bodhisattva. But, you see, I don't have that certainty or confidence, so it is very risky. The more reliable, the safer thing is complete nonviolence.

CI: So unless someone is a fully developed bodhisattva, then complete nonviolence is the better way.

DL: Of course. No doubt. And that story of the bodhisattva is talking about one person's action. But when communities are fighting, it involves many people. One or two persons may have genuine bodhisattva altruism, but at the same time there are many people who do not have that kind of altruism. Then there's every danger to be motivated by anger. Very dangerous. Very risky.

CI: Besides the principles of nonviolence, are there other aspects of Gandhi's work that have influenced you?

DL: One thing, of course, is his simplicity, his way of life. Also, I think, the level of modern education he achieved. At the same time he remained a true Indian. As a citizen of a modern nation it was necessary for him to have Western education, but he personally remained a typical Indian within the tradition. And that's good.

CI: He maintained his own cultural identity.

DL: Yes. You see, after all he was Indian. Nobody can change that. If an Indian requires Western education in order to develop India, or his own future, I think that is a genuine way. But, for example, when a Westerner is utilizing Tibetan Buddhism, sometimes it appears as if the person himself or herself becomes "Tibetanized." Similarly, sometimes when a Tibetan or an Indian has had a Western education, the person himself becomes half-Western. Education and techniques are tools. But if you are an Indian, no course of study can change that. A person who, by gaining a Western education or by studying Tibetan Buddhism, becomes half-Westernized or half-Tibetanized, in a way, loses half of his own identity. But, on the other hand, if he can develop all these different skills—he receives a Western education and he learns other technical skills—yet he maintains his own identity as an Indian or a Westerner, that is as it should be. Gandhi was a good example of this. But I don't know why he always had a goat with him! [laughing]

About nonviolence. Many ancient Indian masters have preached *ahimsa*, nonviolence, as a philosophy.[7] That was a more spiritual understanding of it. But, Mahatma Gandhi, in this twentieth century, produced a very sophisticated approach because he implemented

---

[7] *Ahimsa*, Sanskrit, "nonharming." In Patanjali's 2,000-year-old *Yoga Sutra*, *ahimsa* is one of the five practices which constitute the "great vow" of the moral disciplines.

that very noble philosophy of *ahimsa* in modern politics, and he succeeded. That is a very great thing.

CI: It has represented an evolutionary leap in political consciousness, his "experiments with truth."

DL: In human society, in the human community, I think the value of truth is very important. In the early and middle part of this century, I think many people may have been confused or may have lost respect for truth, because if you have power and money, then truth is sometimes seen as not of much value. I think now we can see that way of thinking is changing. Even the most powerful nations who have everything are seeing that there is no point in neglecting basic human values, basic human faith.

Many places have been totally changed through the use of police force and the power of guns—the Soviet Union, China, Burma, many communist countries, countries in Africa and South America. But eventually, you see, the power of guns and the power of the will of ordinary human beings will change places. I am always telling people that this twentieth century, our century, is very important historically for the planet. There is a big competition between world peace and world war, between the force of mind and the force of materialism, between democracy and totalitarianism. And now within this century, the force of peace is gaining the upper hand. Still, of course, the material force is very strong, but there is a kind of dissatisfaction about materialism and a realization or feeling that something is missing.

CI: Especially for people who have experienced a lot of material wealth, such as people in the West.

DL: That's right. As we are ending this century and entering the twenty-first century, I think the basic concerns are human values and the value of truth. I think these things have more value, more weight now.

This is true in the case of Tibet also. Now it's forty years [since the Chinese invasion] and we are beginning a new decade. The next twenty years will be another period. Now in this fourth decade, again it's human will—the truth—which is all we have in dealing with China. Despite their brainwashing, despite their using every atrocity and propaganda, and despite all of the resources they have utilized, still the truth remains the truth. Our side has no money, no propaganda, nothing except weak, feeble voices. Yet now most people have lost faith in the strong voices of the Chinese. Their strong voices have lost credibility. Our weak voices have more credibility.

CI: Martin Luther King, Jr. said "No lie can live forever."

DL: Yes. So you see, the history of this century is confirming the nonviolence that Mahatma Gandhi and Martin Luther King, Jr. spoke of. Even when it is against a superpower who has all these awful weapons, the reality of the situation can compel the hostile nation to come to terms with nonviolence.

CI: It's a slower process sometimes, but a very effective one.

I was happy to see that your Five Point Peace Plan has a forceful ecological component to it.[8] Even if we manage not to blow ourselves up with nuclear weapons, or if big countries don't just obliterate smaller countries into extinction, there is an ongoing ecological destruction happening on the planet. I am referring to problems such as the greenhouse effect, the global warming due to

---

8 Point Four of the Dalai Lama's Five Point Peace Plan reads, "Restoration and protection of Tibet's natural environment and the abandonment of China's use of Tibet for the production of nuclear weapons and the dumping of nuclear waste."

entrapped pollution in the atmosphere; our air and water supplies being polluted at a staggering rate; and the huge holes in the ozone layer letting in dangerous levels of radiation, which not only threaten us with increased cancers, but in a short time could kill all the plankton in the seas and thereby destroy all life in the oceans. Do you foresee the planet surviving this ecological crisis? Do you think we'll make it?

DL: That's difficult to say. I don't know. You see, it is very clear the planet is our own house, and without this we can't survive. That's quite certain. Ultimately, we are the children of the mother Earth, so ultimately we are at the mercy of the mother planet concerning environment and ecology. This is not something sacred or moral. It is a question of our own survival. I think—at least, I hope—that it may not be too late if we realize the importance of the natural environment. In some cases, we may be required to sacrifice some kinds of comfort for a reasonable contentment and therefore treat the natural environment more respectfully. I think it may not be too late, but I don't know. Some scientists today say it is very serious.

CI: Your Holiness, I know that you are interested in the new sciences—in brain research, molecular psychology, physics, and so on. With genetic technologies scientists are finding that they can splice cells from one animal into another and form a whole new animal. They are also experimenting with tissue taken from fetuses and put into old people to inhibit geriatric diseases, such as Parkinson's and Alzheimer's.

In molecular psychology, the study of the molecules of the brain, researchers are using chemicals to radically alter mind and behavior. These scientists look forward to a day when anything abnormal will be treated with chemicals or by genetic manipulation. It seems that life is becoming more of a mechanical proposition—it is as though we are so many interchangeable parts. What is the essence of life? What is sacred about it?

DL: Through genetic or chemical changes, one could see changes in the moods of a person or in his way of thinking, as you have said. Still, I feel that the essence of the person is not altered.

When we talk about people, we are thinking about a certain level of consciousness. That is, whether young or old, men or women, educated or uneducated, mentally normal or abnormal, still we call them a human being. Even if a person is totally crazy, his essence is the same. The human identity remains there.

So now some people say that eventually some very sophisticated computer may produce some kind of mind, some kind of consciousness. But you see, like with the mother's egg and the father's sperm—basically nobody regards the egg or the sperm itself as a living human being. Yet they come together, and there are certain circumstances which act as a basis of human consciousness, we believe. Once that has happened, then we call that either a human being, or we say it is conceived as a human. So similarly, different matter can be combined and may reach such a stage that it can act as a basis of consciousness. Then under that circumstance, consciousness enters and becomes a living sentient being.

CI: And would still be subject to the laws of karma and...

DL: Oh yes. Of course, this is something very new. Now, you see, today a human being to us is something very normal, but suppose there were a very old person who existed before our world as we know it—I think such a person would find our people today very strange. So similarly for us, if something like the arising of consciousness happened with the computer and a living being could be created, that would be astonishing at the beginning—very unusual—but eventually, it would be considered normal, just another form of sentient being.

CI: So we would say that there is a life force and that it can be provoked in any number of ways. It could be through a natural egg and sperm or it can be created in the laboratory...

DL: Yes, I think it's possible. In Buddhism we talk of four types of birth: spontaneous birth, birth from a womb (which is the natural one), birth from eggs, and birth from heat or fluidity. The delicate question is whether certain actions or movements are motivated by consciousness or not.

One might use a computer, and due to certain compositions of mechanical things or matter it might begin to act almost like a sentient being. If you take something like a plant or flower, due to certain chemicals, they react to light or dark. The process of the living human body is more or less the same. But generally people don't consider plants to have consciousness. There is life, but not sentient life. The demarcation is that so long as the existence of consciousness is not there, we do not consider it as a sentient being. So now, you see, with a computer in the future which starts to speak and to do things like us humans, what we have to find out is whether the actions performed by the computer are motivated by what we call mind consciousness or are due simply to mechanical functions. Once it is confirmed that there is the existence of consciousness, then we can consider it a sentient being.

CI: I know that the Tibetan system has a very elaborate understanding of the death process. I wonder, Your Holiness, whether you have personally had any glimpses into what is taught in *The Tibetan Book of the Dead.*

DL: I have no experience, really. Once I fell into the water at the Norbulingka Palace and I had the experience of seeing stars for a few seconds. But no, I have no time to meditate on these things lately. Some practitioners who have spent more than twenty years meditating on this have extraordinary experiences on these different levels of consciousness. In some cases, they stopped their breathing for a short while. That is not a natural process, but due to meditation. Due to practice, they deliberately induced that level of consciousness, and they experienced exactly what is described in the texts.

CI: A few days after you announced the Five Point Peace Plan, the Chinese took retaliation against the people in Tibet. Even when you speak out for peace, this kind of thing can happen. Does this make you hesitant to talk about these things publicly? Do you worry about reprisals when you speak about things that may adversely provoke the Chinese?

DL: Actually, you see, the Five Point proposal was made public, I think, at the end of September last year [1987]. Then the Chinese reacted negatively and called me a reactionary. That caused the demonstrations in Tibet, and then the retaliations occurred. So, of course, we were very much concerned and anxious.

You see, on the surface, whether it is very rough or not, there is basically a grave situation in Tibet. I think the Chinese in their way are a very civilized nation. At the same time, they only know force. They do not understand truth. I think now as the time goes, it seems better. There has been a positive change during the last nine years.

Actually the basic content of my Strasbourg proposal [presenting the Five Point Plan to European Parliament] was already known by the Chinese leaders before the statement was made in the U.S. Our delegation had on one occasion or another explained these basic things to the Chinese government, but they had always neglected our situation and, in some cases, they openly told us, "You are outside of Tibet, and while you remain outside you have no right to make suggestions on these things."

You see, the Chinese are hard of hearing; they are deaf to our voices. As a human being with a human voice, one wants to express or talk to another human being. That's quite logical; it's common sense. But, if there is no listener, then there is no use talking. If there is someone who is willing to listen, then there is more desire to explain. Now in the outside world there are more and more people taking notice of the Tibetan problem. Since our Chinese friends' ears are not so sharp, when we shout loudly it only makes our own voices hoarse. [laughing] So I made these proposals not in Peking, but in the outside world. As a result, in the last twelve months the Chinese attitude toward us is more positive than in the past nine years, because of outside world pressure.

CI: But inside Tibet they have been quite repressive.

DL: Yes, for the time being. In the short term, since last year, there has been some setback; it is more rigid. But now I am very glad to know that the Tibetans themselves are very prepared for that fact. So despite the Chinese's harsh methods, the national determination of the Tibetan people is very strong. Yesterday I met one young monk who actually participated in the first October demonstration of last year [1987] and who escaped a few days back. Something remarkable. I really admired their determination, the ones who participated. But then I asked him, "Do you really feel strong anger towards the Chinese?" and he began weeping, and he said that, yes, he was very angry with the Chinese. And there were some other young children—ten years old, thirteen years old—I met a few months back. One boy who participated in burning some Chinese vehicles had escaped. He also expressed strong anger. Very sad. Very sad.

CI: So understandable though. Of course, Gandhi and Martin Luther King, Jr. knew that what they were doing sometimes provoked violence against them and their people, but they understood that this was necessary to call attention to the situation. Sometimes the nonviolent way may provoke violence. It's good to hear from you that the people inside Tibet understand that you are doing what you have to do, and that it sometimes may cause harsher repercussions.

DL: There's no choice.

CI: Your Holiness, if you were to be able to live your life over again, would you do anything differently with regard to the decisions you've made?

DL: Under the same circumstances, no, I wouldn't do anything differently. Of course, there are certain minor points; occasionally we have discussions about this. But, you see, in the last forty years' experience, except for some minor things, there is almost no action which today has brought regret.

CI: You have lost very much in this life. You have lost many people who were close to you, and, of course, you have had to deal with the loss of your homeland for these nearly forty years. Do you find a place for grieving in your life? Can you say anything for people who are facing grief—something which we all have to face sooner or later?

DL: There are two ways of losing someone. One is the natural process. I have lost my mother, teachers, brother. That's natural. Unless old friend disappears, there is no possibility to receive new friend. [laughing] As a Buddhist practitioner, one accepts this kind of loss as part of nature. Nothing special. Nothing extraordinary. So there is not much grieving. Of course, for a few days there is some strong feeling of missing someone. But not much effect.

Then there is another category of loss which is due to tragedy, due to disaster. We lost our country, we lost many reliable good and spiritual friends, so many friends, lost. Suddenly, and beyond our own control. But in our case, the tragedy began in 1950, so that also is some help. This tragedy has come as a process, and we have become accustomed to it. Much before the actual situation happened, we were already fully convinced that sooner or later, this kind of thing would happen, definitely.

CI: Your predecessor, the previous Dalai Lama, thought so.

DL: Oh yes. But nobody believed him. People simply thought that he was just scaring them, and they didn't pay much attention. But when the Chinese so-called, "liberated" Tibet in 1950-51, and at the end of '55 and '56 more trouble started in the northeastern part of Tibet with all sorts of brutalities, then it became very clear. Still we tried our best. So, you see, for me personally it was very helpful that before the actual thing happened, we knew that it would happen.

CI: So you expected the worst.

DL: Yes, but of course, sometimes we feel sad. There is more sadness when I hear that many Tibetans, despite their misery and terror, show us so much trust, so much expectation. That gives us a heavy responsibility and sometimes makes me feel sad. So much trust, so much expectation is upon us, and so little can be done here. There are a lot of limitations. We try our best, and as far as possible we have clear motivation, but whether we achieve or not is a different matter. And, as a Buddhist, you see, when there is a difficult thing, we can easily blame our previous karma. We try our best, but due to our previous karmic force... [laughing] No need to blame God. We can easily blame our own karma.

CI: Do you find that you have people whom you consider your peer group? Are there people with whom you can really relax?

DL: Yes, of course. I think generally everybody is my peer group. My attitude is that if somebody is open and straightforward and very sincere, then very easily we can get this close feeling. If someone is very reserved, very formal, then it is difficult. Usually, you see, my nature is very informal. So I think that is helpful.

CI: If you weren't in your position of being the spiritual and temporal leader of Tibet, do you think there would be some other kind of social activism you would undertake, or do you think that you'd prefer to be a monk living quietly in a monastery?

DL: Nowadays, I think if I were not the Dalai Lama, I would desire time in some monastery or in some remote place to practice deeper meditation. In my twenties, thirties, forties, I had a great desire for spiritual practice. These ideas come after contact with Buddha's teachings or as a result of some knowledge about Buddhism. But suppose I still remained in my own place as a farmer's son, then I don't know. As soon as my birth took place, my father decided that I should enter a monastery, that I should become a monk. If those circumstances had been different, most probably I would have become a technician of some kind because I am very interested in mechanical things.

CI: Given the other problems in the world, would there be one which compelled you to help out more?

DL: I think at the moment, because of the title Dalai Lama, that is the primary factor. Another factor is my own personality, as we already discussed—very open, informal, sincere motivation. From that it seems as if some people might get some kind of mental peace or some benefit.

But if I were not the Dalai Lama, I don't know. According to basic Buddhist philosophy of interdependency, or co-dependent origination, how things are is the reality. So we must make best use of the real situation and choose the best way from among the possibilities which exist.

CI: You have spoken about returning to Tibet. Do you think that you will be able to go back to Tibet in this life?

DL: I think so. But this is not a serious matter. The main serious matter is freedom. Whether as the Dalai Lama or as a monk, Tenzin Gyatso, I want to have freedom to contribute whatever I can in a maximum way for Tibetans as well as other people. So in that respect, if I feel more opportunity outside Tibet, I will remain outside. If opportunity remains equal, then I will return. Either to Tibet or to China. China is a very beautiful country. And anyway, in the Chinese mind, Buddhism is not alien, not something new. Traditionally there are a lot of Chinese who are Buddhists. There are Buddhist shrines, Buddhist temples. Not like in Western countries where there are only new Buddhist centers and where Buddhism itself is entirely new. In the Chinese mind, it's not that way. So you see I am quite sure that if the Chinese people have the free opportunity to have contact with Buddhism, to learn and practice Buddhism, I think many young Chinese will be attracted to it and will benefit. If such an opportunity happens, of course, I am willing to contribute. The Chinese are also human be-ings.

My real concern is whether something would go wrong with that possibility. There is no use in returning to Ti-bet or to China if that causes damage or if there is no real opportunity to help. But it really doesn't matter much to me. Much depends on change in China-proper.

CI: Do you think there will be another incarnated Dalai Lama?

DL: At the moment it is difficult to say. The next ten or twenty years will determine this. I think Tibetans still want to have Dalai Lama. Actually, this is not my con-cern, but if the Tibetan people want to have another Dalai Lama, then Dalai Lama will come. If circum-stances change and the majority of Tibetan people are not much concerned about Dalai Lama, then I will be the last Dalai Lama. That is not my responsibility. Those Tibetans who are now age five or ten, it is their respon-sibility. So in twenty, thirty years when I have passed away, then they will decide.

CI: I hope you will live a long life.

DL: According to my dreams, the maximum years would be 110 or 113. But I could not live that long. So perhaps I will live until I am 90, between 80 and 90. Then I would become useless, an old Dalai Lama of not much value.

CI: I must respectfully disagree, Your Holiness.

Mubarak Awad

For forty days in the spring of 1988, Mubarak Awad awaited his fate in an Israeli prison. Held in solitary confinement, the Palestinian nonviolent activist could not have known that the world was watching as Israel prepared to expel him from the land of his birth. Private messages from President Reagan and Secretary of State George Schultz flickered over the air waves to Israeli Prime Minister Yitzak Shamir concerning Awad's case. The U.S. Ambassador to Israel told Shamir, "You need more Awads in Jerusalem, not fewer."

Despite the appeals from the highest level of the U.S. government, the Israeli High Court ordered the expulsion of Mubarak Awad. Awad was led from his solitary prison cell directly to an airplane bound for New York City. Upon his arrival he was inundated by the international media, who told the world the story of his cause and of his nonviolent strategies for the uprising of the Palestinian people against the Israeli occupation.

* * *

Since Paleolithic time, the Old Stone Age of about 200,000 years ago, people have lived on the land now known as Israel and previously known as Palestine.[1] The recorded history of the region dates back nearly 5,000 years to a time when pagan, nomadic tribes wandered the land, many of whom had migrated from the East. The story of Abraham, which is central to the present Israeli claims to this land, comes to us from the Bible and begins around 2000 B.C.

---

[1]The word "Palestine" is derived from the Greek, meaning "Syria of the Philistines" or southern Syria.

Abraham and his family, for unknown reasons, left the Babylonian city of Ur, crossed the river, and headed northwest. The word "Hebrew" refers to the people "who crossed over" or were "from the other side of the river." When Abraham reached Haran in what is now Turkey, he had a religious experience as described in the Book of Genesis in which he and God entered into a pact. If Abraham would agree to circumcision for all males on the eighth day after their birth, God, for His part, would look upon Abraham's descendants as His "Chosen People" and would promise the land of Canaan (now Israel) to them.

Although Abraham's people began to settle in the vicinity of the "Promised Land," it was not until about 1200 B.C. that the Israelites[2] were able to conquer the idolatrous Canaanites and win the land for themselves. Two centuries later, King Saul and his successor, King David, forged a strong empire with extended borders and a thriving political capital called Jerusalem. It was not to last.

Feuding Hebrew kingdoms, Judah[3] and Israel, weakened the empire, and a series of takeovers occurred during the next few centuries. Many of the Jews scattered to faraway lands. Those who stayed were often subjected to lives as slaves, and they occasionally suffered mass slaughters. For hundreds of years, Persian, Roman, and Greek rulers lorded over the Jews with varying degrees of tolerance or oppression.

Meanwhile, out of the Arabian Desert, strong tribal people migrated to the Promised Land. By the seventh century A.D., Bedouin and Quarish Arabs began to dominate the region, which they named Palestine. From these Arabic people, Mohammed, the founder of Islam, was born in the city of Mecca in 570 A.D. Through his

---

[2] The word "Israelite" derives from the Hebrew *Yisro-El* which means "Man who fought God." As the story goes, Jacob, a grandson of Abraham, had a strange encounter with an otherworldly being. Because of this he was given the name *Yisro-El*.

[3] The word "Jew" comes from the Hebrew *Yehudi* which means "citizen of Judah."

influence and his mighty armies, Muslims, Islamic believers, came to rule not only Palestine, but a vast empire which stretched from North Africa to Indonesia.

The historical stage was now set for the fight between the Arabs and Jews for the Promised Land. Although other conquerors—the Seljuk and Ottoman Turks, the Christian Crusaders, the Mongols from Asia, and the Mamelukes from Egypt—ruled the land during the next millennium, the Arabs in Palestine continued to multiply as the dominant inhabitants of the region. Into the nineteenth century, the Jews, who were now scattered all over the world, kept alive their longing to return to the Promised Land. Equally hopeful, Arabs dreamed of expelling their present Turkish conquerors and claiming Palestine as their own once again.

Arab hopes were fueled by what they took to be an agreement with the British in World War I. In exchange for Arab support in driving out the Turks from the Arabian Peninsula, the British allegedly promised Arab independence and the creation of Arab states after the war, including one in Palestine. However, the Jewish community in Europe and the United States had mustered strong support among the Allies, and a Declaration was drawn up by the British and approved by the U.S., France, and Italy, which proposed the creation of a Jewish homeland *within* the land of Palestine. Jews began to immigrate in large numbers into Palestine. The Arab world was shocked. Tensions between the Arabs and Jews in Palestine mounted, and fighting sporadically erupted.

The turning point for the Jews came after World War II. Nearly the entire civilized world, stunned by the deaths of 6 million Jews in the Holocaust, wanted to assist in creating a Jewish homeland. A United Nations Special Committee convened in 1947 and proposed a partition plan for two separate states in the land of Palestine, one for the Arabs and one for the Jews. The Arabs flatly rejected the plan, noting that it called for giving fifty-five percent of the land (and, they believed, the best of the land) to the Jews, who made up only one third of the population of Palestine at that time.

As its future was being settled, Palestine was under a British Mandate, but chaos reigned in the region. When war became imminent, the British quickly left Palestine, and on May 14, 1948, the Jews celebrated the birth of Israel, uniquely declaring it the state of the entire Jewish people, no matter where they lived. Immediately afterward, the Jews surprisingly triumphed against the armies of Egypt, Jordan, Iraq, Syria, and Lebanon, which had united in attempting to "drive Israel into the sea" and secure Palestine for the Palestinian Arabs.

Joyous and proud, the Israelis announced to the world that after 1,800 years of wandering, they had found "a land without a people for a people without a land." Unfortunately, the Israelis' pronouncement omitted mention not only of the millions of Arab Palestinians who lived there and made up the majority population of Palestine, but of their Arab ancestors who had lived there for the previous thirteen centuries.

In a brutal and well documented wave of force, the Israelis swept through Arab communities in rural and urban areas causing approximately 700,000 people to flee. Four hundred villages were destroyed, and thousands of Palestinian Arabs were killed or made refugees. Many Palestinians took to makeshift settlements either in neighboring Arab countries or in the West Bank and the Gaza Strip. In the Yom Kippur War of 1967, Israel acquired what was left of the Palestinian homeland, and Jewish soldiers and settlers came to occupy the West Bank and Gaza.

Into this troubled region, Mubarak Awad was born on August 22, 1943 in Jerusalem, in the home in which his grandmother had given birth to his father. In 1948 Mubarak's father, who refused Israeli orders to vacate his home, was shot and killed while attempting to carry a wounded friend to safety. Mubarak's only memory of his father is his "throwing me in the air."

Awad's mother was left with seven children, the youngest being forty days old, the oldest, ten years. After threats that her children would be lined up against a wall and shot, Awad's mother gave up her home and put all but two of her children in orphanages. She had no means to support them. Although Mrs. Awad visited her children regularly and refused to give up legal custody, she was never again able to provide a home for her family. Nevertheless, Awad's mother exerted tremendous moral influence on her children as they grew up, instilling in them Quaker and Christian values of service and love and telling them "never to seek revenge." She exhorted them to work "so that other mothers don't suffer as I have."

Mubarak was "one of the lucky ones." He was placed in the orphanage home of Katy Antouns where he lived until he graduated from high school. One of Katy's friends, a young American who had come to visit, asked how he might be of help to the Palestinians. She suggested that he provide funds for Mubarak and his brother to attend the private school of St. George's in Jerusalem. The American agreed, and the two young boys found themselves in one of the most prestigious schools in the country.

During his school years, Mubarak became interested in religion, particularly Christianity. After high school, he determined to study for the ministry. He won a full scholarship to Lee College in Cleveland, Tennessee, and went there in 1959. But Awad became unhappy at Lee when he saw the way black people were treated in the South, and he disapproved of the college's evangelical approach to religion. He returned home to Jerusalem to work in a Mennonite orphanage school for boys where he taught English, math, and religion until 1969.

Awad returned to the United States in 1970 to attend Bluffton College in Ohio. By this time, he had become deeply interested in Mennonite and Quaker beliefs about nonviolence and the Peace Testimony.[4] His education

---

[4] The central document of the Quakers, the Peace Testimony originated in 1660, saying in part: "We are a people that follow after those things that make for peace, love, and unity; it is our desire that others' feet

focused on practical aspects of these beliefs which he subsequently implemented in his work with juvenile delinquents in Bluffton. While obtaining his Masters Degree in counseling from St. Francis University in Indiana, Awad practiced as a group and family therapist for delinquent children. Afterwards, in 1978, he began the Youth Advocate Program which helps delinquents by providing support systems for them within their homes and schools.

Because his work with juveniles was successful, Awad decided to take what he had learned back to his homeland. In 1983, he returned to Jerusalem and started the Palestinian Counseling Center to work with Palestinian youths in a therapeutic context. Awad had always been proud of the young Palestinians who fought against the Israeli occupation. Several years earlier, he had written a book in praise of their bravery called *Children of the Stone*, in which he hailed the youngsters who threw stones at Israeli soldiers. He explained that the stone, generally the only weapon the Palestinians have, had become a symbol for their people. Years later Mubarak would regret his earlier thinking on the subject, saying that "Stones make people run away."

Awad soon discovered in his work at the Palestinian Counseling Center that Palestinians were more concerned about their political situation than about therapeutic approaches to their problems. Inspired, he wrote a lengthy article, which was published in Jerusalem, suggesting 120 nonviolent ways to end the occupation by Israel. "We needed to make it economically, psychologically, and morally expensive for Israel," he explained. In the article he pointed out that the Palestinians had the choice of whether to be under occupation or not. He believed that the Palestinians had "internalized the occupation," and that they blamed everything from poor health care to juvenile delinquency on the Israelis. Rallying them to take responsibility for themselves, Awad

---

may walk in the same, and we do deny and bear our testimony against all strife and wars and contentions."

told the Palestinians that they and only they must decide their future.

Awad had learned nonviolent techniques through his own studies and on several trips to India, where he had immersed himself in the ideas of Mahatma Gandhi. He had also been greatly inspired by Martin Luther King, Jr. and the American civil rights movement. After writing the article, Awad organized a three-day workshop to discuss the ideas in it. To his surprise, several hundred people showed up, including some who strongly believed in an armed struggle for the Palestinian people.

Mubarak Awad returned to the United States to continue his work in Ohio, but a seed had been planted in Jerusalem which was destined to take root. Mubarak knew that the next step was to form a nonviolent study center in Jerusalem, but he had no funds to begin such a project. However, Awad's article had been widely read, and had fallen into the hands of a Palestinian-American professor, Hisham Sharbi, of Georgetown University. Reading Awad's words awakened Sharbi's childhood memories of his own Quaker training in Ramallah, north of Jerusalem. He contacted Awad and offered financial support to start the center in Jerusalem. Once again, the generosity of a stranger would help realize Mubarak's dreams.

In 1985, Mubarak Awad returned to Jerusalem to found the Palestinian Center for the Study of Nonviolence. His aim was to cull from Arabic literature and Islamic texts anything to do with reconciliation, peace, justice, and nonviolence in order for Palestinians to understand these ideas from their own cultural heritage. Awad believed that from this study people would bring forth their ideas, and that "their ideas will be beautiful."

Although Awad's early intention was merely to create a study center, the Israelis found ways to thwart him. He was often arrested, sometimes for such small infractions as having no turn signal, or for simply being in the street. Several times he was tortured while in custody. "The more I organized, the more the Israelis started to feel threatened. I think they didn't want anyone to believe that even one Palestinian would be interested in nonviolence."

Soon, the Palestinians who had been studying nonviolent strategy felt that the time had come for action. Although it may be too much to credit Awad with the *intifada* which began on December 8, 1987, his influence has clearly permeated the uprising.[5] According to Awad, this uprising of the 1.3 million Palestinians living in the West Bank and Gaza is "eighty-five percent nonviolent." It is organized and run mostly by women.

As taught by Mubarak Awad, the Palestinians have earnestly engaged in a campaign of civil disobedience which includes refusal to pay taxes or to obtain required permits for business transactions. For many months, the schools were closed and the children were educated underground. Teachers who were caught faced a ten-year jail sentence, deportation, or the destruction of their homes. Palestinians are raising their flag, writing freedom slogans on the walls of their homes, boycotting Israeli goods, and burning tires in protest of the occupation. The Israelis have responded with massive arrests, beatings, killings (hundreds of Palestinians have died in the uprising so far) and curfews, but the flame burning in the hearts of the Palestinians is strong. They know that for the first time, they are winning the sympathy of the world.

Mubarak Awad explains that they seek a "two for two," (two states for two peoples) solution to the problem, as proposed by the Palestine Liberation Organization, the government-in-exile of the Palestinian people. Although this is seen as too conciliatory a position by more radical Arab factions, most moderate Palestinians believe that it is the only realistic hope for them to establish a country of their own.

Mubarak Awad was deported from Israel in April 1988. However, from that moment to now, he has been tirelessly and effectively working to inspire nonviolent

---

[5] *Intifada*, Arabic, literally, "the shaking" (as in shaking oneself free or awake) refers to the Palestinian uprising which continues to this date.

continuation of the *intifada*. He regularly consults with high levels of the United States government and the PLO on the issue, and, along with others, is forming Nonviolence International, an organization of trained people who will advise governments or institutions interested in nonviolent struggle. Awad's main organization, The Palestinian Center for the Study of Nonviolence, has branches in Washington, D.C. and in Jerusalem. Awad resides with his second wife in Maryland.

I met Mubarak Awad when he came to Berkeley to give several lectures on nonviolent strategies in the Palestinian uprising. The following day I went to interview him in San Francisco. Within a few minutes of our scheduled time together, I was convinced of his nonviolent approach to problems. My tape recorder inexplicably went on the blink as soon as I turned it on for our conversation. After I had given up trying to get it going, Mubarak patiently fidgeted with all the knobs and plugs, fully engaged in attempting to fix it. Twenty minutes later, we were forced to borrow recording equipment from the American Friends Service Committee where Mubarak was staying and where our conversation was taking place. More time was spent on changing locations within the building. Throughout this interval, I had no sense of pressure or impatience from Mubarak. To the contrary, somehow my technical problem had also become his problem. As we sat down for the interview, instead of being embarrassed or anxious about not having tested my equipment, I had the feeling that Mubarak and I were triumphant comrades in perseverance.

Interview with Mubarak Awad
April 7, 1989 • San Francisco, California

Catherine Ingram: Mubarak, how do your spiritual convictions play a role in your work in the world?

Mubarak Awad: I think the most important thing in my early life had been not so much to look toward the world, but to look toward the individual, to look at the family—my brothers and sisters and my mother. That was my spirituality; it wasn't intended to look beyond my community at all. But then, what we saw as Palestinians, with the Quakers and Mennonites and other missionaries who came to help, forced me to ask the questions, "Who are those Quakers? Who are those Mennonites? Why are they helping us?" I needed to see if there was a political reason behind them, or if there was a religious reason. And what I found was that many of those people help just because people are in trouble and in need. That's when I started studying more about the Mennonites and the Quakers.

CI: So you felt inspired by seeing not only what they were doing, but by seeing their motivation in doing it.

MA: Very much so.

CI: Are there specific beliefs from either your Quaker or your Christian background that keep you going in your work?

MA: What affects me most as a Christian is the idea of forgiveness and the idea to help others. That's why my professional field is social work—counseling, psychology. I have the ability to help others in that way and to teach others to help themselves. I'm good at that.

The thing that I learned about spirituality is that there is a part of God in everyone; this is a Quaker concept which I feel strongly. I used to think, "How could there be a part of God in someone I didn't like, someone who had done wrong, or even in myself when I am angry? Where is God in me when I need him most?" But then I would learn that there is God in everybody. That's where we have to make a distinction between a fellow and his actions. There is no bad individual; there is no bad boy or bad girl, it is their actions that may be bad.

Some people have more problems than others, so we work with the problem rather than say to the person, "You are a liar," or "You are a thief." Instead we say, "You have a problem of lying," or "You have a problem of stealing."

CI: Gandhi said something like this which had its origins in Christianity: "We should hate the sin, but not the sinner." Nevertheless, we tend to personalize sin.

I wanted to talk with you about Islam as I know that you have studied Islam in your work and you grew up with many Muslims. Many people believe Islam to be a violent religion because they think of it as advocating conversion by force, severe punishments, and intolerance of others' beliefs. As you know, the press on Islam has been quite negative.

MA: I think the aim of Islam, like Christianity or Judaism or other religions, is to help people live together in peace. In Islam there is a great deal of concern for social justice. For example, Islam traditionally does not discriminate between black and white people or between rich and poor. When Muslims go to pray in Mecca, they all have to wear the same thing so that nobody can look at another and see whether they have money or not.

Islam has enlightenment in it. Mohammed's message from God was for people to love each other and to understand each other. When Islam came along, in that time in the Arab world they were burying girl babies alive because they didn't want girls. Islam stopped that practice.

However, in our lifetime we start seeing Islam as represented by the Khomeini, or we see only the violence of Islam. Yet, in every religion there is violence—in Christianity or Judaism. We cannot say about people that because they are Muslims they are violent or because they are Christians they are violent. When Islam began, it was like Christianity in its beginning. But Christianity became an institution and then Christians started carrying the banner of the cross. They became crusaders, and they invaded those who were not Christians to make them become Christian. The same is true in Islam. Unfortunately, Islam and the Muslim religion have not been studied carefully in the West.

CI: Do you think that the media has to be present for nonviolent strategy to work? For instance, when you had the fence problem in Tekoa, it was the media which ultimately helped attain your success.[6] In nonviolent action and work, it is important to rally large numbers of people into feeling morally concerned about injustice in order to inspire them to stop it from continuing. Is it possible to do this without media attention?

MA: I think the media helps tremendously. In nearly every action, we use the media. In our time now, we have the TV, we have the video camera, we have cassette tapes. In one minute a radio reporter is here, and in the next minute you can hear the story all around the world. So in our situation, the ability to use the media, to be honest with the media, and to make sure that the media understands what is going on has been a good weapon for us, a very powerful weapon.

Anybody who uses nonviolence and civil disobedience in a nonviolent struggle has to have a media. If they don't have the media, they should have their own cameras because they need to show what has happened—to themselves as well as to the rest of the world.

In our case, in front of the media, the Israelis have to show that they are civilized, that they are people who believe in justice and fairness.

CI: What about the groups who do not have media coverage, for instance, the Tibetans in occupied Tibet, who

---

[6] In January 1986, Jewish settlers moved a fence in the area of Tekoa in order to encroach upon five acres of Palestinian land. Mubarak Awad came to the area and peacefully negotiated with Israeli soldiers to disallow the encroachment. Although initially sympathetic, the next day the Israeli soldiers turned their backs on the Jewish settlers' encroachment. Mubarak Awad notified the press and, when the story hit the papers, the settlers were forced to retreat from the Palestinian land.

have been carrying on a primarily nonviolent struggle for nearly forty years, but who have received little coverage during most of that time?

MA: Well, it's important to somehow record it, because for the whole of our history we have not been recording nonviolent struggle. We have been recording the violent struggle. And the ones who have been writing about the violent struggle for history have been those who were maybe in the army or who were a correspondent in war. We have very few correspondents in nonviolent struggle.

CI: You wrote in a booklet on nonviolent resistance: "During this particular historical period and with regard only to the 1.3 million Palestinians living under the Israeli occupation, nonviolence is the most effective method to obstruct the policy of Judaization." Does this statement mean that you see alternatives to nonviolence in other situations? You have pointed out that in Jerusalem, because it is the Holy Land, if only twenty people demonstrate, it is reported in *The New York Times*. Yet, for many people struggling in the world, their nonviolent resistance seems of no direct consequence to their situation. They just offer up new lines of unknown martyrs.

MA: Well, when I really started thinking about our situation, the Palestinians in what we now call the West Bank and Gaza—occupied Palestine—I realized that we don't have weapons and we cannot get weapons to fight the Israelis with. We have so many people who are inspired to struggle against the occupation, but there are only a very few of them who are either trained or could get hold of weapons. Now, I believe that for the Palestinians outside the occupied territories they should make their own choice. They could get weapons and they have the right. But for the Palestinians inside, through the nonviolent struggle we have been able to stop the Israeli settlements, we have been able to stop the Israelis from taking our land, and we have been able to stop the continuation of occupation, not only on the level of land, but on a psychological level—really to stop occupying oneself, to feel that he or she is under occupation.

Now if there have been any victories in this, and in the Palestinian struggle I think there have been, it will help any nonviolent struggle around the world. They will start looking at the Palestinian case and they will see that after using armed struggle for forty years, the Palestinians have realized that they are able to use nonviolent struggle, and they have been achieving something with it. So another reason that I hope that the Palestinians can achieve is so that others will look at them and say, "We can do it this way too." The similarity in the mentality of people is always there. As much as you want to struggle, you don't want to be killed. And if you don't want to be killed, you also have to make it clear that you don't want to kill. This is the beauty of nonviolence.

CI: You have said that some of the leaders of the Arab world are frightened by the *intifada*, and that they have approached you to talk about your nonviolent strategy. Given that these are the traditional allies of the Palestinians, why are they afraid of the uprising?

MA: I think a powerful part of the uprising is that it has eliminated leadership of one man or one king who can say to the people, "Do this," and the people do it. When a lot of people start taking the initiative by themselves, this is dangerous for the ruler. Here is a government which does not have the power; the people have the power. And when people have the power, you don't need a policeman in the street. In these sixteen months of the *intifada*, we don't have policemen, we don't have stealing. People are taking care of themselves. And, really, we don't need a government!

Now imagine, if you are a king, and people say, "We don't need a king," or if you are president and they say, "We don't need a president." There would be less and less need for government to tell the people what to do if the people are doing it themselves.

One of my beliefs is that the less the government rules, the better the government. The more government regulation, the worse the government. In the Arab world, everything is run by the government. Everything. And the people do nothing because all the regulation is by the government. When the Palestinians decided that they didn't want to listen to those government regulations, the other Arabs started to get scared. They are afraid that this *intifada* will say to the Arab population in every Arab country that we have the guts, we have the strength, we have the empowerment to tell the ruler that we are not willing to follow your orders. If you are a king, your power comes from the people who give it to you, and when people don't give you the power, you're not a king anymore. It's a very strong revolution.

CI: People say that there is an outbreak of peace in the world. Do you see a growing movement toward the idea of nonviolence? Do you see other nonviolent *intifadas* around the world, and if so, to what do you attribute this?

MA: Yes, if I would speculate I would say that it is partly because the tension between America and the Soviet Union has lessened. Now there is no Cold War between the superpowers. They are coordinating together, so they don't need to use small countries to make trouble for the other. This is one thing.

CI: Gorbachev gets enormous credit for that, I think. The joke is that the U.S. administration is having a hard time taking "yes" for an answer.

MA: Maybe they will get used to it. The other thing is that there have recently been a lot of settlements; the Iran-Iraq conflict was settled, Namibia got its independence. I think that people are starting to see that they are able to have negotiated settlements and that war is too destructive. No matter who you are in any country, even if you are *winning* a war, with the weapons we have now you are going to lose probably one third of your population. So there's no winner in any war.

People are also seeing that there are chemical weapons, biological weapons, nuclear weapons. Enemies can get hold of these weapons.

CI: Chemical and biological weapons are sometimes called "the poor man's atom bomb" because they are cheap and relatively easy to acquire.

MA: Yes, and don't think people would not dare to use those weapons. They *will* dare to use them. We cannot protect ourselves from all of those, so it becomes obvious that people who need to struggle for their freedom will have to use other methods. Nonviolence is one of those methods.

CI: People call you the "Gandhi of Palestine." What has it meant for you to be held in such high esteem?

MA: I have very much difficulty with that. I am not Gandhi. He is in a class by himself. My idea was to promote nonviolence and Gandhi's teachings with the hope that someone else would come and pick it up, because I think this is going to take ten to fifteen years before the Palestinians will be able to accept the struggle in a nonviolent way. So when a lot of reporters and even Palestinians started giving me this title, well, I felt uneasy. Gandhi did that work for so many years, and here I am just starting. I am not Gandhi, I am Mubarak. Gandhi was a different man; his spirituality was different. He was a greater man than me, and I am not in his league.

CI: But you might be willing to be in his footsteps?

MA: [Laughing] Yes, I am in his footsteps, but not in his league.

But you know, I will also do whatever I want. Gandhi took things from an attorney's point of view. He tried to see what aspects of court could be used, what rules and regulations. I am opposing all rules and regulations. I don't care for rules and regulations, I don't follow rules and regulations. I don't respect any rules at all. And I tell Palestinians not to respect the rules. Gandhi had respect for the British rule.

CI: If Gandhi looked at things from a legal point of view, would you say that you have more a psychological point of view?

MA: Yes, exactly. What I did over there was that I merged my training in psychology and my love of nonviolent struggle to bring a different ideology. For example, when I say to people that we are under occupation because we *choose* to be under occupation, it's as though you are talking in therapy to a person and saying, "Look, you have to understand that those problems are *yours* and you are the only one who can work on the problem." So what I do is to give alternatives. One alternative is an armed struggle. Let's look at other alternatives. Another is the nonviolent struggle and there are other alternatives as well. And then you make a choice.

CI: You have said that if one is to talk to people about their going to prison, one has to be willing to go to prison himself.

MA: Yes.

CI: And I know that you were in an Israeli prison for forty days...

MA: The last time was for forty days. I have been in their prisons many times.
  I think you have to experience what you talk about. If you are a teacher, that is when you become a good teacher. You know beforehand the consequences of what

you say. You tell people your own experience such as what happened to you in jail, and then people make their own choices. If someone is weak, not strong enough, then there is no need to come to the demonstration. You don't have to impress anybody. When we say, "Let's fill the jails," it is important to understand what the consequences are for you personally in jail. So when you have already been in jail, then it becomes obvious that you are not talking of something that might happen or would happen—this has already happened to you.

I got beaten, I got electric-shocked, I got harassed with tear gas thrown at me, so I know what it is to have those difficulties.

CI: You have said in your talks that the first time is the worst. After you had those terrible things happen to you, was it possible for you to go to jail again and experience less fear than the first time?

MA: Yes, because the fear is not from the punishment of the body as much as it is a psychological fear—the fear of the unknown, the fear of what's going to happen to you. Those people come to you and threaten you with, "We will do this," or "We will do that." After the first time you know that for two or three hours they are going to do this to you. By knowing it, you will have a psychological level of stability. So you will say, "All right, I am going to be beaten." And, knowing that you are going to be beaten, sometimes your body will understand that, and you will have your body and your mind working together.

The Israelis or anybody else who wants to torture you or to make you afraid will try to separate you from your mind. You may be in a room with a few of your people and they will take one out and beat him up and come back, and you will think, "Oh, I am next." You start to know that every oppressor wants to have the element of fear to maintain his oppression of someone else. And if you understand that, then you yourself will be calm. You don't need to be alarmed if you are going to be beaten. So you just have to contain yourself and somehow meditate within yourself saying, "All right, they are going to do it, and I feel sorry for them." Openly tell them, "I feel sorry for you. You can beat me and do whatever; I am not going to tell you anything, and I feel sorry for you that you have to do this."

CI: When I think about the Israelis in this position, given that these things happened to them not so long ago in Germany, I think of an abused child becoming an abusing parent.

MA: Exactly.

CI: I was inspired to hear you say that one of the things that the Palestinians have going for them is that their opponents happen to be Jews and that the Jews are basically a good people whose sense of goodness can be appealed to. Given that you've had horrible experiences in Israeli prisons, one could allow you to feel a great deal of resentment toward the Israelis. What qualities in particular are you speaking of when you say they are a good opposition to have?

MA: First, there is the quality of their being Jewish. A Jew has to have justice as part of his belief. When they go and pray they will say, "God, give me the strength to help my neighbor and to do justice and to give to the poor." This is Judaism. To be a good neighbor.

The Jews have also been morally fighting for equal rights, for women's rights, for black rights, and against slavery, against oppression everywhere. And they have not only been doing it in action, but they have been writing about it. They have been the champions of this. What can Jewish writers who have been writing about how beautiful it is to free the slaves say when we ask, "Why is it not so beautiful to free the Palestinians?" And they are sensitive to this.

CI: You have said that the enthusiasm in the *intifada* has been based on a lessening of fear on the part of the Palestinians. How has this occurred?

MA: I think that when you have 1.3 million people who suddenly decide that they want freedom, when a whole population—you, your parents, your neighbors, everybody that you know individually, your friends, your cousins—when you see them resisting and demonstrating in the street, you don't feel alone in your struggle. And when you don't feel alone, there is that unity which creates a confidence in you. When you start creating confidence, you then have the empowerment to say, "I am not afraid." That's why Palestinians—knowing that the Israelis have the guns, knowing that some of the people are going to be killed—are not afraid.

I'll give you a story. A woman who was working with my wife at Friends School in Ramallah was preparing to go to a demonstration. My wife said to her, "Hey, be careful." And the woman said, "It doesn't matter. I am working for freedom; I am not afraid anymore. If I die, at least I die for my freedom, and if I live, I live to be free. Either way I'm working for my freedom."

You see, fear is part of occupation. The Palestinians are not afraid of the Israelis now, and that's what the peace process is about. You cannot have peace when people are afraid. You have to have peace between strong people. The Palestinians are strong now, and Israel could have peace with them. If the Israelis come and crush the *intifada*, the Palestinians will be putting their heads down again, and there will be no peace.

CI: Let's talk for a moment about the PLO and the famous Palestinian National Covenant.[7] Although some of

---

[7] The Palestine National Covenant, the basic document which has guided the Palestine Liberation Organization since its inception under Ahmed Shukairy, was accepted in 1969 by Yassir Arafat, the current leader of the PLO. The document says: "The establishment of Israel is fundamentally null and void." It also suggests that the destruction of

the leaders of the PLO talk of a two-state solution now, I have read that the Covenant is the number one reason that most Jews resist discussing "two for two." After twenty years of violent tactics, many people associate the Palestinian cause with terrorism. Even though there's been a departure from the use of violence by the PLO, who is to say that they won't revert to the use of violence once they get what they want?

You have been trained in the principles of nonviolence from childhood. As you well know, the training in nonviolence is difficult and not practiced by very many people. It's hard to imagine that suddenly, after all these years, the PLO would not use violence once it was in a strong position. Do you have any assurances about this?

MA: It's not necessary. I think that when the Palestinians use nonviolence as a means of struggle, it doesn't mean that they are nonviolent people. And I say it loud and clear: it doesn't mean that the Palestinians later on would not use violence. I'm one of those who will tell the Palestinians, "If nonviolence doesn't work, you can always turn to the gun, so why are you afraid to try nonviolence?" It is my hope that if nonviolence works, this idea would not only be a strategy with the Palestinians against the Israelis, it will move inside the Palestinians so that a teacher would not hit a student, or a parent would not hit a child. The idea would be to use this training as part of our community, as part of our daily life to be nonviolent. But this will take time.

CI: How do you see this happening? What will prompt people to behave in such gentle ways with each other?

MA: The first thing, in our case, is to see that on a political level, nonviolence works. And then to see that on a personal level, it works as well. For me it is for a personal level, but for the majority of Palestinians it is for

Israel would not only be legal, but would benefit the Arabs, the Palestinians, and humanity in general.

the political level. Right now they are seeing if it works. However, if it fails, it fails for both levels, personal and political. The people will then say, "Why do we have to do this?"

I don't think it's easy for the Palestinians to be nonviolent, and I don't want to take the credit to say that I introduced nonviolence there at all. What I did, really, was bring the ideas together and say to the Palestinians, "Look, fellows, your grandfather, your father, your mother, everybody has been using nonviolent methods all along." These were already there. I just called it nonviolence. I started saying that "nonviolence" is not a bad word, it's not a passive word. I didn't invent nonviolence. Believe me, a lot of the villagers are nonviolent people. Their entire life has been nonviolent. I mean, what else do you expect from a farmer?

CI: Still, I think many people credit you with helping the *intifada* organize in a nonviolent way.

MA: Yes, that's what I did.

You asked about the PLO. I'd like to come back to that because not a lot of people understand what the PLO is. The PLO is our only government. It's our government in exile. And when somebody attacks the PLO, it is like attacking the Palestinians. For example, the Israelis don't want to talk to the PLO, not because of the PLO, but because they don't want to acknowledge that the Palestinians have a nationality and that their leader is the PLO.

After the 1982 war in Lebanon, almost everybody in the West Bank and Gaza became a PLO member to support the PLO military in its time of defeat. But when people talk about the PLO, they don't talk about the women who are in the PLO or the workers in the hospitals, or the lawyers and doctors. These are all part of the organization of the PLO. Most people think of it as only a military group involved in an armed struggle.

CI: Well...in America, especially, the PLO has been portrayed as a terrorist organization.

MA: Yes, they look at that armed-struggle group as if this is the whole PLO. But imagine if the Palestinians were seen to be fighting communists, what would the PLO be called then? Freedom fighters! But since we are fighting the Israelis, and the Israelis are allies to the U.S., we are terrorists. When people say to me, "The PLO are terrorists; how could you support them?" I must say that I don't see the PLO as terrorists. I see that the PLO has done terrorist acts—one cannot deny that—but you cannot say that when a Palestinian baby is born, he is a terrorist.

CI: Did you openly disapprove of the terrorist acts—hitting civilian targets, and so on—which the PLO has claimed credit for?

MA: Of course I disapproved. But there is also something else which must be looked at, a sad thing. In any conflict, when you are my opponent, I will say that you are a terrorist, that you are a weird individual, that you are a cockroach. Why? Because when I kill you, then I don't feel so bad because I am killing a terrorist, and a terrorist is less than a human being.

CI: The Nazis used a similar brainwashing technique to train the executioners to see Jews as subhuman.

MA: Exactly. And now the Jews are doing it to the Palestinians. It is from the mouth of Shamir himself to say that we are cockroaches. So it is all right to step on your enemy and crush him because he is like an insect, and you don't feel guilty about it.
That's why for people who are enemies, it is better not to meet in person because it is easier to kill someone if you don't see his eyes. For us Palestinians now, we always ask, "Who are the Jews?" We give them names. We used to think of them as just people who have money behind them, and that they themselves were worth nothing. We used to do this to build our psyche. If you see

someone else as bad or as dirt, then it's all right to get rid of the dirt, to clean the dirt.

CI: It's very different from, say, the Dalai Lama referring to the Chinese as "My friends the enemy." How do you think of the Israelis?

MA: I am one of those people who reminds the Palestinians that the Israeli is a human being. And we must see them, as well as ourselves, as human beings. The more you destroy another human being, the more you destroy yourself.

There are some hopeful signs. For instance, when we do any program between Palestinians and Israelis, each group has to work with the other. On one occasion we were planting olive trees in a village north of Jerusalem. We had an Israeli group who had volunteered to help us, and since they would be there during lunch time, we asked the Palestinians to prepare lunch for them. It took quite a while for the Palestinians to agree to this. Next we asked that they eat together, and that also took a lot of persuasion. And then when we asked the Israeli group to please not bring any food, explaining to them that the Palestinians would provide the food and that we would all eat together, some of the Israelis said, "No, no, no, we will bring our own food. We are afraid that some of the Palestinians will poison us."

So even in a small group where people are trying to help each other, there is a lot of mistrust; there is a lot of fear of the other. As it happened, when we planted the olive trees, the Israeli soldiers came and pulled all of the trees out. Still, I felt that the project was a success on the human level because the Israelis and the Palestinians did sit and eat together. Even some of the Israeli soldiers ate the Palestinian food.

But I don't think we are even close to calling the Israelis friends yet. There is still so much hatred, so much sadness, so much killing. I mean, imagine, we have over 500 people dead and 45,000 people in this uprising who have been hit—either maimed or punched or hit with bullets, or whatever. Now, those 45,000, when they look at the Israelis, will think, "You did this to me." So the longer the continuation of the *intifada*, the less we will be able to keep seeing the Israelis as human beings. That is a difficulty. That is why I am putting all my effort into going around the world to say that we have to support the peace process.

CI: What will happen if the nonviolent strategies fail?

MA: If we fail now with this uprising as a nonviolent struggle, then the individual whose brother or sister or somebody died will say, "Look, I tried to contain myself with all my discipline; now I am fed up. I'll go and get my gun, or I'll get ten or twenty bombs around me, and I'll go to a movie and let it go, and I'm willing to take two, three, or four Israelis with me."

So we are either going to have a disaster later on, or we are going to have peace. I think that now there is a change in the Israeli society, in the Israelis themselves. What is happening to us has happened to them. When, after waiting nearly 2,000 years to have their own nationality, they then deny ours and take our nationality away from us, it is painful for them. And in every Israeli, it is coming out now. Every Israeli has to deal with himself about this.

One day a young Palestinian boy, maybe thirteen years old, came to me crying. He was from one of the refugee camps and he had been throwing stones at an Israeli soldier. Three times he had thrown stones at the soldier and three times the soldier had beaten him up, the third time quite badly. On the fourth time, the boy again threw the stones and again the soldier chased him. When he was finally caught by the soldier, the boy expected to be really severely beaten this time, but instead the soldier hugged him. This boy came to me weeping, angry, not understanding. He said to me, "He hugged me!"

I said to the boy, "That Israeli soldier was a human being."

Joan Baez

Joan Baez's first act of civil disobedience occurred when she was a teenager in Palo Alto High School. The school had planned an air raid drill and had instructed the students to, upon hearing the alarms, walk home and wait in their cellars until after the estimated time an atomic blast would take.

Joan, who had a physicist father, and who, in addition, had studied the teachings of Mahatma Gandhi, decided that the air raid drill was "ludicrous." Having consulted her father's books, she determined that the time it took for a missile to get from Moscow to her high school was not time enough to walk home and get into the cellar. Furthermore, the concept of winning an atomic war went against all her beliefs. She boycotted the drill, staying in her seat at school while everyone else went home. The next day the story of her protest was on the front page of the local paper, which prompted letters to the editor saying that the high school had Communist infiltrators in it.

It is now some thirty years since that event. Recently I noticed a small news item in the San Francisco Chronicle *entitled, "Joan Baez Breaks the Rules." It seems that Ms. Baez, while on tour in Czechoslovakia in June 1989, invited the banned singer Ivan Hoffman to join her on stage. During her concert, she also dedicated songs to Czech prisoners and various political groups. For these transgressions, Czech authorities turned off the microphones at the folk festival where Joan Baez was performing, and the singer was charged with breach of contract by the concert organizers.*

* * *

Joan Chandos Baez was born on January 9, 1941, in Staten Island, New York. She spent much of her early childhood in upstate New York, where her father worked as a research physicist at Cornell University. Joan's mother became interested in Quaker meetings, and led her small flock of three girls and husband to the local meetinghouse each Sunday. As a young girl Joan thought the Quaker meetings were "a horror! A room full of drab grown-ups who sat like ramrods with their eyes closed."

Through contact with the Quakers, Joan's father, Dr. Albert Baez, became a pacifist. Rather than make money in the lucrative defense industry, he chose the route of the scholar, taking teaching jobs and working for UNESCO, helping to build a physics lab at the University of Baghdad in Iraq. It was during their year in Baghdad that Joan felt her "passion for social justice was born." She would later write of this experience in her autobiography *And a Voice to Sing With*: "In Baghdad, I saw animals beaten to death, people rooting for food in our family garbage pails, and legless children dragging themselves along the streets on cardboard, covered with flies feasting on open sores, begging for money." As a young girl she wrote in her journal, "When I think of God, I think of the earth as a very small thing. Then I think of myself as hardly a speck. Then I see there is no use for this tiny dot to spend its small life doing things for itself. It might as well spend its tiny amount of time making the less fortunate specks in the world enjoy themselves."

Another social awakening took place when the family moved from Baghdad to southern California. Joan attended a school which had a large Mexican population of immigrants and illegal aliens. Although she is half Mexican, Joan found herself ostracized by the Mexicans because she didn't speak Spanish, and by the whites because she looked Mexican and had a Mexican name. In time, the discovery of her singing voice began to drastically change her status with the students. She would take her ukulele to school and hang around at lunchtime waiting to be asked to sing. Soon she became something of a "jesterlike star" at school, and her days of being ostracized were over.

The next phase of her social conscience developed when Joan was a junior in high school. By then her family had again moved, this time to Palo Alto, California. Joan attended a three-day conference on world issues, sponsored by the Quaker's social action branch, the American Friends Service Committee. The main speaker at the conference was a twenty-seven year old black preacher from Alabama named Martin Luther King, Jr. "Everyone in the room was mesmerized," Joan wrote in her memoirs. "He talked about injustice and suffering, about fighting with the weapons of love...and about organizing a nonviolent revolution." After he finished speaking, Joan was on her feet, cheering and crying.

The following year Joan met Ira Sandperl at a Quaker Meeting. He was to become her "spiritual/political mentor for the next few decades." Ira was a Gandhi scholar and a proponent of organized nonviolence as the most important tool of the twentieth century. His dedication became infectious for Joan, who developed a solid foundation in nonviolence which she felt was both "moral and pragmatic." This foundation has informed the rest of her life's work.

After high school Joan moved with her family to Boston, where she attended Boston University's School of Drama, the only school which would accept her. Soon she was a regular at the coffee houses around Harvard Square in Cambridge, and eventually she was offered a job singing at a club in the middle of the Square. Within a short time, she became locally famous as a folksinger and dropped out of university forever. In the next few years her life rocketed to stardom and riches. By age twenty-one, she was on the cover of Time magazine, and cavorting with the likes of (then unknown) Bob Dylan and, soon thereafter, the Beatles. Nevertheless, her values remained true, even in choosing to sign with the obscure but high-quality company of Vanguard Records over the impersonal, super-successful Columbia with its glittering walls of gold records.

Joan Baez also worked for the civil rights movement in the early sixties. She marched with Dr. King in Grenada, Mississippi, and counts it as one of the medals she has awarded her own heart that she sang, "We Shall Overcome" to 250,000 people on that day in Washington in 1963 when King gave his "I Have a Dream" speech. Several years later Dr. King visited Joan Baez and Ira Sandperl when they were in jail in support of the anti-draft movement. In one year from that time, Martin Luther King, Jr. would be dead from an assassin's bullet. Joan Baez wrote these words to him in her autobiography: "You, more than anyone else who has been a part of my life, are my hope and inspiration."

In protest of the Vietnam War, Joan Baez began to withhold the sixty percent of her annual income taxes which would have gone to armaments. The decision, which she boldly explained in a letter to the Internal Revenue Service and simultaneously to the press in 1964, was financially costly to her for the duration of the war. Over the next years the IRS put a lien on her house, her car, and her land. IRS representatives came to her concerts and took cash from the register before the promoters could touch it. Although the government got the taxes, plus fines, Joan refused to voluntarily pay them; she knew that the efforts to which the IRS went to collect the money from her were also costly to the government.

In 1965 Joan Baez and Ira Sandperl co-founded the Institute for the Study of Nonviolence in Carmel, California. During the first four years of its inception, Joan served as a "teacher's aide" to Ira in the study of "nonviolence in all its aspects, from use in personal relationships to internationally organized methods of fighting oppression." Joan was giving about twenty concerts a year at this time. Most of the money she took in from her tours and record royalties she gave to nonviolent causes.

While serving time for refusing to support draft induction in 1967, Joan Baez met David Harris, also a war resister serving time. They fell in love, were married, and had a son, Gabriel. David Harris went on to do ten months in prison for draft resistance. Shortly after he returned home from prison, the couple split up. Joan has mostly lived alone since then. She is reconciled to solitude and writes in her autobiography, "I am made to live alone."

In 1972 Joan Baez visited Hanoi as a guest of the North Vietnamese for thirteen unforgettable days during the famous Christmas bombings. Night after night she spent huddled in shelters as B-52s carpet-bombed the city. The woman who had sung to a crowd of 500,000 in the middle of the night at Woodstock found herself singing in the middle of the night to frightened fellow refuge seekers in the strange city of Hanoi, while being bombed by her own countrymen. The album that came from that experience, "Where Are You Now, My Son?" made it on to the charts in 1973 and is one of which Joan Baez is most proud. The effects of her time in a war zone have stayed with her. To this day, she sometimes jolts out of deep sleep when she hears a plane overhead.

Seven years after her visit to North Vietnam, Joan Baez published an "Open Letter to the Socialist Republic of Vietnam" denouncing her former hosts' abuses of human rights and their failure to abide by the "principles of human dignity, freedom, and self determination that motivated so many Americans to oppose the government of South Vietnam." This letter provoked intense criticism of Joan Baez by American leftists, but like Gandhi, Joan Baez remains committed to truth, not to consistency.

It was also in 1972 that Joan Baez first became interested in the work of Amnesty International, the esteemed human rights organization. She later spent a year organizing Amnesty International West Coast. Over the years she attended vigils, concerts, and demonstrations for Mothers of the Disappeared in Argentina and dissidents all over the world, once phoning a surprised Andrei Sakarov and Elena Bonner in Moscow to sing, "We Shall Overcome."

In 1979 Joan Baez established her own organization, Humanitas International, in Menlo Park, California to "address human rights issues that other organizations could not take on." Her goals for Humanitas are to see the world "through both eyes" and to speak out "against repression anywhere in the world without regard to ideologies of either the right or the left." Under her leadership, Humanitas has lent support to Desmond Tutu's nonviolent freedom struggle in South Africa, Lech Walesa and the Solidarity movement in Poland, the Nuclear Weapons Freeze Campaign, the freedom fighters in Afghanistan, and many other causes on all sides of the political spectrum. Humanitas has also been outspoken in opposing U.S. intervention in Central America and has worked to expose human rights abuses in that troubled region. In 1981 Joan Baez traveled to Latin America on a human rights fact-finding tour where she spoke with activists, torture victims, and relatives of the "disappeared." A PBS documentary, "There But for Fortune: Joan Baez in Latin America" told the story of her journey.

As a spokesperson for nonviolence she has faced violence. The most recent event occurred in May 1988 when she was attacked by right wing Israelis who hurled eggs at her as she took part in a rally at a military base near Tel Aviv. Baez was there in support of Israeli soldiers who refused to serve in the occupied territories of the West Bank and Gaza Strip.

After an eight year hiatus from recording in the United States because she was unable to find a record company willing to back an album, Joan Baez has again been in the studio and on tour. Her new albums *Recently*, *Diamonds and Rust in the Bullring* (recorded live in Spain) and *Speaking of Dreams* (commemorating the thirtieth anniversary of her music career) continue to reflect her commitment to social issues.

I met with Joan Baez on a couple of occasions, although the day we were to do the interview she became ill and we were forced to do most of it by phone. A few months later, however, we spent a long Sunday afternoon in her home in Woodside, California. She lives simply in a rustic house with stained glass windows, surrounded by flowers and a garden. Joan made tea for us and we sat by the fireplace in her kitchen, gossiping about love and lamenting about the state of the world. She smiles easily with beautiful, sad eyes and sometimes seems lost in a private world of memories or reflections.

Her life has been entirely shaped by what she calls her "greatest gift," a singing voice. Yet her talent has been not only a boon on its own merits, but has put her in a position to give back in myriad ways through her concern for others and through her nonviolent social activism. Whether singing to a crowd of thousands, talking to the President of France about Mahatma Gandhi, or soothing a Vietnamese woman whose son lay dead under rubble left by a bomb, Joan Baez's voice is indeed a gift.

Interview with Joan Baez
September 8, 1988 • Woodside, California

Catherine Ingram: For a long time you've been deeply involved with organizations such as Humanitas and Amnesty International. Why have human rights been so compelling for you?

Joan Baez: The things I am involved with and that have been the priority for most of my life all have to do with nonviolence. For most of those things, I won't see any results in my lifetime; the end of the nation-state—we all have a good chuckle about that; nonviolent armies in place of the armies that do what they do now, etcetera. These are perfectly intelligent things that are not going to happen in my lifetime. But they will probably have to happen one day if there is going to be a human race.

I think that what is so compelling about human rights are the tangible results. One occasionally meets a prisoner...that's been a very powerful thing in my life.

I've learned lots of things—from the Russian dissidents to the Chilean prisoners. Probably the first one who was so moving and tangible to me was Mario Serundas from Brazil. I knew what he'd been through...

CI: In terms of torture...

JB: Yes, and then I met him, and he was all the things that I think people should be. And I can't understand how anyone would have done to him what they did. He wasn't ideological, wasn't rhetorical.

I met a wonderful man in the Gaza Strip, Nafez Assaily, from the Palestinian Center for the Study of Nonviolence. I could tell after twenty minutes of talking with him that he was a Gandhi type. He had been beaten and tortured while in police custody, and I asked him, "How did you relate to that?" He said, "I loved. I did the only thing they couldn't cope with. I actually loved the people who were torturing me, and I told them so. I forgave them consistently, and they were absolutely at their wits end of what to do with me."

The work of Amnesty International is something which continues to be really available to young people. It allows them to feel as though they can actually "do something." You see thirteen-year olds running around a U2 concert with a petition to get thirteen Guatemalans out of jail. Very tangible.

I think that during the course of my life, nonviolence is the most deeply rooted issue and it has to come up in everything. I couldn't work with Amnesty International, for instance, if they didn't have that clause about nonviolence, because that really is the foundation and the root of everything that I've ever done.

CI: Can you talk a bit about what you see are the salient points of nonviolence. I know you've studied this subject for nearly thirty years. Why does nonviolence make sense?

JB: I think the bottom line is—and this is probably a quote from Ira Sandperl—nobody should be allowed to kill someone over his or her idea of truth. It's the murdering that we've been doing in the name of wonderful things, such as truth.

Maybe I wouldn't be a nonviolent advocate and fanatic if it hadn't been for Gandhi, because up until then it really was dreams and talk. Ira always kidded in saying there was probably a caveman who refused to carry a club and everybody said, "Look at that nut." They didn't have communism yet so they had to call him something other than a communist!

What Gandhi said was, "Let's take this extraordinary idea and organize it." It hadn't been organized on a massive scale before. He proved that a moral argument is really enough. In fact, only when people are morally steeped in nonviolence to their own satisfaction—that what they believe is correct, when that's what they'll do until death—that's really the only time nonviolence holds. As a tactic, nonviolence will wear out if you don't really have a moral and spiritual foundation to it. It'll wear out when you want to do something a little bit flashy or expedient.

CI: What about in situations such as stopping a Hitler or stopping a Pol Pot?

JB: Well, you know what's extraordinary about us is that we are so unimaginative that we say things like, "You either had to let Hitler murder 6 million Jews—probably 13 million people altogether—or kill him." And that's as far as anybody can think. Never mind the fact that he never could have done what he did if people hadn't followed him around, saluting him.

I was having a discussion with somebody the other day about the American public and the silly candidates that we have running. I said, it has nothing to do with the candidates. It has to do with what the people want or what the people are willing to let go by because they don't care or are not interested. It was obviously the same thing with Hitler. For whatever reasons, he was allowed to flourish rather than being locked up in a padded cell or taken to a hospital or given some...

CI: ...love therapy or something. It's interesting to explore whether there are any exceptions to a nonviolent path. It sounds like you're saying no, that it's the way.

JB: Well, when you say it's the way, then you're obligated to come up with alternatives. For instance, when somebody says to a pacifist, "What would you have done in World War II?" or when somebody said to Gandhi, "Would nonviolence have 'worked' against Hitler?" Gandhi said, "Of course, but there would have been monumental losses." Yet there were anyway. People don't consider that a problem because that's war.

I always think of this example. Say in Latin America the priests begin to get revolutionary, and they start carrying guns. They get involved in armed struggle, the struggle continues on, and people start to die. It's considered part of the program. You kill people and some of your people also die. It's never considered anything out of the ordinary. If the priests, on the other hand, decide they're not going to use arms, they're going to organize nonviolently, as soon as somebody is killed in that context, generally the public reaction is, "Aha, I told you it wouldn't work." It takes only one death for them to say, "I told you that nonviolent stuff wouldn't work."

I was in, I think, Grenada, Mississippi and in one of the churches was a little list of names of people who had been killed in the civil rights struggle. It must have been four or five years into the struggle and there were only four or five names on that list—as opposed to 3,000 or 50,000, or whatever it might have been had it been a violent revolution. In practical fact, the history of nonviolent warfare is really in the favor of minimizing losses, despite what people would like to think.

CI: I'm sure you know the kind of courage and bravery that it takes to be nonviolent in the face of those who would harm you. It's so rare, because the animal instinct in us tends to rise up and fight back.

JB: The image that comes to my mind is of the hero of "Platoon," shivering in terror in the jungle with mosquitos all over his face. He had to be trained to be able to do what he did. Gandhi talks about meditation being as important to the nonviolent soldier as drill practice is to the conventional soldier. Nonviolence doesn't just happen. You don't just suddenly walk into the middle of conflict and know what to do.

I've discovered that the people who impress me with their nonviolent behavior in violent situations are inevitably people who have trained themselves and been involved in nonviolent strategies for awhile. You can't do it in a weekend workshop.

I agree that nonviolence is harder. I think that's why it takes so long to get it started. That's why people forget Gandhi or forget King or they belittle the concept of nonviolence. We've got thousands of years of training in organized violence, so we just assume that's what works. People say, "Well you're either a fighter or you're passive." But one must accept nonviolence as a form of fighting, and that's very hard for people to understand. However, compassion and joy can be as contagious as war fever.

CI: Let's talk about your spiritual practice, what your process has been, and what it is for you now.

JB: When my spiritual practice has been formalized enough to, say, take ten days of silence at Tassajara Buddhist monastery or someplace where I can be really quiet, or when I've gone regularly to Quaker meeting, or when I haven't been touring so crazily, then I can tell the difference for me in keeping my head on straight. It's really difficult on tour, but I find I need quiet time. Silence has been enormously important to me in whatever I'm doing because it keeps me from doing too much. It keeps things somehow calmed down. So I suppose the answer to your question really has to do with silence and my Quaker upbringing. Sometimes I prefer to do meditation and introspection in a group with people— Quakers, mostly, because they're trained in it. It's useful to not have somebody start thumbing through a magazine because they're not used to the silence.

CI: Isn't that amazing? Silence is like a mind bath, quite necessary for most of us.

JB: It is amazing. But some people simply can't handle it. They start drumming fingers, you know, or they say, "Oh I was silent on the way in to work."

CI: I've read somewhere that you've expressed concern for the increase in human rights violations in the world. What do you attribute the increase to? Do you have any sense of why this would be happening, or are we just more informed about it now?

JB: I would assume it has some direct correlation to the acceptance of worldwide violence. The violence is just monumental. Yet at the moment some people are very optimistic about some changes in the world, and I would have to agree. Some of the changes are very exciting.

CI: Such as those in the Soviet Union, Iran-Iraq...

JB: Yes, and the rise of the U.N. out of obscurity. I do think it has to be connected with the major powers deciding to play chess for awhile rather than blow each other's brains out. I think that's all good. Yet at the same time, all of these spin-off wars where people are gassing each other and slitting each other's throats are just extraordinary. There have been 127 wars since World War II ended, with war defined as a conflict in which 1,000 or more deaths occurred. They are called "active conflicts," but they are actually wars where people are killing each other. This contributes greatly to human rights violations. When I first started working with Amnesty, one of the phrases we used to emphasize was that there was more torture worldwide now than there had been since medieval times.

CI: In terms of percentages?

JB: I think so. The hopeful thing at the moment is that most governments respond to pressure—most don't want to be exposed, and Amnesty does expose them—and that respecting human rights is now obligatory. The issue of human rights is on the agenda of all major powers when they meet to talk about anything. They no longer ignore it or make it a separate issue.

CI: That's certainly an historical breakthrough, isn't it.

JB: I think so.

CI: As you know, the First World is living largely on the energy and resources of the Third and Fourth Worlds,[1] and that has also produced tremendous violence. It is probably why the policy in Central America, for instance, is so dictatorial and repressive. We live lives of such luxury here in this country. As Americans, we live in the courtyards and palaces of the world. In our cultural context, it's very hard to live simply, to really renounce beyond a certain point. Will you speak about this and about our individual responsibility?

JB: I have my questions about all of that. It seems to me that the people who live the most contentedly with themselves and with the world are those who have made an effort to come to terms with the question of inequality and of who gets what. They're people who make use of their own property, who grow things and who are

---

[1]Generally speaking, the Third World refers to the developing poor nations, such as India or Pakistan, while the Fourth World refers to the poorest countries which are not considered to be in a stage of economic development, such as Ethiopia.

very conscious of ecology. My father lives in a marsh which is an ecological reserve. He told me something the other day which was very moving. He said that in spite of his many years of Quaker training, he had always somehow felt that human beings took priority over the other animal species. As he studies more, he has begun to see that all the birds in the marsh and all the animals heading for the list of extinction are a part of the whole. It's not that easy to separate them out anymore. I feel very unqualified to talk on the subject as I'm flapping around the world on airplanes which pour out their fumes. I'm living in two different worlds—at home trying to conserve on gas and various things, and then getting on an airplane. Or I face conflicts such as, do I stay in a luxury hotel, which I love, or do I...

CI: ...rough it and be exhausted in third class.

JB: Exactly. And I generally opt for luxury. Not on a mega-level, but I like to stay in nice, comfortable, clean places. In other words, I'm jealous of Gandhi's ability to be able to really shift from poverty to whatever without batting an eye.

CI: That kind of simple non-attachment to luxury is a value that you would like to inculcate more in your life?

JB: Well, I tell you, I am involved in it to some degree or I probably would be living in Beverly Hills, but I find that distasteful. I live the way I'm comfortable, which always shocks people when they get here, because it's rustic. It usually has nothing to do with the images they had in mind, but for me it's luxury. I have everything I need. And then, you see, I think that how I live at home isn't the most important point. In other words, it's what I do in the world that matters.

There are times when one must be willing to give things up, and I have been. A time of going to Israel, say, is a time when you know it's not going to be luxurious. It's going to be work. Yet, it's something that I love.

When I traveled for three months in the Mideast, the places I wanted to go back to were Turkey and the Gaza Strip. It has to do with what Gandhi said: he found God in the eyes of the poor. Those are the places which were so moving that they were just unbearable. And it had nothing to do with luxury.

CI: You've also visited the refugee camps on the border of Thailand.

JB: It's the same thing. You're reminded: bare bones. My mom worked in the Somalian refugee camps in Ethiopia and in the Cambodian camps in Thailand. I asked her which one she preferred, and she said the Somalian camps, and when I asked her why, she said it was because they were simpler.

CI: Our dilemma is that even though we're aware that we're part of the problem, it's hard to be a greater part of the solution at the same time.

JB: But I think you have to find priorities in everything that you do. I remember getting very cynical at one time. I spent a few years feeling very guilty about not living in voluntary poverty because many people around me had begun that whole process. And then I realized that a lot of them were a real pain. All they did was live in poverty. I then discovered that I was much more interested in other people's *in*voluntary poverty than in my own voluntary poverty.

My personal interest in this comes and goes in waves. I used to give away everything and then buy it all back three months later.

CI: What about other people's projections about you? Does being well-known and visually recognizable hinder your activism? Do people meet you and only see the persona of Joan Baez?

JB: Oh probably, but I've made it one of my hobbies to just break that down in every situation of meeting new people or being seen on the street. It started years ago when Dylan and I were approached by two screaming fans. Bob's reaction was very traditional—Let's run, let's get outa here. And I said, "Don't be silly," and I put my hand out to them to shake hands. Well, it sort of wrecked the fun, you know, because they were into being screaming fans, and I was into saying hello. Then after the balloon had deflated, I think they liked it because then we just chatted.

As soon as you defuse those situations, everybody realizes it's much more intelligent. It almost always works. Sometimes in a case where there are lots of people, the steam engine is already going and you can't control it. But even then it can turn out fine. Once in Turkey we had 26,000 people at a concert, and they all began to come onto the stage. They were so starved for recognition that when I sang a Turkish song to them, they began standing up and shouting in Turkish, "Freedom, Peace, Love." Nobody could arrest them for it because the police were all immobilized by this concert. It was really a massive demonstration; they just couldn't hold themselves in. Kids walked out on the stage—one tied a kerchief around my neck and gave me a kiss; another gave me a hat; another gave me a flower. And then at the end, the crowd just started moving onto the stage, so I said, "Please, everybody stay. Everybody stay." The police were useless. They were used to either doing nothing or beating everybody up, so we asked them to do nothing. But those big crowds are a wonderful challenge. That's also training—to try and get a sense of the crowd and give them as much room as possible. Recognize them, and usually it works.

CI: That's brave.

JB: Oh, it was exciting. I was so teary that visit. I got a letter from the woman who engineered my stay there. She's a very left-wing Turkish lady, a well-known writer. Her letter said that after I left she put an article in the paper asking, "Did you hear her?" which she addressed specifically to the students who are in jail in Turkey. And she has received hundreds of letters, ninety percent of them from the prison, saying, "Yes we heard her." Now she's doing a TV special called "Yes we heard her."

CI: You're fortunate to have both the opportunity and the talent to be able to give in that way.

JB: I have been given such a gift. This last weekend a very close friend of mine lost her sister-in-law to suicide. She had lost her son to suicide twenty-five years ago, and I had been there. So I took the guitar and I went down. It's not easy for me because I can't allow myself to feel anything, or I won't be able to sing. So I sang and everybody sobbed, and there were rivers of tears, and wet hankies. But I realized the way they responded had nothing to do with me at all. It was to the power of the gift that they responded.

CI: Another part of having a gift like that is the understanding it brings of one's own emptiness, the experience of yourself as an empty vessel which something is pouring through. I would think that the understanding of emptiness is the greater gift actually.

Do you feel that people in the public eye should speak out, and do you see any trend in that direction? It seems that a lot of movie stars and people who are well-known are starting to take up social causes.

JB: Well, I'm awfully cynical about most of them, frankly. Of course they should speak out, but the likelihood of them having anything to say is pretty dim. If we're talking about training, their training has been in limousines. However, people such as Sting and Peter Gabriel are truly connected. Gabriel is a very serious man, running up and down the hotel lobbies when we were in Atlanta on the national tour [for Amnesty International] and getting signatures to save the life of a mentally retarded black kid on death row.

But, I'm dubious in general because these are very empty times. They're so empty that when somebody says anything of substance, everybody says, "Oh, wow, golly, gee whiz, that person's really committed." On the one hand, to be cynical is useless because it's not going to encourage anybody to do anything. But on the other hand, to be dewy-eyed about situations that are really self-serving isn't useful either.

CI: Joan, you have been on the scene for a long time. What has happened since the sixties? Do you have any historical perspective on where the hope and the idealism and the commitment went?

JB: Well, I've never studied history, but I can assume that it has something to do with the fact that things go in cycles. I also sense that America has made itself into a cocoon partially to protect itself from its own reaction and world reaction to the war in Vietnam. We simply never handled it. We literally had a homecoming party for the Vietnam veterans twenty years after the fact.

I also think that being a country which has sustained this "We are the greatest superpower in the world" image for a very long time is taking its toll, because we're not going to come to terms with the fact that we're slipping.

You know, when I was in Turkey I met a Kurdish rug dealer who was very bright. And at one point he said, "What's the difference between the American public and yoghurt?" I said I didn't know. And he said, "Yoghurt has culture." It's no small secret—it's a widely known fact—that it's falling apart here, culturally, educationally, spiritually, not to mention...

CI: ...economically.

JB: Right, which is the only thing that people basically relate to. It has them so terrified that they're just not going to look at it or deal with it. But I think a lot was invested in the war in Vietnam and trying to protect our image, and then all these years afterwards in not admitting what a mistake it was.

And it's such a land of plenty that it is bound to produce laziness. Why bother? People wonder why hasn't another song been written like "We Shall Overcome" or "Let It Be." It's because those songs don't come out of nothingness. They come out of struggle and concern and despair, and also out of groundswells of togetherness, movements. I mean, "We Shall Overcome" was a part of the most powerful movement and the only nonviolent movement in this country.

CI: You were part of that movement. What were some of your impressions of Martin Luther King, Jr.?

JB: Well mainly, the fact that he was funny. I've seen lots of footage of him, but only once, on some obscure documentary, have I seen his clowning. But that's how he survived, and that's how they survived. He also survived with prayer, but his funny part, it's just a pity that people didn't get to see that. I understand him thinking that he couldn't afford to do that. He was a minister and a preacher. He had this thing he had to do, and I think that in that society and in those times, maybe it would have been incorrect for him to loosen up. I know that's how I felt for years about myself. I was afraid to clown around because maybe I wouldn't be taken seriously in all the political and social work.

CI: Your instincts on that may have been right. It's a little sad that humor would have to be concealed in order for someone to be taken seriously. I would have loved to have seen Martin Luther King being silly.

JB: Oh yes, he was absolutely human. Just lovely. As for me, I simply couldn't tolerate the fact that he had died. I wouldn't deal with it until eight years after his death. At the time of his funeral I said, "Funeral! Phooey on all that. I hate funerals. I'm going to go write a song."

Thich Nhat Hanh

Thich Nhat Hanh sits talking to a group of students under the Bodhi tree in Bodh Gaya, India. It is believed that Gautama, the Buddha, was enlightened at that spot, that all Buddhas previous to him had been enlightened there, and that all future Buddhas will one day be enlightened there as well. Adjacent stands the Mahabodhi Temple, built by Emperor Ashoka over 2,000 years ago, around which Tibetan pilgrims circumambulate and do hundreds of thousands of prostrations. Buddhist practitioners come here from all over the world to seek the state of wakefulness exemplified by the life of the Buddha. For more than 2,500 years, this spot has been a beacon for people committed to understanding their minds.

Thich Nhat Hanh, or Thây as he is affectionately called, is speaking today about dependent co-arising, or the interconnectedness of all things. This was a favorite theme of the Buddha's, one which is said to have been the cornerstone of his enlightenment. Scholars spend entire lifetimes studying this doctrine, a twelve-link schema of cause and effect which describes the interrelatedness of all aspects of life.

Thich Nhat Hanh presents dependent co-arising in a uniquely simple and elegant way, so that even a newcomer can grasp it. "Can you see the sun in a grain of rice?" he asks. "For without the sun on the rice fields, there would be no rice. Can you see the cloud in a wooden table? For without the cloud there would be no rain to water the tree, and there would be no wood to make the table."

As he spoke I looked around at the group of friends and students sitting with him. They were on a month-long pilgrimage led by Thây to the seven Buddhist holy spots. Half of the group were Vietnamese refugees; half were Westerners, mostly Americans. Although our native countries are many thousands of miles apart, we were clearly intercon-

*nected. What links existed between us? What links of pain?
What links of understanding? And what forces had
brought us to sit here under the auspicious Bodhi tree and
listen to a talk on interconnectedness, while nearby a
group of young Tibetan monks watched us, giggling all the
while, and an old Tibetan woman, who had gone mad,
danced crazily on the temple grounds?*

* * *

The most obvious reason we found ourselves together in
this place was Thich Nhat Hanh. Zen master, poet, and
peace activist, Nhat Hanh in his straightforward presentation of Dharma has become one of the most important
Buddhist teachers in the West. His presence is elfin, yet
confident; ephemeral, yet rooted, like a tree. Richard
Baker Roshi described him as "a cross between a cloud, a
snail, and a piece of heavy machinery."

Thich Nhat Hanh was born on October 11, 1926, in a
village in central Vietnam. His childhood was happy,
largely due to the support of his loving mother. At the
age of sixteen, he and four close friends became monks,
because they "thought that would be an enjoyable thing
to do," and he was given the Buddhist name Thich Nhat
Hanh. *Thich* is a transliteration of *Shak(ya)*, the family
name of the Buddha, and all Vietnamese monks and
nuns take this name. *Nhat Hanh* means "one action."

As a young monk, Thich Nhat Hanh assiduously studied the way of mindfulness, noting carefully each movement of his body and mind, using meditation practice
and short verses to help remind him to return to the
present moment. However, much of the monastic system
of training seemed archaic to him, and when he suggested to his superiors that the education of the clergy
include modern Western philosophy, science, and literature, they were unresponsive. So Thây and a few friends
left the monastery and went to Saigon, where they lived
in an abandoned temple.

During that time Nhat Hanh edited several publications, including the official monthly magazine of the six

largest Buddhist associations in Vietnam. He also published four books before he was twenty years old,
including a tract entitled *Buddhism for Today*. He even
wrote short stories and novels at a time when monks
were prohibited from reading novels. His first two books
of poetry, *The Autumn Flute* and *Buddhist Teachings in
Folk Poetry Form*, were also printed during this time.

In the 1950s Thich Nhat Hanh founded the first Buddhist high school in Vietnam, offering an alternative to
the French colonial system of education. He also
founded a monastery in central Vietnam, which served
as a place for monks, nuns, and laypersons to renew
themselves spiritually. Within a few years, the church's
leaders recognized the importance of the curriculum
Nhat Hanh had suggested, and they invited him to help
found Van Hanh Buddhist University in Saigon.

In 1961, at the age of thirty-five, Thich Nhat Hanh
left Vietnam for the first time and came to the U.S. for
graduate study in comparative religion at Princeton and
Columbia. He greatly enjoyed his studies and teaching
responsibilities, but after two and a half years, his
monk-colleagues in Vietnam urged him to come back to
help them with their work for peace in the country. Nhat
Hanh returned home to his war-torn land.

In 1963, Thich Nhat Hanh wrote *Engaged Buddhism*,
coining the term that described the Buddhist nonviolent
work for peace and social justice. The monks and nuns
were confronted with a choice of continuing to meditate
in their temples while hearing the cries of those injured
and dying just outside, or to help those in need. They resolved to do both, to meditate while in service to others.
With the help of a number of young people, Nhat Hanh
founded the School of Youth for Social Service in 1964,
which by 1975 had attracted 10,000 members. Under its
auspices, college-age monks, nuns, and students went out
into the countryside, first to provide education and
health care, and later to care for the wounded and help
rebuild the villages. One village was rebuilt four times,
and each time it was bombed again.

In 1966, Nhat Hanh was invited to tour the United States by the Fellowship of Reconciliation and Cornell University to educate Americans about the conditions of the war and to plead for an end to the fighting. He met with Secretary of Defense Robert McNamara, renowned Trappist monk/scholar Thomas Merton, Senators William Fulbright and Edward Kennedy, and perhaps most importantly, Dr. Martin Luther King, Jr. One fruit of this visit was the publication in English of *Vietnam: Lotus in a Sea of Fire*, a book which became an underground classic among Americans and Vietnamese seeking a truly peaceful solution to the war.

The meeting with Dr. King began a friendship of mutual respect. In fact, soon after their initial conversation, Dr. King began to speak out against the war in Vietnam, an effort which provoked criticism both from people inside his support base who felt that the Vietnam issue was diversionary from civil rights, and from his opponents who felt it was traitorous to question the U.S. government's role there. King, of course, remained undeterred from his commitment to the issue, although he recognized that he had likely escalated his own personal danger. In January 1967, Dr. King nominated Thich Nhat Hanh for the Nobel Peace Prize, saying, "I do not personally know of anyone more worthy of the Nobel Peace Prize than this gentle Buddhist monk from Vietnam."

But Nhat Hanh's frankness in America and in Europe, where he met with Pope Paul VI, prohibited his return to Vietnam, as he would have been imprisoned upon arrival. Having been granted asylum in France, he has now lived in exile from his country for twenty-three years.

Following the war, Thich Nhat Hanh sought to find ways of helping his destitute countrymen still in Vietnam, as well as those attempting to escape. He and his colleagues tried to send support to hungry children, but these efforts were thwarted. As a result, they developed an underground network of Buddhist social workers, who delivered parcels of food at the risk of imprisonment. Nhat Hanh and his colleagues also endeavored to rescue boat people in the Gulf of Siam, an effort which did not come to fruition for reasons he explains in the following interview. Uncertain how to continue, Thich Nhat Hanh entered a five-year period of retreat at his hermitage in central France, where he spent the time meditating, gardening, writing, and occasionally receiving visitors.

During this time, Nhat Hanh was told about many human rights abuses in Vietnam, and he, in turn, encouraged his colleagues to investigate and expose these violations. His advocacy for human rights won him the respect of many people in Vietnam, and he became a symbol of inspiration there. Consequently, the Vietnamese government viewed Thich Nhat Hanh as a threat and twice spread rumors that he had died, once in 1982, prior to government efforts to establish their own Buddhist church, and again in 1984, just before the arrests of a number of prominent monks, nuns, and writers.

In 1982, Thich Nhat Hanh again came to America to attend a conference. That trip impressed on him the enormous interest in Buddhism among Americans, and he agreed to return the following year to lead meditation retreats and give a few public lectures. The next trip to America would be the beginning of a new phase of Thich Nhat Hanh's life and would inspire Westerners and Asians alike in "engaged Buddhism." Teaching them meditative sitting and walking, conscious breathing and smiling, Nhat Hanh exhorts students to be wakeful in their actions in the world—not only in helping others but also in the small details of daily life—and to recognize how each of our lives impacts on others. He has begun to attract thousands of students who find inspiration in his simple presentation, in his lucid insights, and in the quiet power of his person, as when he says: "The real miracle is not to walk on water or in thin air, but to walk on the earth."

It was on his second visit to America, in 1983, that I first met and interviewed Thich Nhat Hanh at the Zen Center in Mt. Tremper, New York. Over the years I have kept up with his teachings (through friends) and his writings (through his numerous books), and so it was with special delight that I traveled to Bodh Gaya, India in November 1988 to spend one week of the Buddhist pilgrimage with Thich Nhat Hanh and to interview him a second time. We spoke for about an hour in his room at the Vietnamese Temple.

Nhat Hanh is, at this writing, sixty-three years old. Seeing him, this is almost impossible to believe, as he has a youthfulness of face and movement that suggests someone fifteen years younger. But his words evince the wisdom of his years. Moreover, he speaks in poetry, even in a language which is not his own, the poetry which comes from inner stillness.

Interview with Thich Nhat Hanh

November 10, 1988 • Bodh Gaya, India

Catherine Ingram: Thây, in our last interview you spoke of how the bananas grown in Vietnam are used in exchange for arms from the Soviets. What are other examples you see of these kinds of interconnections, socially and politically, in which the superpowers benefit from exploitation of Third World countries?

Thich Nhat Hanh: The eating of meat and the drinking of alcohol have to do with this, because to reduce the consumption of meat and alcohol by fifty percent could change the situation in the Third World. So much grain could then be shared. Even small things have to do with exploitation—drinking your tea, using toilet paper, or picking up your newspaper. You know, the Sunday edition of *The New York Times* is very large and heavy. It represents the destruction of a forest.

But I think that the Third World is also trying to exploit the First World. Each is trying to do his or her best to exploit the other. It is only a matter of who is more clever and can succeed.

CI: We do see those situations being here in India. We often feel that people try to exploit us.

TNH: That's true. We must all learn to benefit from the good things other people can offer, but without making them suffer. There are many things that I wish the First World could "exploit" and "profit" from the Third World. For example, here in India people are so very poor, and when Westerners arrive they have the impression that they are superior. But if we look deeply, we may see that some of those who have a superior attitude are not as happy as those who are extremely poor. I saw a young man in Benares trying to sell something to a Westerner. He acted as if he would die if he could not sell this thing. But I noticed that when he was not successful in selling to the Westerner, he turned away and he sang a song to himself. He wasn't sad at all.

CI: He went away singing.

TNH: Yes. Selling seemed to be a kind of theater to him.

And when I arrived at the airport, the immigration officer looked at my passport, then he looked away and talked with someone over the desk, and he sang a song, and then another. He only put the stamp on my passport after singing two songs. [laughing]

In the West, some people commit suicide because of emotional problems or due to stress. People here seem much more relaxed. They don't run fiercely after things. They can be happy with very few things. If the First World could exploit this attitude from the Third World, that would be great.

Here in India, I am especially aware of the children. I think that if we want to help them, we should not just give them rupees. Instead, we should help with things like family planning, so that one woman will not give birth to more children than she has the capacity to bring up. If the children had adequate medical care, especially preventative medicine, I think people would be much happier than in the West. With family planning and medical care for the poor, I think that life here would be much more enjoyable.

And the children, of course, try to exploit the tourists in their own way. I would not blame only Westerners as exploiting. People exploit each other.

There are many other ways of exploiting. We exploit the soil, the land, but we can also preserve the land. A farmer is exploiting the land; there are two ways of doing that, and one is better because it gives back to the land. In order to live happily with another person or with nature, you have to try to preserve its beauty, its resources.

It's similar to begging. You know that I am a beggar myself, because *bhikkhu* in Pali means "beggar."[1] We beg for food, and in doing this we cultivate our humanity, our modesty. We try to learn and to practice the spirit of equality, because when we are begging we have no right to choose just the rich houses. The Buddha told his disciples to look on every house equally. We have to stand in front of one house and then move to the next one, and if the next one is very poor, we see it equally. We may have the opportunity there to meet with people in order to share the Dharma.[2] Begging has many qualities like that. Begging can make life beautiful. We do not condemn begging; it is the way it is done which matters.

CI: The motivation when someone is begging...

TNH: Yes. So when, as tourists, we behave in a way that encourages children to beg, I think that is bad. Things are not good or bad in themselves, but we make them good or bad...

CI: ...by our intentions.

---

[1] *Bhikkhu* generally refers to a Buddhist monk. In most Buddhist traditions, monks receive only the food which is offered to them by laypeople. Pali was the language in use during the time of the Buddha.

[2] "Dharma" is the Sanskrit word for "the truth," or "the law."

TNH: Yes. Or by our lack of insight. If we make another person poor, we become poor ourselves. If they lose their dignity, we lose our dignity.

CI: We also see exploitation by the big pharmaceutical and chemical companies' sales of drugs and chemicals which have been outlawed in Western countries and are now being dumped in poor countries where they have not been banned. In addition, there is the problem with infant formulas. Women all over the Third World have been told that in order to make their babies healthy, they should use infant formula. So the mothers mix this extraordinarily expensive formula with contaminated water, which is often all that is available, and the children die from the contaminated water. Instead they should be drinking their mothers' milk which gives them the natural immunities they need and is much healthier for them. Infant formula is actually causing the deaths of babies in the Third World. There have been occasional boycotts in the West which have stopped some of this, but infant formula seems to be coming into fashion again.

These are other examples of how sometimes the greed of large corporations, for instance, can exploit the poor, less educated societies.

TNH: That has to do with the ethics of consuming. By consuming, we participate in that kind of destruction and exploitation. To me, practicing mindfulness in the act of consuming is the basic act of social justice. The exploitation of markets in the East is something most of us do. But the consumers play a very important role if they are aware of what is going on. If they learn how to consume properly, through their way of consuming they can stop that kind of exploitation. So it's not useful to protest verbally—"You should not exploit people in the Third World; you should not pollute." Saying things like that will not help. Only by attacking the problem at the roots can we make a difference—that is to educate our-selves in the way of consuming.

CI: So that we would perhaps boycott certain goods.

TNH: I think we should be very careful in selecting the kind of items we consume, and learn to consume less. That is the Buddha's teaching. You can be satisfied with fewer things and be happier.

Happiness is not an individual matter. You cannot be happy individually. Let's talk of a married couple, for instance. How can one person in the couple be happy if the other is not happy? It's very clear. The only way to be happy is to make the other person happy, and then you will be happy, too. Our situation in the world is like that. People know quite clearly that if the Third World collapses and cannot pay its debt, then the whole mone-tary system will collapse, and the First World will col-lapse also. So taking care not to exploit the Third World and trying to help them stand on their own feet also helps the First World.

Happiness is not an individual thing. Many people have seen that. Only, how can we practice it? We must sit together to find ways to educate ourselves, to educate our friends and our children.

CI: In our last interview you spoke of a kind of karma which exists between your country and mine, Vietnam and the United States. Joining you on this pilgrimage are many Vietnamese and many Americans. You are planning to do a retreat for Vietnam veterans. Will you speak more about this karma between our two coun-tries? Do you see a healing taking place?

TNH: Healing is the topic of the retreat. Really, I don't think that I have to reconcile myself with Americans, because I have no anger toward them. I see that both countries are victims of a wrong perception of each other's reality. Vietnamese don't understand Americans, and Americans don't understand Vietnamese. Maybe by trying to help each other, we make each other suffer, like husband and wife. [laughing] You love, yet you make the other suffer. You say to the other, "You should be like this in order to be happy." Or, "We should liberate you like this so that you can become happy."

The problem is not really to reconcile but to heal. To heal and to try to look more deeply to see the roots of our suffering, because the suffering continues in Vietnam as well as in America. And it will continue for a long time if we don't make a root diagnosis in order to give the proper kind of care. A retreat like that will be a chance to sit together, to breathe together, to walk together in order to look back. To look back not on the past but to look back at ourselves, because looking deeply on ourselves we see all the roots; we see the past and the future. And seeing that way, we would not continue to blame each other or blame one side or the other. We see that because of a lack of understanding, we have caused suffering to ourselves and to others.

A person once asked me about the problems in Central America and about what America should do. I said, "Well this time, try not supporting the anti-communists; support the communists—because your money will destroy the people you want to support. Because of your money, the anti-communist government in South Vietnam became corrupted. Therefore, this time try it the other way. Give the money to the communists, and they will become corrupted, and the other side will win!" Although I said this as a joke, there are veins of truth in it. It is an invitation for us to look back.

Without being too involved with your money and your technology, try to be humble in your way of looking. Be aware that you may have a wrong perception of what has happened. Try to look more deeply. Consider a government under pressure, preoccupied with so many urgent things and people who feel they have to fight. When you have the kind of insight that that government would need, then you can work for the government from your heart, advising them what to do in a kind way so that they will listen. To love your government may be one of the most important things you can do. But the peace movement often just hates the government, shouting and trying to...

CI: ...bring it down.

TNH: Yes. If we love our government instead, what we tell them, what we write to them, will be in a kind of language they can understand. If we have understanding and if what we say is important, our government will have to listen to us, not because we threaten them but because we are a source of energy to help them realize important matters. All these things we have to consider. It should be a popular movement.

CI: Do you still see this antagonism toward the government today? I know that in the late sixties and early seventies, that was much the case, but now it seems there is a lot of apathy. Do you feel that this kind of split between the peace movement and the U.S. government still exists? That perhaps the peace movement hasn't quite learned "being peace"?

TNH: Do you see the peace movement or any peace organization trying to be supportive of the government, trying to advise the government on what to do and what not to do in a spirit of peace? If so, then there is a difference.

I think there *are* people who see that way. We have to bring them together in a conference where we drink tea and practice walking meditation and smile, and breathe, so we can consider these things.

CI: I know that you influenced Martin Luther King, Jr. in his understanding of Vietnam and what was happening there. Can you say how he influenced you?

TNH: Yes. Prior to meeting him I had written to him from Vietnam. The letter was published with the title, "Searching for the Enemy of Man." A year later, I met him in Chicago and we held a press conference together.

It was then that he came out against the war in Vietnam. At that time, many of his colleagues did not think it was wise, but he did it anyway. We were very close after that. The last time I saw him was in Geneva for the *Pacem en Terris* [Latin: Peace on Earth] Conference. He invited me to have breakfast with him one morning, and we had a long conversation. I said to him, "You know, Martin, in Vietnam they consider you a bodhisattva." I was glad that I had the opportunity to tell him that, because three months later he was assassinated. The day I learned of his assassination I was quite angry because we had a person like that and we did not know how to preserve him.

It was so easy to communicate with Martin. You could tell him just a little and he understood the things you did not say. I was also very influenced by his understanding of nonviolence, but it was not through words. His enthusiasm, his sincerity, his presence made me believe in the path of nonviolent action.

To me, people's general understanding of the principle of nonviolence is very superficial. People tend to think of nonviolence more as a technique of action, rather than a source of strength. There is so much focus on the distinction between nonviolence and violence, between nonviolent people and violent people. But in reality it's not easy to take sides like that. One can never be sure that one is completely on the side of nonviolence or that the other person is completely on the side of violence. Nonviolence is a direction, not a separating line. It has no boundaries.

When I eat a vegetarian dish, I might think that I am nonviolent in my eating. I do not eat living beings such as chickens or cows, and I may be proud of eating only vegetables. But if I look more deeply, I see that my way is not entirely nonviolent. When I boil the vegetables, I boil a lot of living beings. Nevertheless, by being vegetarian, I am going in the direction of more nonviolence, less violence. I cannot say that I am completely nonviolent. Even the Buddha, while he was walking and

drinking and eating, could not be entirely nonviolent
due to what it takes to be alive.

So when we look at the Pentagon or the Army and see
them as our enemy, that's not fair. That's not true.
There are army generals or army commanders who conduct military operations to avoid the killing of innocent
people, and there are others who only want to succeed in
their military operation and are ready to sacrifice any
number of civilians. So considering these two kinds of
people, we can see that one is more violent than the
other and that it is still possible to practice nonviolence
as an army officer.

Why not be a friend of the army in order to help the
army to commit less violence? So, too, you have to be a
friend of your president, a friend of your congressperson.
You cannot draw a limit and say that these are people I
oppose, and these are people I support.

CI: Basically, you are saying that we are all participating
in some degrees of violence and nonviolence. Everybody
is at whatever stage they're at, and each is not that different from any other.

TNH: Yes, so that we do not leave anyone out, so that we
do not consider anyone as an enemy, even the person
who is very violent. We have to go to him or her. If not,
who will be helping that person become more nonviolent? If we work for nonviolence on the basis of anger,
we go against ourselves.

You know, the peace movement is supposed to be nonviolent, but somehow it has gathered strength from its
anger. If you are angry, you can shout, and so on. That's
not peaceful, because peace is the *way*, not an aim, not
an end. If you think that non-peaceful means bring
peace, you're wrong.

To have a good foundation, a peace movement must be
based on insight and the understanding which is the
foundation of love and concern. There must be those in
the movement who really practice looking deeply. If they
are too busy, they cannot do that. It does not mean that

they have to spend a lot of time in the meditation hall, but it means that while writing something, saying something, doing something, looking at something, they have to look deeply.

CI: What was Gandhi's influence on you?

TNH: Maybe if Gandhi had not succeeded, my being influenced by him would have been less in the beginning. That early influence was not in terms of theory or insight, but of success—which is not the deepest kind of influence, because you cannot judge the value of an action based on whether or not it brings success. You have to judge the value of an action in relation to the action itself. At that time I could not do that, so I was influenced in that more superficial way. That is not such a good thing.

I think we may fail in our attempt to do things, yet we may succeed in the correct action when the action is authentically nonviolent, based on understanding, based on love. But sometimes we need a few more conditions to be successful, and if the time is not right we cannot succeed. For example, in Vietnam our nonviolent struggle for peace was participated in by many young, educated people. Sometimes we took suffering on ourselves in order to move other people, such as when some of my monk brothers committed self-immolation, and so on. But we were caught between the two major powers of the world. And although from time to time our voices could be heard from outside, those outside who were strong enough to support us were divided also. You Americans wanted to join this side or the other side. You wanted peace, but you thought that a victory by one side would bring peace more quickly. So it was kind of lonely, and we needed a few more conditions, such as your support, in order to succeed. Looking back, I see that the nonviolent struggle for peace in Vietnam was a beautiful one. It did not succeed very much, not because it was wrong, but because it did not have all the conditions needed.

CI: Unlike Gandhi who happened to have a lot of conditions which were right in that historical moment in time.

TNH: Yes, unlike my action in the Gulf of Siam. In 1977, I conducted an operation to rescue boat people. At that time, not many people knew about the presence of the boat people. But we knew. So we secretly started a project in which we sent out boats to pick up refugees. The Singapore government, the Malaysian government, the Indonesian government did not know what we were doing or they would have chased us away. We picked up hundreds of refugees and we hoped to secretly ship them either to Guam or to Australia. We planned that on their arrival, we would inform the press so that the world would pay attention to their plight and they would not be chased away and sent back, as had been practiced by Malaysia, Indonesia, and other countries. They had sent back thousands of people who subsequently died in the ocean.

We were about to succeed, but because of some kind of leak made by one of our friends to the press, the press spoiled everything. They tried to hunt down our action, and they published information about what we were doing, and then we were exposed. The police came at midnight and quartered me and my associate. I had to hand over the refugees to the UNHCR [United Nations High Commission on Refugees] who kept them for months and years in the camps in Malaysia. It was very painful. Yet, we had conducted the operation in meditation. We lived, I can say, like holy people, in the mode of prayer, of meditation, all the time, because we knew that human lives depended on our mindfulness. If we were not mindful, people could die. We sat late into the night every night, reciting the *Heart Sutra* after the sitting, and we lived as though in a monastery.

So I am still very content and pleased with the operation, but the conditions were not right. The press is sometimes frivolous. They just want to write a story.

CI: And they don't care that human lives are sacrificed. It is very sad.

We are living in dangerous times. There are a number of threats to our world: in the environment, in political tensions between nations which have weapons of unparalleled destruction, in an escalation of the numbers of people which the planet has now to support. At the same time there's a flourishing of Dharma. A lot of people are seeking light in this darkness. Do you have any sense for our future as a planet? Do you have any vision about what is to come? I know that you practice being in the moment, but perhaps sometimes you think of the future. Do you see a future that is livable?

TNH: You can have the answer to that question by just looking at the present. The future is contained in the present. We can see that how we are and what we are and what we will be are the outcome of what we are and how we are now.

CI: I'm not so much worried about you and me...

TNH: I know.

CI: ...but rather about how we are as a human race. There are so many people motivated by greed and by hatred and by delusion, and they now have tools to destroy all of us, unlike any time in previous history.

TNH: Well, to say whether we have a future or we don't have a future will not help. Either way it will not help. To say there is a future may make people have false hope. It's not good. And if we say there is no future, then people will have more despair, and that's not good. So I would be inclined to say that the future is in the present. Look and see for yourself. I would add that we should try to live happily in the present moment, and if there is real happiness then we will have a future.

People, in consuming a lot and trying to be rich, believe that they are happy, but we have to help them to

see that their life may not be happy. We should try to
help them find real happiness from looking at the blue
sky—really looking—or looking at a child or a flower.
When people have a base of real happiness, they will
abandon the other things. Maybe that's the most important thing to do now in order to have the future and the
present. If we have the present then we have the future.

CI: So, in other words, if people could understand what
really leads to happiness and peace of mind...

TNH: ...they will abandon things that destroy.

CI: Have you had any new insights being here in the land
of the Buddha, in the place of the Buddha's enlightenment. Any new feelings or moments of *satori*?[3]

TNH: I try to be simple. Last time I was here was twenty
years ago, and it was more simple. I liked it better. The
children were more simple—not like what we saw today.
This morning I said that the hardest thing was to go
through the begging children in order to go to the Bodhi
tree. But if you do not see the children, you will not see
the Buddha. I explained to people that these children are
living Buddhas. Yet these Buddhas are difficult to approach, because we put them on another level which ob-
scures their Buddhahood.

One of the things that I have been meditating upon is
how to come to the land of the Buddha and appreciate
the Buddha without destroying the children or Buddhism. I saw an announcement that Holiday Inn is going
to open very soon in Bodh Gaya. I am afraid of things
like this. They will not help the children. Some people
may get jobs, but that will not compensate for the damage.

---

[3] *Satori*, Japanese, is the Zen term for the experience of enlightenment.
In the above context, it is meant to describe a powerful moment of insight.

It is time to bring Buddhism back to India. Not any kind of Buddhism but the kind of Buddhism that India needs now, because Buddhism is a universal religion. There was a time when Buddhism was just for India, but after that it evolved into something of a universal nature. Now Buddhism should be tested in laboratories in the West to develop effectiveness for modern life, to help the people of our time in social, political and psychological problems. Our success in developing that kind of Buddhism will determine our success in bringing Buddhism back to India.

CI: It is ironic that it needs to be reintroduced to the land of its origin.

TNH: Yes, it's because the Indian intellectuals and young people now are different. The kind of Buddhism they would need is different from the Buddhism of ancient times.

CI: Buddhism has taken root in America much more than when we last spoke. Can you say what you've observed as the particular flavor of Buddhism in America? Can you say what America's influence or coloring has been for Buddhism?

TNH: I think the patterns of different kinds of Buddhism are flowering in America. We can learn from many traditions there. Last year we had a retreat at Mt. Madonna in California with the "floating *sangha*." I said that Buddhism in America may be mostly lay Buddhism. The family should become a field of practice, and the Buddhist center should be a center for families to come and practice. That does not mean that monastic Buddhism should not exist. But it should exist in a way that has a very close link to other kinds of Buddhism. Democracy, science, and art should contribute as well. We should build Buddhism with the local materials. In your country, there are so many avenues that should be used to build Buddhism.

CI: Such as...

TNH: I think everything. Music, literature, the arts, everything. I said this morning that Buddhism is made of non-Buddhist elements. With mindfulness, you know what to draw upon. You count your resources in order to make Buddhism.

Take the telephone, for example. The telephone sound does not seem to be very pleasant, but I have introduced a Buddhist element to it.[4] We have found that "driving meditation" is very effective. Many people are practicing it and they feel much better. In New York City, we practiced a "subway meditation." We had to go in the subway from the meditation hall to practice walking meditation in Central Park. I invented subway meditation so the people would not hate it but would take pleasure in it, and it was very successful. One person told me that he had used the subway for twenty-five years, and this was the only time that he had enjoyed riding on it. As with anything, if you are conscious, if you are mindful, if you are skillful in what you are doing, you can make it pleasurable.

CI: Do you feel that at this time in history there is still a place for monasticism or that it is appropriate for people to withdraw from the world and simply do their meditation practice?

TNH: Many people have taken action, but if their state of being is not peaceful or happy, the actions they undertake only sow more troubles and anger and make the situation worse. So instead of saying, "Don't just sit

---

[4] The ringing of the telephone can be a reminder to be mindful. To practice the "telephone meditation" introduced by Thich Nhat Hanh, when the phone rings, wait for three rings before you answer, all the while breathing and smiling, calmly and consciously. "You can afford to do this," Nhat Hanh says, "because if the other person has something important to tell you, he or she will wait for at least three rings. If you do this, the quality of your conversations will noticeably improve."

there; do something," we should say the opposite, "Don't just do something; sit there." We sit there and we get more lucid, more peaceful, and more compassionate. With that state of being, our actions can become meaningful to the world. Then action and being are not different. If you are caught in a storm crossing the ocean in a small boat and everyone on the boat panics, the boat will sink. But if there is one person who remains calm, that inspires confidence. The boat can get out of danger because of that one person's attitude. That is the meaning of being awake, or meditation.

CI: You have lived for many years as a refugee from your own country. As a monk you are trained in non-attachment, and as you said, the Buddha's way is to treat every house equally. But I wonder if you long to go back to Vietnam, if you miss it very much? I've just spent time with the Tibetans living in exile in Dharamsala, and they feel that India is not really their home, although they've been here for nearly thirty years. What are your feelings as a refugee?

TNH: Well, in a way I miss my country very much, because I used to work almost exclusively with Vietnamese. I wrote books for Vietnamese to read, I spent time in the Vietnamese classrooms for monks and nuns and students. So that is a habit. When I got out, during the first year I often dreamed of going home, but in the dream there was always something preventing me from going home to my monastery. That dream repeated itself a number of times, but I continued to practice. I see now that other places are also beautiful. The French, the English, the American people are kind to me, and they are willing to learn the Dharma. And I have learned to appreciate the fine herbs in the West. I feel fortunate to live with trees which do not exist in Vietnam, such as magnolias and so on. After some time, that dream of going back to Vietnam just stopped. I feel at home where I now live. But I am privileged because at the same time I am still very present in Vietnam since people continue to

read my books there, and, even in the communist
regime, we are able to send back books I write in Vietnamese.

CI: Are they allowed in or are they smuggled in?

TNH: They are smuggled in, and people over there hand
copy them to pass on to others. So I have continued to
offer my insight, my instruction for the practice of Buddhism there, and it is helping people because they are
suffering from the present regime. They appreciate my
offering even more than before. I feel very present in my
own country. I am still in Vietnam, and Vietnam is in
Thây. So I don't feel the pain of that loss, but my countrymen and countrywomen have not arrived at the same
state of peace. Many of them still suffer.

CI: What advice do you give to them, and beyond that,
what advice do you give to all people who live as
refugees—Cambodians, Tibetans, Central Americans? So
many people now live with not much hope of getting
back to their own countries. Many people are not as fortunate as you in feeling at home where they are now and
in being able to practice Dharma. Many of them have
different belief systems from those of their host country.
As a monk and refugee who has adjusted very well, do
you have any advice for these people?

TNH: I think the only way is to share with them my experience, my suffering in the first one or two years, and
then the way I adapted, learning to see that the Earth is
my home, not just a portion of the Earth. And that is
possible.

I wrote a story, "The Moon Bamboo," in which a
young lady was mistreated by her step-mother and,
climbing on the bamboo tree, she went to the moon. She
got married on the moon, but her lover from her former
home missed her and tried to climb up. They met, and he
used tricks to get her to come back. Then her husband on
the moon had his turn to miss the young lady. Moon and

Earth become a symbol of Vietnam and outside of Vietnam. I wrote this story for the refugees.

The mindfulness gong rings at this point in the interview, and we sit silently for three breaths. During the pilgrimage, the gong is rung periodically throughout the day.

TNH: I think that every person should look and see that he is his own country, his flesh and bones are his nation. By adapting and contributing the value of his country to the place where he lives, he can get back the beautiful things. That way people can be happy and they can also contribute to the richness of the country where they live.

Cesar Chavez

When Cesar Chavez was thirteen years old, he participated in his first field strike near El Centro, California. His
father, Librado, had organized the hundred men who
would also participate. They had made their demands to
the farm manager clear: they wanted a minimum wage of
fifty cents per hour, overtime pay after eight hours of work,
no child labor, and separate toilets for men and women.
They also wanted free drinking water while picking in the
fields, instead of being charged a nickel per ladle. It was
dangerous to even approach the farm manager with such
demands, and when they did, the manager accused Librado Chavez of being a communist. He also warned the
men that the company had ways of dealing with trouble-
makers.

The grapes hung full on the vines, beckoning to be picked
immediately or they would rot. The strikers formed a picket
line in front of the vineyard's main gate. On the other side
of the entry way, state troopers, labor contractors, and
farm supervisors waited forebodingly, periodically glancing
down the road.

Suddenly roaring trucks descended on the vineyard
amidst clouds of dust. More than a hundred braceros,
Mexican peasants, arrived to work the fields. They and the
families they had left behind in Mexico were desperately
poor and hungry. The braceros were willing to do the
lowliest jobs for long hours with little pay. Librado Chavez
pleaded with them in Spanish not to cross the picket lines,
but although the braceros understood the plight of the
grape-pickers, their own needs came first and they sadly
crossed the lines.

The following day, it was the striker families' turn to
face hunger. Labor contractors refused to hire anyone
who had participated in the strike, and the Chavez family
was forced to move on—to another field in another town,

to another shack that would become home for a picking season.

In that time, there were few precedents for a successful strike by farm workers. The National Labor Relations Act which Congress had passed in 1935 insured the right to organize of almost every labor group in the country, and it required that industry bargain with organized labor "in good faith." Agriculture was an exception. No protection under the law existed at that time for farm workers; a union was unthinkable. Many years and a "mighty hard road" later, Cesar Chavez would become the first man in the history of the United States to organize a successful union for farm workers.

* * *

The Chavez family had not always been migrant workers. They had once owned a 160-acre ranch in Yuma, Arizona, which had been given by the government to Cesar's grandfather. Cesar Chavez was born in the family home on March 31, 1927. Cesar's parents, Librado and Juana, whose families had come from Mexico, farmed the land, sold fruits and vegetables, and ran a small market near the ranch. Grapes were their most prized crop.

Cesar's father had always given jobs to migrant workers, telling his son, "Some have different skin colors, some speak different languages; some are old, some young. But they have one thing in common—poverty."

When Cesar was ten years old, the ranch was auctioned off due to his father's inability to pay back taxes owed on it. Incredibly, the Chavez family found themselves homeless almost overnight, five children and two adults living in their old Studebaker, heading for the fields of California to labor as migrant farm workers. Looking back at the strange course of his life from the time he left the ranch, Cesar Chavez told his biographer, Jacques Levy, "If we had stayed there, possibly I would have been a grower. God writes in exceedingly crooked lines."

Life on the road was shocking to the family. In a surplus labor market, agribusiness thrived, and competition among field workers created poverty-level wages. Child labor, though illegal, was standard practice and expected by labor contractors, middlemen who hired field hands and took a cut of their pay. Cesar's most vivid memories of his youth are not of school days but of crawling under twisted, scratchy vines for hard-to-reach bunches of grapes, choking on chemical sprays used on the fruit, breathing the hot dust of the fields as sweat poured into his eyes, and spending much of his day in a back-breaking stooped position.

Following the crops from the Imperial Valley in southern California to the San Joaquin Valley in the central part of the state, the family lived mostly in one room huts in the labor camps or in their car. They often went without food, yet in moments of real desperation, the kindness of a stranger nearly as poor as themselves often pulled them through. The respite of the year came during the rainy season when the Chavez family stayed in a small rented house in Delano and enjoyed a semblance of stability from December to March. In Delano, Cesar met Helen Fabela, his future wife.

As World War II got under way, many farm workers left the fields to serve in the armed forces or in the war industry. As a result, farm workers' pay went up, and Cesar Chavez, then fifteen, managed to earn a whopping dollar per hour wage in the fields. In 1945, when he was eighteen years old, Cesar was drafted into the Navy. Although the war had ended, Chavez spent twenty-eight months patrolling the Pacific Ocean before receiving an honorable discharge in 1948. Cesar returned home to marry Helen and start a family. They both labored in the fields, sometimes earning as much as $100 per week, sometimes going for weeks on end with no work and no pay.

By 1951, the first three of the Chavez's eight children had been born. Living in poverty, they dreamed of a better future for their family. At that point, Fred Ross, an Anglo, entered their lives. Ross worked for Community Services Organization (CSO) and had developed service projects for inner-city Mexican-Americans. He had been told that Chavez might be of help in organizing farm workers into a CSO chapter. Fred's idea was to provide a catalyst for the workers to help themselves in securing better living and working conditions. He had hoped to find one among them who could lead the others. Soon after their first meeting, Cesar Chavez proved to be that man. Three years later, Dolores Huerta, a housewife and mother, would join this team and become a leader in the movement as well.

Chavez volunteered to work for the CSO free of pay at night while keeping his day jobs in the fields. Chavez watched Ross carefully and soon became a competent organizer in his own right. Ross and Chavez quickly recognized that the Mexican-Americans would be a strong citizens group if they exercised their right to vote, so Chavez undertook the task of voter registration for the Mexican-American community. Local officials, also aware of the political power of a Chicano voting bloc, made it as difficult as possible for Mexican-Americans to register. Chavez tirelessly provided education for the community, teaching reading and writing skills, leading citizenship classes, and establishing lengths of U.S. residency for qualification to vote.

Although his own education had taken him only to the seventh grade, Chavez began to study in his spare time; he spent hours in libraries, devouring books such as *The Grapes of Wrath*, Jack London's *People of the Abyss*, and the poetry of Walt Whitman. But the most influential book for Chavez was Mohandas K. Gandhi's autobiography, *The Story of My Experiments with Truth*. Chavez began to theoretically understand the power of *ahimsa* in achieving social and political goals.[1] He had not yet had a chance to test the theory, but he would.

---

[1] *Ahimsa*, Sanskrit, literally "non-harming."

After volunteering for a year with Community Services Organization, Chavez was hired to work full-time
with the organization. His leadership abilities became
honed over the next few years as he organized sit-ins
and pickets at ranches and worked with hundreds of
people. He learned how to enroll others in *la causa*, the
cause. "Once you help people, most people become very
loyal. The people who helped us back when we wanted
volunteers were the people we had helped." Chavez also
understood how to build a pyramid of workers. "The
primitive stage of organizing is like the performer in
vaudeville who has sticks and plates. He spins a plate on
top of a stick, then spins a plate on top of another and
another. Pretty soon he's got nine or ten plates spinning
on separate sticks. Well, there's a law of diminishing re-
turns. At a certain point, he reaches his peak. In organizing, before you reach your peak, you get another
spinner to help you spin."

Over the next five years, Chavez began to realize that
the goals of CSO could take the workers to a certain
point and no further; what the farm workers most
needed was a union. Chavez approached the Board of
CSO with plans for a union, but the directors vetoed the
idea, citing their strict dedication to non-political service and noting the futility of the plan. In 125 years of
attempts, a farm workers union had never been organized. Sadly, Chavez decided to leave his job. He was
thirty-five years old and earning $4,000 per year with
CSO. He had managed to save a little money, but he
knew it would quickly run out. He had a wife, eight children, no financial prospects, and an impossible dream.

The next period of Chavez's life was again a struggle.
He missed his job with CSO, and his family had to make
enormous sacrifices. Yet Chavez remained determined,
driving all over the state, holding small house meetings
to "really talk to the poor," and accepting hand-outs of
food along the way. Slowly, a solid community began to
coalesce. With the help of his brother Richard, his wife,
Helen, his cousin Manuel, and old friends Dolores
Huerta and Fred Ross, Cesar formed the National Farm

Workers Association on September 30, 1962. While Helen worked in the fields, Cesar recruited members for the
new organization. Within a year he had signed up nearly
a thousand farm worker families, who paid $3.50 per
month in dues. The Association began to attract notice
and help from individuals and other organizations sympathetic to *la causa*. Chavez welcomed such support but
carefully refused to accept money as a gift, saying,
"Sooner or later, whoever offers money will want something in return—a vote, a promise of support, maybe a
change in our thinking."

By 1964, the union had voted Chavez a salary of $35
per week and Chavez had started publishing a weekly
newspaper. As its numbers and reputation grew, the organization began to win a few small battles, but
agribusiness was still winning the war. By September
1965, however, momentum had developed for the first
big strike. Filipino grape-pickers, concerned about un-
equal pay, had begun striking vineyards. The National
Farm Workers Association joined them in support. As
the strike went on, tensions mounted and violence
erupted. Some workers were badly beaten, a few were
killed, others were harassed and intimidated. Cesar
Chavez began to notice that a police car followed him
everywhere he went. And there were numerous threats
on his life.

It was not until three years later that the tide began to
turn for the workers. The historic grape boycott had
been under way since 1965, but the farm workers were
demoralized after such a protracted fight with the growers. There was talk among them of striking back with
violence. Chavez decided to fast as a reminder to the
workers of their commitment to nonviolence. The fast
lasted twenty-five days, during which time Chavez saw
groups of farm workers from all over the state for twelve
hours each day. Usually too weak to get out of bed, he lay
on a cot and repeated the same message thirty to forty
times daily: stay true to nonviolent means; we shall
overcome. Extremely sick, his vital signs down, Chavez
ended the fast on March 10, 1968, flanked by his wife,

Helen, and friend Senator Robert Kennedy. "Nonviolence is action," Chavez asserts. "If you really want to do something, be willing to die for it." The fast infused the movement with determination and pride.

By 1970, *la causa* had become a national concern. For the first time in American history, consumers understood the plight of the farm workers, and 17 million of them stopped buying grapes. The growers conceded the battle to the workers and negotiated contracts that insured better wages, improved working conditions, and recognition of the union. The union came to be known as the United Farm Workers (UFW).

In a sense, the grape boycott was only the beginning of the struggle for farm worker rights. Teamsters, the government, and the growers fought the workers for every inch of ground over the next decade. Chavez was at the center of all of it. He has fasted, he has remained true to nonviolent strategies, and he has not given up. Under California Governor Jerry Brown, the farm workers made solid gains, particularly with the establishment of the Agricultural Labor Relations Board, designed to oversee violations of agreements between workers and growers. Since that time, however, Governor George Deukmejian, who succeeded Brown and was heavily financed by California agribusiness, has appointed only pro-grower members to the Board, and it has consistently hurt *la causa*.

The most volatile recent issue and the current grape boycott concerns the use of pesticides on crops. According to the farm workers, 8 million pounds of pesticides are used annually on grapes. The poisons cling to the leaves and are absorbed through the skin. Some of these sprays are so toxic that they affect workers weeks after the spraying has occurred. Farm workers in California have the highest incidence of job-related illnesses. In 1985, Governor Deukmejian vetoed a bill that required posting warning signs when a field has been sprayed.

Aside from the spraying of grapes, 300 million pounds of pesticides are used on food crops in California. Most of these residues cannot be completely washed off. Aerial spraying of crops deposits only some of the poisons on its target, the food. The rest of it drifts for miles in the air, sometimes landing in nearby water sources or leaching into underground water supplies. The current boycott asks for the banning of five of the most deadly of these pesticides.

Beginning in July 1988, Chavez undertook his longest fast ever—thirty-six days—to raise public awareness of pesticide use. The fast was also an act of penance, according to Chavez, "for those in positions of moral authority and for all men and women activists who know what is right and just, who know that they could or should do more, who have become bystanders and thus collaborators with an industry that does not care about its workers."

A reporter once suggested that Chavez sounded like a fanatic. "I am," Chavez replied. "Those are the only ones who get things done."

Being a fanatic would also explain his willingness to die for *la causa*. My first impression on seeing Cesar Chavez was that he had laid his body on the line. His is a body that has worked, fasted, and suffered long years; much of its strength is now sapped. Yet he has one of the sweetest countenances I've ever seen, with deep brown eyes and a beautiful, genuine smile. He was immediately warm, casual, and talkative, the result, no doubt, of a lifetime of knowing and working with thousands of people.

I had driven from San Francisco to Chavez's retreat headquarters, La Paz, near the tiny town of Keene (a general store and post office, as far as I could tell) in the Sierra Mountains east of Bakersfield. I arrived early in the morning for our appointment. Chavez had been up and working for some time, and was leaving for Canada shortly after our talk. We spoke for about an hour in his simple office where everything seemed ancient—the desk, the telephone, the several thousand books shelved on the wall. We then walked to another office to get a video tape which he wanted to give to me called, "The Wrath of Grapes." In watching him walk, I again noticed

his frailty. Chavez has had severe back problems for
years. He is a true martyr, I thought to myself. And suddenly I pictured the many thousands of California farm
workers laboring in the hot fields year after year. They
are also martyrs, dying on the "front lines," as Chavez
points out in the following interview. They are the most
heavily exposed to the pesticide toxins which go into the
production of half of the nation's food supply.

Driving back through California's Central Valley, the
fertile fields on one side of Highway 5, the barren brown
hills on the other, several times I watched with disquiet
as small planes spewing gray spray swept out of the sky
and covered the green fields—of rice, celery, strawber-
ries, onions—with an invisible blanket.

Interview with Cesar Chavez
April 22, 1989 • Keene, California

Catherine Ingram: Do you see any similarities between
the civil rights struggle in India and the struggle of the
farm workers? For instance, Gandhi struggled to eliminate the caste system, and, in a way, we experience a
modern caste system here with the poor minorities of
color.

Cesar Chavez: Oh, there are a lot of similarities. Gandhi
was dealing with the powerless and the poor and the
ones who were discriminated against, and we have that
now—the poor, and the people who are discriminated
against. We have classism, racism. Gandhi was also
working against a foreign domination, and this is similar to our situation in that agribusiness is really like a
foreign domination. They don't live here.

CI: They don't?

CC: The multi-nationals, more and more, are being controlled by foreigners—Japanese, Germans. People don't

realize what Japan owns here—they own subsidiaries of subsidiaries, a lot of California. They own a great deal of the wine country.

The other similarity is that people Gandhi dealt with tended to be religious, and the people we deal with tend to be religious as well.

CI: What aspects of Catholicism inspire you in your work, and what aspects have inspired the people you work with? Are there particular teachings that you focus on?

CC: Well, Christ's teachings. The Sermon on the Mount is the most inspiring, and that was one of Gandhi's inspirations also. The message of Christ is all about love, all about loving—not only God, but also one another. I think that's the point.

CI: The teachings of love.

CC: Yes, but what love is, that is to be interpreted. In our work, you know, love is really sacrifice. It's actually not vocal. Although it can be enunciated, it has to be practiced. You need both.

I think part of Gandhi's greatness was that he didn't want to be a servant, he wanted to be of service. It's very easy to be a servant, but very difficult to be of service. When you are of service, you're there whether you like it or not, whether it's Sunday, Monday, or a holiday. You're there whenever you are needed.

CI: I know that a lot of your current work has to do with raising people's awareness about the use of chemicals and pesticides on our food. What is happening to the farm workers who are exposed to these chemicals, and what is happening to the people who are eating the food on which they are sprayed?

CC: Our struggle with pesticides goes back more than thirty years. We raised this issue a long time ago, because we were the victims. In fact, right after the Second World War, I was a victim of pesticide poisoning. I knew very little about it at the time and it took me a few years to learn more. But when most of the people were worried about how thick the eggshells were on the birds, we were talking about human beings—about workers and then about consumers. For many years people would laugh at us, or they would ignore us, or they would just stare at us as if we were crazy. But today, everybody knows about pesticides.

We've been raising this issue a long time. In fact, we were successful in banning the use of DDT about nineteen years ago. We got it banned on grapes, but they came back with other poisons. Those were the ones that Rachel Carson wrote about in *Silent Spring*.

You know, either we ban these poisons and get rid of them, or they will get rid of us. These are deadly, deadly agents. They are organophosphates, nerve gas poisons. That's how they kill the insects; they affect their nervous systems. And so, too, they affect our nervous systems. Pesticides have killed a great number of workers and incapacitated many others; they have wrecked the health of the workers, their families, their children. See, now these pesticides are everywhere—in the water, in the soil, in the atmosphere, every place. And what we've learned is that body weight is a kind of buffer, and the more weight you have the more you can buffer; the less your weight, the more you are at risk. So it is children who are suffering the cancers and the birth defects. The number of miscarriages of women working with grapes is very high. We now see lots of cancer and lots of birth defects—terrible, terrible examples of birth defects—children born without arms or legs.[2] Oh, it's just horri-

---

[2] For example, in the town of McFarland in the California Central Valley which is a crop-growing area regularly sprayed with pesticides, childhood cancers are eight times the normal level. Dr. Marion Moses, a leading medical researcher among farm workers, cites cancer cases as the "hardest data," and she says that she has "soft data" on stillbirths and miscarriages. However, Dr. Moses suggests caution in concluding culpability and feels that lengthier studies are needed. She also adds that while body fat can more safely harbor chemicals than lean tissue,

ble. We did a video about this, "The Wrath of Grapes."[3] It is just incredible what is happening. We've been campaigning to the point where we now have our workers pretty aware of it, and I think we've played a major role in the awareness of the issue all over the country, all over the world.

CI: I think your fast of last year raised awareness on this issue.[4]

CC: It did a lot. The fast is a great communicator. Like Gandhi, because we don't have the economic or political force, we have to appeal to the moral force, and the boycott is the best instrument. Gandhi said that boycotts were the most near-perfect instrument for social change.

CI: People's pocketbooks often awaken their conscience.

CC: And beyond that, it really is a moral force. Gandhi worked this out for all of us, because it's the moral force that compels, and then it translates into economic pressure. It starts from a moral stance, but it takes time.

CI: When you do these fasts, what gives you inner strength?

CC: That's a good question. I really don't know. Sometimes I fast for only one or two or three days and have a difficult time. In fact, I tried to fast two days ago and I couldn't do it. I'm trying again today, and it's very difficult. Then at other times, it just happens.

---

weight loss or expended energy poses a danger as the chemicals are released.

[3] According to the United Farm Workers Union, fifty-four percent of table grapes tested by the government contain pesticide residues, but the government does not test for forty-four percent of the poisons used on grapes.

[4] In 1987 Cesar Chavez fasted for thirty-six days on water only to "identify himself with the many farm worker families who suffer from the scourge of pesticide poisonings."

CI: Do you think it has to do with the issue you're fasting for or the amount of support you have around you?

CC: I don't know. I've never been able to tell except that, well, Gandhi spoke about the door, or the window, the light. I can't really talk about those things, but sometimes it is *comparatively* easier than at other times. There is...there is a force there. I don't quite know what it is.

CI: For a long time your family has had to sacrifice with you for the cause. They've had to watch you go without food, they've seen you be put in prison. There were times when you were so poor you couldn't buy food for them. And when your children were growing up there were many times when you had to leave at crucial moments. I read in your book *La Causa* that even on the day of your daughter's wedding, you had to leave after just one dance with the bride in order to negotiate a contract. This is similar to Gandhi's situation as well. A lot of times his own family had to be relegated to a lesser priority.

CC: Oh, with him it was pretty bad. But I've been very lucky in that I've been able to keep the support of my family. You don't have to be present to spend time with them when you engage in the same struggle, because you are together when you engage in the same project. I think the strength in our family comes because it's always been directed away from ourselves.

When I was growing up, my dad and my mother instilled in us a really strong awareness of doing something for other people. It was preached, and it was practiced by them. We grew up in that way. We thought nothing of doing for other people, and we also saw the great advantages of doing things for others. The great payback comes in feeling good about helping people, and we understood that from the time we were very small. I don't think I have done this as much as my mother did, and I don't think I preached it as much. I think I acted on it quite a bit though, and so my kids—most of them—

picked it up, the idea of helping, putting others first. If you do for somebody else, it's really doing for yourself. You can't explain it, but you understand it through doing it and once we experience it, it becomes a lot easier. I think this is what has happened in my home.

Now, with my mother it was planned. For instance, when we were growing up we were very poor, and yet my mother would send my brother and me—we were just small boys—to look for hobos or for people who were hungry and bring them home to eat with us, even though we had barely enough food for our own family. Those are very strong impressions, lasting impressions, to see people willing to do that. I often think that the reason that I discovered and became interested in Gandhi was because of my mother. I was predisposed because of the training at home. Anyway, my kids, most of them, have picked up some of this. Some of them are working with us here, but even those who are not working with us are committed to the ideals of being of service and helping people.

CI: It's been passed down in your family.

CC: Yes, even to the grandchildren. What happens is that they see it in the home. It's like anything else; if they see dope or drink at home, they do that. If they see making money, they do that.

CI: What changes have you seen for the farm workers in all these years?

CC: [Laughing] Our work is like two steps forward, and one and nine-tenths back. We've been able to accomplish quite a bit in terms of increasing society's awareness. We made the plight of the farm workers a household word throughout North America. We have developed a broad understanding of the problem and a network of support. Some polls show that as much as eighty percent of the public know about the work we do. That's the biggest thing we have accomplished. And as a result of that, a limited number of workers now have traditional union benefits—better wages and so forth—but not a lot of the workers. We still face a day to day battle.

It has taken most unions between thirty and fifty years to get established. We're pioneers in this field, so it's going to be awhile before we really get established. Once we break that barrier, I think it will go very fast. But it's been back and forth and up and down—a long, long struggle.

We've been subjected to so much hardship, legal maneuvering, you name it.

CI: Yes, there's that 1987 lawsuit of $1.7 million, in which a vegetable grower claims that a farm worker strike cost him the loss of a harvest. I don't understand how you can be sued for that. Isn't potential loss the leverage for any strike?

CC: Yes. The claim against us is illegal. That law is unconstitutional. We continually have to challenge the unconstitutionality of such claims. That was the reason for my second major fast back in 1972, a twenty-five day fast, and that was a hard one. I ended it and they took me to the hospital; my vital signs were down. I was in bad shape. Only twenty-five days, but it was hard. We saw even back then that we couldn't get the legislation we needed on this.

Now with the most recent case, it has gone back to the state courts from the Supreme Court to see how they would interpret it. Unlucky for us, it was interpreted with a $5.6 million judgment against us.

Well, the bond itself is $5.6 million to appeal. We don't have $5.6 million. You've got to put up at least the exact amount of money that the judgment is for. So we recently went to court and got a judge in Yuma, Arizona to set the bond at $250,000, and then the growers appealed too. Oh they drain you. They use the courts.

CI: In other words, even though the growers know that eventually they may lose the case, they can just wipe you out in the meantime with expensive legal tactics.

CC: Yes. Our system is not as democratic as people think. It's not as free as people think. We're quick to make judgments about other countries, but we're pretty bad ourselves. For eight years under Reagan, we were harassed with federal investigations here. It was so bad that we even assigned a room for the investigators. In fact, the last group that was here said, "We've looked at these books three times!" And they left.

See, if they find that I've taken one penny, I can be thrown out of the union. And they've done that to a lot of union leaders. They can't believe that I don't take pay, or that I don't have an expense account. I have to sit here and tell them how I live. If I go somewhere, I don't stay in hotels, I don't buy my food. People give it to me. That's how I do it, so what do I need money for? The investigators at first didn't want to believe that, but finally we convinced them. Well, they laid off of that, but it's always something else. We've been harassed up and down by the authorities.

Our power is with the people. That's where our power is. People—all shapes, all colors, all sizes, all religions. We have people who are very conservative who support what we do, people who are even anti-union. See, everybody interprets our work in a different way. Some people interpret us as a union, some people interpret our work as an ethnic issue, some people interpret our work as peace, some people see it as a religious movement. So we can appeal to broad sectors because of these different interpretations.

CI: How do you organize nonviolently around the issue of pesticides? It's an unseen enemy. I suppose you can say that the effects are seen, but the actual substance is unseen.

CC: It is immediately unseen, though in the long term, it is seen. But it's a lot harder to make people aware, because for the consumer, if you eat this grape, it won't harm you now, but it may harm you ten, fifteen years down the line. But you take the same grapes that may harm you in five, ten, or fifteen years, and you see that they are harming people instantly—you see what the pesticides are doing to the work force and their children. You carry the message by showing the impact on the people in the front lines.

CI: So the workers are the front lines, and in their exposure and subsequent harm from the pesticides, they represent what is to come for the consumers down the line.

CC: Right, the workers get it instantly, but the consumer is going to be affected later on, because it's cumulative. Now people know this, but for years and years we were just the laughingstock when we spoke of this. Or we would hear things like, "Without pesticides, we'd starve." Well, they didn't have pesticides many years ago, and if people starved, they starved for other reasons. The thing is that about twenty years ago, about twenty percent of the crops of the world were lost to pests and today it's twenty-seven percent with jillions of more pesticides.

CI: The pests get more immune.[5]

CC: Yes. And then they need to use much more poison to kill them. Take, for example, the deadly nerve gas, parathion. Twenty years ago they were using about two pounds per acre. Today they are using up to six pounds per acre.

CI: I have a feeling that we are going to see a lot more immune-deficiency problems in our lives because we're being saturated with these poisons. What must the soil be like after all this spraying?

---

[5] According to Professor George Georgehiou of the Department of Entomology, University of California, the number of species of insects resistant to pesticides increased from 224 in 1970 to 447 in 1984.

CC: The soil is becoming like a piece of plastic; you just stick plants there and you grow them artificially.

CI: Who or what would you say is the biggest enemy of the farm workers?

CC: The biggest enemy is the system. Agriculture has changed from the time that our founding fathers laid out the foundation for our country. But the perception about ownership of land hasn't changed. There is something peculiar the world over about owning land. Land gives you power beyond its wealth, beyond liquid cash. Land has a powerful, powerful influence on people. You're dealing with landowners who literally own where you live, where you walk, and where you breathe. That power is awesome. And power tends to corrupt, and the system gets corrupted.

Agribusiness in California has developed on cheap labor—and not by accident; it's been planned. To maintain cheap labor the growers have worked out a horrible system of surplus labor—a surplus labor pool that they are experts at maintaining. Experts! See, agribusiness controls immigration policy, and it has for years. So much so that not long ago the Immigration and Naturalization Service was part of the Department of Agriculture. They control it.

CI: Do they turn a blind eye and let people get in illegally?

CC: That too. But they also set the immigration policy and control how it will be carried out and how it will be interpreted. They have tremendous influence.

CI: How does that work to benefit the growers?

CC: Let me give you an example. The beginning of agribusiness, the way we know it now, started back in the late 1800s. Curiously enough, unlike most systems, the workers were here before the jobs were. See, all the railroads, like the one running right by here, were built by the Chinese. And after the railroads were built, there were thousands of Chinese without work. So the early entrepreneurs, that's what they were in agriculture, came and saw this tremendous amount of labor, and that's why they developed labor-intensive crops in California, unlike in the Midwest and other places. It was because the labor was here. Other places had the climate and the water, but here they had a tremendous surplus of labor. So that was the beginning. It was in that system the labor contractor system started. And as in all systems, they polished it, they honed it, and now it's...

CI: ...big business. I never realized that California produced so much of our food because of the surplus labor rather than the actual soil, climate, and water.

CC: Oh yes. There are other parts of the world that have the same or an even better climate than we have, although California has about fourteen climatic regions.

Then, too, everything is interwoven with agribusiness, so when you take on the growers you're also taking on the large insurance companies who also happen to be owners of land, and you're taking on the large banks, and the railroads, and the pesticide and fertilizer companies. Talk about a power base against you. That's why legislatively and politically there's no way we can do anything. They've got it clamped.

That's what Gandhi realized and why he went over to the boycott.

CI: I still don't understand exactly what agribusiness does in manipulating immigration policy to create a surplus labor pool.

CC: Well, what agribusiness does is often outside the law. They would recruit in, say China, and then they'd send recruitment teams into Japan (the Japanese didn't last too long, they had different ideas and they came with their families—the only other immigrants who came with families were the Mexicans). Then after that they sent recruits to India, and then they tried the Philippines. After the revolution in Mexico, people came. And then during the Dust Bowl, they went to Mexico and recruited for the Dust Bowl and then there was the Brassario program during World War II.[6] Now they're recruiting in Mexico, Asia, Africa, Honduras, Nicaragua, El Salvador, Guatemala. This is all recruitment for agribusiness, and that's how they do it.

CI: So they bring in all of these foreigners and it's to their advantage that the people remain illegal.

CC: Oh yes, because they exploit them and the illegals can do nothing about it. They cannot make a move. They have to accept whatever they are given. It's terrible.

CI: In your life, in your work, and in all that you have struggled for, is there something you could say about how life is?

CC: Well, not really. Life is so many things. But we're here playing the record every night and finding out everyday whether we did what we're supposed to do. The message was clear from Christ, Gandhi, all the good people who said exactly what has to be done. So every night you've got to think, "What did I do today?"

Life is very complicated. But we try to keep it simple. Get the work done. We're essentially activists. We have our precepts and our principles, and then we act.

I was never for writing on nonviolence. What can you add? It's all been written. In the very early days, we gave the impression that nonviolence was sort of saintly, like saints who go around lightly stepping on eggshells. But now over the years we see nonviolence is not that. It is not that.

---

[6] The program was implemented to recruit Mexican farm workers who, after working the fields, were then sent back to Mexico.

So we don't write about nonviolence, we don't preach it. We never talk about nonviolence to the workers unless there's a need to talk about nonviolence. In other words, if we're negotiating a contract, I'm not going to talk about nonviolence, but if we're in a picket line I'm going to talk about nonviolence. Because if you talk too much about it, it becomes...

CI: ...less authentic.

CC: Yes, exactly. And we were very worried about that. Now we have legions of people who are nonviolent out there, the workers. But in the early days it was very hard. Now people know how to act, what to do. And not because we have said to do this. We haven't had one hour of teaching; it's all been by example.

We want to be men and women of the world. We want to work. We just want to do things nonviolently.

CI: How did you first come into contact with Gandhi's ideas?

CC: Oh, it was very interesting. As I recall, I was eleven or twelve years old, and I went to a movie. In those days, in between movies they had newsreels, and in one of the newsreels there was a report on Gandhi. It said that this half-naked man without a gun had conquered the might of the British empire, or something to that effect. It really impressed me because I couldn't conceive of how that had happened without guns. Even though I had never heard the name of Gandhi before, the next day I went to my teacher and asked her if she knew anything about him. She said, "No, but I have a friend who knows quite a bit about him." Then she gave me the name of her friend, a construction worker who was studying Gandhi. He gave me a little book on Gandhi. As I grew up, I started learning more, and ever since then, I have made a life project of reading about Gandhi and his message.

CI: What about Gandhi's life and message has most influenced you?

CC: His activism. He was a saint *of the world*. He did things, he accomplished things. Many of us can be so holy, you know, but we don't get very much done except satisfying our own personal needs. But Gandhi did what he did for the whole world. Not only did he talk about nonviolence, he showed how nonviolence works for justice and liberation.

CI: In your own life and work, have you experienced any new thoughts or new ways of seeing how nonviolent strategy works?

CC: No. It was all done by Christ and Gandhi and St. Francis of Assisi and Dr. King. They did it all. We don't have to think about new ideas; we just have to implement what they said, just get the work done. Gandhi offered everything there is in his message.

As I said, what I like about Gandhi is that he was a doer. He did things. He had thoughts *and* actions. Also he did a lot that he is not recognized for but which also has a lot of meaning. You know, he organized quite a few unions—there's nothing much written about this—but even today those unions are active. My biggest disappointment with the movie "Gandhi" was that it mentioned nothing whatsoever about the unions that he built. He organized the clothing workers, as you know, in Ahmedabad. In fact, I had a chance to meet one of the people from that union.

Gandhi was also a fantastic fundraiser. He raised millions of rupees, and he had a huge network of social services. He had probably the largest circulation of any newspaper in the history of the world. Even though there were only one or two thousand copies printed in the original, everybody reprinted it. So the message for me is that of his nonviolence and the fact that he was a doer. He made things happen.

CI: Does the fact that he was successful influence you in your appreciation of him? A lot of people attempt to do similar things, but for whatever reasons—their time in history, or circumstances beyond their control—they're not as successful.

CC: No, what influences me is not whether or not they're successful, it's that they don't give up. I lose faith in someone who doesn't continue a project, who starts something and then leaves it. The world is full of us quitters. Even if Gandhi had not liberated India, he stayed with the project all his life. And that is my great attraction. He just didn't give up.

A.T. Ariyaratne

Soon after his self-help organization in Sri Lanka had become a nationwide movement, A.T. Ariyaratne learned of an assassination plot on his life. The notorious Choppe, a powerful lord of the underworld, based in Sri Lanka's capital city of Colombo, had been hired to kill the grassroots leader, and the plan was to be carried out at a Buddhist center where Ariyaratne would be speaking. Ariyaratne heard of the plan the evening before it was to happen. In the dead of night he went to Choppe's house and stood before the man known as the King of Killers. "Choppe Aiyah, I am Ariyaratne whom you are planning to kill tomorrow," he told the surprised gangster. "Please do not desecrate that sacred Buddhist seat of learning with the blood of a beggar like me. Kill me here instantly." The killer looked into the eyes of the brave science teacher who was organizing the poor in hundreds of villages. "I cannot kill you," Choppe told his midnight guest. From that moment on, Choppe became a great admirer and supporter of Ariyaratne and the Movement, referring to Ariyaratne as "Our Sir."

When I first met and interviewed him during a conference at the United Nations in 1983, Ariyaratne told me that according to Mahatma Gandhi, when one tries to effect change, one must go through five stages: "First, people will greet you with indifference; next they will ridicule you; then they will abuse you; next they will put you in jail, or even try to kill you. If you go through these four phases successfully, you will get to the most dangerous phase—when people start respecting you. Then you can become your own enemy unless you are careful."

* * *

The lush, tropical island-country of Sri Lanka, formerly known as Ceylon, lies off the southeastern tip of India. The country is now torn by war, but for most of the past two thousand years it has been a land of peace—*Dhammadveepa*, as it was known to its Buddhist inhabitants, Island of the Dharma. Glistening white temples and monasteries dot its landscape where orange-robed monks and nuns silently practice meditation. Elephants, cobras, monkeys, bats, tigers, and some of the most exotic birds in the world live in its wild jungles. White-sand beaches and the deep blue-green of the Indian Ocean surround the island. In the interior, great ruins of former capitals stand as monuments to the glory of ancient times where whole cities of gigantic statues of the Buddha repose as visible reminders of a former tranquility. It is even rumored that other ancient cities of advanced philosophical thought are buried below the earth's surface of this land.

Ahangamage Tudor Ariyaratne was born in the coastal village of Unawatuna in southern Sri Lanka on November 5, 1931. There Ari, as he is known, grew up the son of a businessman who later became a village leader. Before entering primary school, Ari had learned the Sinhalese alphabet from the head monk of the local Buddhist temple, and throughout his childhood, Buddhism was integrated into Ari's education. As a teenager he also enthusiastically engaged in social work in his village. From his earliest youth, Ari had both large-scale dreams and the practical experience of helping others.

Ariyaratne left his village to obtain a degree from Mahinda College in Galle, Sri Lanka, and later a governmental teaching degree in science. He then began teaching at a prestigious Buddhist high school in Colombo which had been founded by the American theosophist Col. Henry Olcott.

It was here that the realization of Ari's lifelong dream had its beginnings. In 1958, Ariyaratne organized a group of his students into a two-week "holiday work camp." The group went to a remote poverty-stricken village of the lowest caste so that students might "understand and experience the true state of affairs that prevailed in the rural and poor areas, and develop a love for their people, utilizing the education they received to find ways of building a more just and happy life for them." To do this, Ari and the students lived in the village in order to learn from inside what the community most needed. The upper-class students shared the local people's huts and food, worked with them in their daily activities, and held "family gatherings" at night to discuss their needs. They discovered that the most urgent need was for sanitation, and they came up with a plan to build latrines. The plan was implemented through the first work camps of what would become a major movement. They called the camps *shramadana*, from the Pali, *shrama*, labor or energy, and *dana*, to give. The very idea of upper-class students building latrines for lower-class peasants aroused much anger in the nearby high-caste neighborhoods. Several times the work of the *shramadana* camps was sabotaged under cover of darkness. Undaunted, the students and villagers repaired the damage and continued their work. By the end of the two weeks, the students and villagers had formed a powerful bond of friendship and accomplishment.

The idea caught on. Within a short time, more camps were organized. Other schools began implementing the *shramadana* idea for students on weekends and vacations, and soon the villagers who had been helped joined in helping other poor communities. Dozens of villages became part of the Shramadana Movement, with the local people themselves initiating projects and expansion. But the real formation of the Movement's principles was yet to come.

Ariyaratne looked to India for inspiration and guidance, and decided to go there to study Gandhian movements, particularly the Bhoodan-Gramdan campaign led by Vinoba Bhave, a close follower of Gandhi.[1] Bhave had

---

[1] Vinoba Bhave (1896-1982) was considered to be Gandhi's spiritual heir. The Mahatma once commented that Vinoba Bhave understood Gandhian thought better than he himself did.

walked thousands of miles during a nearly twenty-year period, holding meetings all over the Indian sub-continent and acquiring land donations from the rich to give to the poor. The Boodan-Gramdan ("land-gift") campaign raised approximately 4 million acres of land for the poor and is considered one of the greatest legacies of Gandhi's followers in India. Ariyaratne steeped himself in the experience of Vinoba Bhave and other Gandhian leaders, and returned to Sri Lanka with a clear vision for the Movement which he now called Sarvodaya (*Sarva* means "all" or "embracing everything"; *udaya* means "awakening"), a name Vinoba Bhave had used in 1948 to describe the Gandhians' new goals for India after independence.

The Sarvodaya Shramadana Movement now began to spread its influence into hundreds of villages not only in Sri Lanka but eventually, Africa and other parts of Asia. Sarvodaya also began to aim at "world awakening" by convening conferences and offering technical assistance and training to self-help movements in the Third and Fourth Worlds.

With a strong emphasis on decentralization and self-reliance, Sarvodaya has implemented programs in education, health care, transportation facilities, agricultural projects, and a wide range of technologically appropriate energies such as windmills and methane generators which convert human wastes into cooking gas. In a one-year period, Sarvodaya built three times as many roads as did the government, linking for the first time many underdeveloped villages which had been neglected under colonial rule. By the 1970s, Sarvodaya had organized more than a hundred coordinating centers, each serving the needs of twenty to thirty nearby villages. In addition, Sarvodaya now serves a rural awakening program of 3,500 communities.

The movement also has a strong spiritual emphasis. Ariyaratne has organized Sarvodaya's 3 million members in the practice of "loving-kindness" meditation[2] which the members do once or twice daily, all at the same times. Ariyaratne feels that so many loving thought forms being sent out simultaneously have a tangible effect on humankind. The religious philosophy of Sarvodaya prescribes Buddhist ideals of kindness and generosity. As Joanna Macy notes in her book *Dharma and Development: Religion as Resource in the Sarvodaya Self-Help Movement*, "It is the chief premise of the Movement that the notion of development can only be meaningful in terms of human fulfillment." Ariyaratne believes that this fulfillment comes from the deepest understandings of interdependence and a commitment to an ever-renewed state of wakefulness. Since the beginning, Buddhist monks have worked side by side with villagers in Sarvodaya Shramadana projects.

For the first decade of the Movement, Ariyaratne's only income was his salary as a science teacher. With this he supported his wife, mother, and six children, and, in addition, financed the basic needs of the Movement. As more people came to know about Sarvodaya, donations flowed in from all over the world. By 1972, Ariyaratne resigned from his teaching post to work full time for the Movement.

Although Ariyaratne says he wants no truck with power politics, as the leader of millions in a country which is coming apart at the seams, he has been forced to address the political issues.

The world press tells us of a civil war between the Hindu Tamils, people of southern Indian origins, and the Sinhalese Buddhists, the indigenous people of Sri Lanka. According to international reports, the Sinhalese, who make up seventy-four percent of Sri Lanka's 16.5 million people, and the Tamils, who make up eighteen percent, are at war over the basic political and economic rights of the Tamil people. Some Tamils advocate secession from Sri Lanka to create a separate state in

---

[2] The traditional word for loving-kindness meditation is "metta," and comes from the Pali, the language in use during the time of the Buddha.

the northeastern provinces, where Tamils are a majority.

In the following interview, Ariyaratne tells a different and controversial story about the causes of violence in Sri Lanka, a story being played out not only on a tiny island country but throughout the entire world. Ariyaratne believes that the sheer speed of economic development and quick changeover to a cash economy are the underlying causes of stress and violence in his country. In his clear and direct way, he implicates the Western powers and the forces of greed within Sri Lanka's own leadership which have encouraged materialism over community and spiritual values.

After our initial conversation in New York, I again spoke with Ariyaratne in Oakland the following year, where he further elaborated on global economic connections, providing me with my first clear understanding of the ways that Third World countries are economically exploited.

Ariyaratne explains all of this in an unassuming, matter-of-fact manner, almost as a friend would speak of a kitchen wall which needed painting. He wastes no time in anger. He is energetic in his speech, unhurried in his movements. The following interview took place after Ariyaratne had given a talk to a group of Buddhist meditators on the subject of social activism within a Buddhist framework. It is a subject he knows well, and he has spoken on the topic to groups all over the world. As the founder of Sarvodaya, Ariyaratne is one of the most successful living examples of blending Gandhi's ideas with the Buddha's.

Interview with A.T. Ariyaratne

October 21, 1984 • Oakland, California

Catherine Ingram: Ari, you say that the world's problems are interrelated. What are some of the ways in which this is so?

A.T. Ariyaratne: We are living in an interdependent world. Communications and various technologies have brought us together—technical things that we are all using, such as this tape recorder—these have become common everywhere, even in places where people have nothing to eat. Also we see that the world's resources are being used interdependently. I've just returned from Japan where I heard that over seventy percent of their food requirements are imported from other countries. The so-called economic miracle of Asia—Japan—is dependent upon the rest of the world and mostly on those countries where people are starving. These examples are one kind of interdependence.

The other ways that our problems are connected is that the superpowers are building nuclear armaments. If anything happens, an accident, it's not only they who are going to suffer, but everybody in the world. Then there are also the drugs which are dumped in our countries from the developed countries—pesticides, experimental pharmaceuticals.

Whatever we are doing in whatever part of the world, we have to keep in mind this global perspective. In the Sarvodaya Movement, while we may be working in the most remote villages in Asia or Africa, we always try to keep a global vision.

CI: Have you seen any decline or any improvement in the economic status of the poor in the last few years?

ATA: I think conditions for the poor are becoming worse. I believe the cause is that the international economy is controlled by so few people, and, furthermore, that the people who are actually the primary producers of food and labor-intensive products are in the poorer communities of the world.

Take Sri Lanka, for example. Maybe a handful of people in Sri Lanka, a really insignificant minority, are benefiting from the economic development or the increase in trade with the West that has taken place in the past few years, while the poor people are becoming poorer, and the numbers of the poor are increasing. This is a phenomenon in all the developing countries. In my country, wherever food is processed, we pay more for the processing than for the food, with the added chemicals and all.

CI: In my country we have to pay more for the food *not* to be processed or sprayed with chemicals.

ATA: If there were a direct exchange between people, all these expenses would be cut down. The whole thing is a pyramid and everything is done to satisfy the upper level.

International trade should be restricted because the injustice this international economic order produces cannot satisfy basic needs of clothing and shelter but satisfies the greed of rich people in rich countries. And we, in the poor countries, get cash in return, and this cash is once again spent to buy media-created wants, desires created entirely by the advertising media. It's a vicious cycle.

CI: What's the answer to this problem?

ATA: What I would advocate is to totally de-link from this international economic system. Now, I do not mean to disassociate from different peoples in the world. We should simultaneously strengthen the links that exist between grass-roots or non-exploitative groups in the world who do not approve of the present affluent social systems which are trying to direct all our energies.

CI: How would you link up all those grass-roots organizations?

ATA: First, we have to think of what we as people, whether in rich or poor countries, have in common. What we have in common is humanity, the spiritual life of people. In this, there are no barriers at all. I believe that spiritual life cannot be centralized. It is possible for us human beings to organize our own lives as individuals, as families, and as communities. If we are to bring about any change in this at these three levels—the individual, the family, and the community—we have to strengthen the spiritual foundation we have. In our Sarvodaya experience, when several hundred of us meet together, think together, work together, share our joys and sorrows together, we feel that we are releasing certain thought processes which give us some sort of protection, some hope, joy, security. We feel those effects, and we believe that our communities are linking together this way. Maybe the scientists will prove it one day, but even if they don't, we don't care.

Now I am here in San Francisco, over 14,000 miles from my home. I don't feel that I am in a strange place; I don't behave as if I am among strangers. Similarly, you didn't treat me as a stranger; you accepted me as a member of your family. In spite of our geographical or economic levels in different parts of the world, people who believe in the small community can always get together. In the cases where people stay apart it is because we allowed the technology to be used and handled by those who believe in huge systems of power or huge systems of economic organization, such as the military or multinationals. Most of the technology available in the world is used by this minority of people who believe in largeness, centralization. So we, as small communities, first building on our own spiritual life, should find those technologies which we can utilize to communicate with each other. Maybe we can't launch satellites straightaway, but we can use the telephone, the postal services, the printed matter. There are ways that small groups in the world keep in contact.

This is what reaches the old societies. When I say the old society, I don't mean the society that existed in the twelfth or thirteenth century. What I mean is a society that is existing in our own time, which is steeped in the "old" values, where they believe that children have a moral responsibility to look after their parents when they are old, where a family has a responsibility to live in cooperation with the families around it, where the food producer has a moral obligation to produce clean food without destroying the environment or polluting the soil with chemical fertilizers.

CI: This concept of an old society certainly differs from the values of Western societies where a high premium is placed on anything "new." What are the philosophical underpinnings of the "old" societies versus the "new" societies?

ATA: Firstly, the biggest blunder Western culture has made is that there is no standard to measure good and bad. It is lost in liberal thinking. In other words, there is nothing called sin and merit. You are not accountable because you do not know whether you will be reborn or not. In Sri Lanka, we believe in rebirth. We believe in sin and merit.

In our society, the old system prevails to this day. I believe that the vast majority of people in the world, at least eighty-five percent, belong to this old society. And some of them are economically well off, of course, but still they retain their old values. It is a mistake for us to forget these values, to want just the modern society and the accumulation of goods, and to think that this eighty-five percent should rush to acquire what the fifteen percent have. This wealthy fifteen percent are not only in the U.S. and Japan; they're in my country, too.

So now, what should we do, those people who belong to the old society, who wish to reject this attitude of trying to become the modern society—energy-consuming, environment-polluting? We say reject it. We want to live in the old ways, correcting the deficiencies we have, satisfying the basic needs of people so that nobody will be poor. We don't want to be rich; we want a no-poverty society, not an affluent society. And we will make a new society bypassing the modern society in the same way that those who are in the modern society bypass the old society. They have unsuccessfully and, well, dishonorably told the people in the Third World, "Come, you can reach our level. We give you the First Development Decade, the Second Development Decade, the Third. We give you the Year of the Children, Year of the Disabled, Year of the Elderly, of Women." All right, now after all these beautiful years, are the disabled looked after? Are women liberated? Is every child fed? No. So this bluff must stop now.

The poor man still cannot find one liter of water to drink while these others have thousands of liters in which to swim. We say, "No, we don't want to reach where you are. Instead we believe in a spiritual foundation, moral relationships, small economic and political organizations in a highly decentralized but highly coordinated way." How to do it? Well, we have to find how to do it. This is why we have to link up all these movements around the world and think together.

CI: With regard to the moral and spiritual values of the old societies, I've heard that in Sri Lanka, the great influx of cash has contributed to a prostitution trade among young people—boys and girls who, in a weekend, can make more money than their parents earn in a year, and that it is turning the Sri Lankan economy and values upside down. Is Sarvodaya addressing this problem?

ATA: Well, now we are doing curative work, trying our very best to save people who have gotten into drugs or prostitution or crimes or other social evils. For example, we have a range of welfare activities to help these people. We have a special program in the south where ex-criminals are being reformed. And at the same time, we have a program to prevent this sort of thing from happening. Our efforts should not be merely palliative or first aid, they should also be preventative. This program has a dimension where people are shown a society in which this sort of thing will not occur. We try to show downtrodden people ways to uplift their general conditions and attitudes. However, our social philosophy in the

Sarvodaya Movement is that a lot of these problems are the result of the unjust economic system that prevails.

CI: Does America play a role in the economic oppression of the world's poor?

ATA: Yes, I think America should take a substantial share of the responsibility. After all, America was a country built with very high principles of equality, brotherhood, and all that. I remember our parents looking up to America as the country which might liberate the rest of the world. But I do not think that America or the other superpowers are playing the role that these big powers should play in the world today. They have no moral right to spend $900 billion a year for armaments when 900 million people are starving. As long as this sort of money is completely diverted for the destruction of people, the economies of the poor people are shattered.

CI: In the process of de-linking your country from the international system, how will you handle the problem of your enormous foreign debt? Is this a way in which the international banks have brought your economy under their control?

ATA: Yes, they have tied the economy of the developing poorer countries to the world economy in such a way that they set the rules and they are in control. These countries have no way out of this situation unless they gather all the courage they have, educate the people as to what has happened, prepare them to face the worst as far as the consequences are concerned, and then tell the banks, "We are not going to pay our debt."

You see, right from the beginning, at the time we were given the money, it was inherent in the system that we were not in a position of earning and paying it back. Now to get out of paying it will have very severe consequences; it's not as easy as what I say. That's why this could be done only by countries whose leaders have the capacity to show an example of selfless leadership in their own style of life, their own fearlessness, and their moral integrity. I am speaking about a leader who could say, "Look here, this is the reality of the situation: we can go on taking loans and being in debt, but we will never succeed in eradicating poverty in our societies. At most we will only increase the rich by a few more people. To eradicate hunger in our country, therefore, we are going to reject this economic theory, this market economy as it works now, and instead pool all our resources to meet the primary needs of the people."

The "basic need" is our first economic objective, not growth, not increasing the per capita income. This talk about growth and no-growth is nonsense when there is no value attached to the whole thing. You should not ask the question, "How much has the economy grown?" You should ask, "How many people are now getting a balanced meal?" You know, a lot of wealth goes into unnecessary, wasteful consumption. But in the old societies, when the primary needs are satisfied, they then build works of art and architecture. Of course, a Marxist would say that this is all from the slave labor of the people, and there have been some societies like that, but not the Sri Lankan society. That *Samadhi* statue of Buddha [at Polonaruwa, Sri Lanka] could never have been carved by a slave. It could have been done only by an absolutely free man who got into that stone and carved the serenity of the Buddha. I remember Pandit Nehru, the Prime Minister of India, would come to just look at it for long periods of time. Only basic cultures produce great works of art and architecture in the world, things that last for centuries.

Now once we satisfy these primary basic needs, next we are going to satisfy needs at a community level. Every house need not have a television set; you can have a bigger television for the whole community. I visited a community in Japan last week; there were only 300 people in the community. They have a day-care center, a preschool, a primary school, a junior secondary school, a senior secondary school, and a university. This serves the entire community—men, women, and children. They live quite happily without a mass educational system which only conditions the people to a society where competition and individual material advancement are the main objectives.

So by filling these larger educational needs in a cooperative way, the resources would be more than enough for every country. The leadership in poor countries has to have the courage to decentralize the economic and political power. Decentralization strengthens the center, really. If the center has the courage to distribute power, to that extent the center is strong. Once the country as a whole has that kind of strength, then they can say to these foreign banks and governments, "Sorry, we would like to pay you because customarily we pay our debts, but we cannot pay. You have taken it back many times more in other ways."[3]

CI: In the last year and a half there has been a wave of violence in Sri Lanka between the Tamils and the Sinhalese. What is going on in this civil strife?

ATA: As anticipated by most of us, there began a big wave of violence in Sri Lanka. This was generally called communal violence, but for us it was the climax of a gradual breakdown of spiritual, moral, and cultural values. This had been happening over twenty or thirty years. Then the communal issue became the excuse for what happened and there was a lot of publicity outside Sri Lanka saying that the Sinhalese Buddhists were killing Tamil Hindus, which is an absolute lie. No Buddhist killed any Hindu as such. There are gangs of fellows belonging to lawless elements and also to political

---

[3] According to a 1988 UNICEF report, Third World debt now stands at more than $1 trillion; debt repayment takes approximately one quarter of the developing world's revenues. Meanwhile, the forty poorest countries in the world have halved health spending over recent years and cut education budgets by one quarter. Lawrence Bruce, president of the United Nations Children's Fund, charges that "the mounting debt repayments of so many of these developing countries to Western institutions are quite literally snatching food and medicine out of the mouths of millions of children."

parties who were waiting for any chance to plunder other people and get money. These are the people who did all this damage—not a single Buddhist monk or what you could call a decent Buddhist.

When all this began, none of the leaders came out to stop it. So the Sarvodaya groups appealed to the people to stop the escalation of violence and help those who were affected. We opened up relief camps and did everything possible throughout the country for relief and reconciliation. I personally went round the country addressing public meetings everywhere and appealing to both Sinhalese and Tamils not to get trapped in this violence involving a few hundred people.

We had seventeen Tamil brothers and sisters living in our house. One day a Sinhalese gang came to the door, and my young daughter went out and said, "My parents' instructions are that if my father is here, he will have to be killed before any Tamil family member is touched. If my mother is here, she will die first. Now, as I am the oldest in the family and my parents are not home, I will have to die before you touch them." Perhaps she didn't realize the gravity of what she was saying, but the people did not harm her. They apologized and went away. This is the type of thing newspapers don't publish. There were many, many Sinhalese women and children who did heroic deeds during that period when there was insanity prevailing in the country.

CI: These were Buddhists who were protecting Tamils?

ATA: Yes, yes, yes.

CI: I know that you organized a Peace Walk which attracted 30,000 of your fellow countrymen. You were asked by President Jayawardene to stop the walk due to fears for your safety.

ATA: Yes, but I did not stop because of my personal safety. I would not stop simply because somebody threatens me. We who take to nonviolent revolution are prepared to die at any moment to help others live. But when the President comes and makes a personal appeal like that, I can't be that stupid or that arrogant to turn it down, so I stopped the walk. I was also concerned that somebody might say that because of us the All Party Conference would not be called. So I continued the Peace journey by car for, I think, sixty-nine days. When the All Party Conference started, we stopped the journey. I had decided by that time that I was creating unnecessary fear in the minds of the political leaders, both for those in power and for those who were trying to come into power. They were not so much afraid of the movement; they were afraid of me, because they thought I could move crowds of people. I decided that it's bad to create fear in anybody's mind, so I left the country for a few months to alleviate this fear.

CI: Were they afraid you would become a political force?

ATA: I *am* a political force. I mean, I need not hide it. But, you see, I will never dabble in power politics. There are more important things to do. Instead of confronting a government, we in Sarvodaya confront the whole system. They may call us sentimentalists or idealists or whatever. We are not interested in sitting in their chairs, but their fear is there.

Anyway, my absence does not affect the movement. Every village is organized. We will double the number of places where we work before the end of one year. Yes, Sarvodaya will go on. My dream is to get 16,000 villages in Sri Lanka to build a truly alternative system without calling it alternative, and then one day to declare our freedom.

As a follow-up to the above interview, I sent a letter to Ariyaratne with questions regarding the civil strife in Sri Lanka which has been ongoing for the four years since the interview occurred. His reply was dated November 11, 1988. —CI

CI: You said in our 1984 interview that the outbreak of violence in Sri Lanka at that time was the result of a breakdown of spiritual, moral, and cultural values over thirty years. Do you still see those reasons as the inherent causes of the civil strife in Sri Lanka?

ATA: Yes. All aspects of spiritual, moral, and cultural life have a value basis. Once this value system is destroyed, more and more coercive instruments of the State, such as the police and the armed forces, have to be used to bring about order in economic, political, and social life. During the last decade, a frantic attempt was made by the government and the local and multinational economic sectors toward materialistic affluence. Liquor shops increased tenfold. Gambling and casinos, with attendant evils, became numerous. Drug addiction became a new and dangerous phenomenon. Earning money and spending money was promoted as the most fundamental value in life. The bad example set by a very small minority was propagated to the susceptible general public through the media of television, radio, and newspapers. Pornographic literature fell into the hands of schoolchildren.

So, when all these evils were introduced to our society, naturally, violence became part of the structure first, and later it came to the community where not only personal disputes but also political disputes came to be settled by armed power. The so-called ethnic conflict was only a symptom. Nobody here talks about the ethnic conflict now; it has receded to the background. The general public is sandwiched between power groups, and they are helpless. Local and foreign troops control most of the life of the people, and anti-government armed groups are having a heyday. We have to work very cautiously to keep the people within the nonviolent constructive programs which Sarvodaya has implemented. Violence will not take anybody anywhere. We believe that when the violent groups have exhausted their energies in mutual elimination, then they will turn to the nonviolent alternatives offered by Sarvodaya.

Joanna Macy

It was one of the happiest weeks of her life. Joanna Macy and a group of Sri Lankans were on a Buddhist pilgrimage to the sacred sites of Sri Lanka. For Joanna the experience provoked mysterious memories, a déjà vu, of ancestors on pilgrimage across Europe. "This is our heritage," she thought. "Pilgrimage shaped our civilization."

A few years later, in 1983, Joanna Macy went to England to lead "Despair and Empowerment" workshops, training people in facing the threats to our world, feeling the sadness inherent in learning to "sustain the gaze" in the face of such threats, and experiencing the power which the release of these denied feelings brings. After the workshops, Joanna visited Greenham Common and other U.S. nuclear missile bases in Europe where people had stationed themselves in "encampments" in protest of nuclear weapons. Macy understood only too well their protest. For years she had been involved in anti-nuclear activism in the States. "Hundreds of thousands of metric tons of radioactive waste have been generated by our production of nuclear power and nuclear weapons," she has written. "The toxicity of these wastes requires them to be kept out of the biosphere for many times longer than recorded history." She is also aware that the waste is leaking into the air, soil, aquifers, and rivers.

Yet for Joanna, being at the encampments produced a strange sense of "being in medieval monasteries." The nuclear sites had become "spiritual places," each encampment having started with a peace walk to arrive there, a kind of pilgrimage.

"And then I got it," she recounts. "It was a déjà vu of the future. If there is to be a future, at every site where nuclear weapons or power has been produced, where there are radioactive remains, shells of buildings, tailings, and so on, people will have set up guardian sites. They will

guard the 'poison fire' for the sake of all beings throughout time. And this spiritual vocation will serve to keep them faithful."

Her vision for the Guardian Sites was born. The nuclear sites will become monasteries of the future. People will come on pilgrimage to honor them, to bring offerings, and to conduct the "great rememberings" of the ways we had nearly killed our world. Pilgrims will keep vigil at the sites, monitoring the radioactive levels, making sure the containment is intact, and creating a sacred acknowledgment of our "technological capacity to commit collective suicide."

"The disposal of radioactive waste calls us into a different relationship with future generations," asserts Macy. For her, radioactive waste serves as a reminder that her "future ancestors are all the children for centuries to come." In her meditations, Joanna Macy holds thoughts of loving kindness for "Beings of the Three Times"—past, present, and future. She believes that we must experience the life of Gaia, the living Earth, as our own life, and that we need to expand our sense of time itself out of compassion for those beings yet unborn, "who are so innocent and so at our mercy."

* * *

Born in Los Angeles on May 2, 1929, Joanna Rogers grew up in and around New York City. Although her father was an investment broker, she comes from a long line of Presbyterian preachers, ending with her grandfather. Joanna attended a French school for primary and secondary education in Manhattan, often as the only American in the class. Perhaps her eventual identity as a global citizen originated in this period of living in one of the world's most international cities, speaking and studying in a language belonging to a country thousands of miles away, and intermingling with fellow students from different nations. She felt a particular fellowship with colonized Africans whose academic training in French history and philosophy mirrored her own, yet, as in her case, had little to do with their ancestry or environmental context.

Joanna remembers her life in New York City as miserable. "We didn't have a happy family life, and there is too much concrete in New York," she would later explain. Joy in those years came through her love of books and her summer vacations when the family went to stay at her grandfather's farm in western New York state. "That saved my sanity," she says. She would spend most of her time there either alone or with her best friends, "two trees and a horse."

As a girl, Joanna was also inspired by her beloved grandfather's devotion to the church. At age sixteen, she had a powerful mystical experience in which she felt that she was present at the crucifixion of Jesus. Through this experience she was startled to discover "our capacity as humans to either inflict crucifixion, or to turn aside from what we know to be true and thereby participate in crucifixion." Looking at her world—at the poverty and injustice in East Harlem, at the effects of the World Wars and the Holocaust—she realized that her vision of the crucifixion was not limited to what had happened to the historical Jesus. After that experience she knew, "My life wasn't 'mine' in the same way ever again."

She turned to the study of religion, majoring in Biblical history at Wellesley College, in the hopes of becoming a missionary in Africa. Her sense of adventure in the spirit of service was further heightened by meeting Albert Schweitzer and serving as his interpreter for one summer day in New York.[1] She began a correspondence with Schweitzer beginning in her college days and met with him again years later in Bordeaux, France.

---

[1] Albert Schweitzer (1875-1965), physician, philosopher, theologian, and pianist, was world renowned for his work in French Equatorial Africa (which later became the independent country of Gabon). Dr. Schweitzer founded a hospital in the African jungle where he worked for the welfare of both people and animals. During his latter years, Schweitzer ardently crusaded against the build up of nuclear armaments, pleading his case in letters to Eisenhower, Kennedy, Nehru, and Khrushchev.

Through Schweitzer she came to understand "reverence for life" for the first time within the Christian faith.

However, this refreshing perspective was not enough to stem the rising tides of religious doubt. In her studies of Christian doctrine she began to experience "intellectual claustrophobia" and found the Christian claims to "exclusivity of truth so absurd that I had a crisis of faith." Since she had no affinity with any other religion, Joanna became an atheist.

As a senior in college she won a Fulbright scholarship and moved to France to study political science, specializing in Marxism and French Communist Party tactics. Her knowledge in this field garnered her a job as an "intelligence analyst" with the State Department in Washington when she returned to the States. She also became active in the civil rights movement and used her influence with the State Department to address discrimination in housing.

There in the nation's capital, Joanna met her husband-to-be, Fran Macy, a Soviet affairs analyst. Fran's jobs would take the couple to places far from their Washington home, although Washington would be their base for the next thirty years. After a five-year period in Munich, Fran Macy was offered a job in Moscow. It was at the height of the Cold War between the super-powers and Fran had grown weary of the tension. Instead of accepting the promising job in Moscow, he joined the staff of the Peace Corps in India, and the family (by then there were three children) moved to New Delhi.

It was the mid-sixties. America was just beginning its involvement in the Vietnam War, and a world away, Joanna Macy, viewing the war events with a wary eye, would discover Buddhism through her contact with Tibetan refugees living in India. The encounter with the teachings of the Buddha, along with the impact of a meditation retreat atop a Himalayan mountain, rekindled Macy's interest in religion in general and re-awakened her personal commitment to a spiritual life. Following a tour of Peace Corps duty in Africa for several years, the Macys returned to Washington. There Fran and Joanna engaged in anti-war activities. Joanna also took a job with the National Urban League in Washington, an organization dedicated to the rights of blacks.

But Joanna's passion for scholarship in religious studies could be put off no longer. She began graduate school at the age of forty-two, first in Washington and then at Syracuse University in central New York. Her doctoral work centered on Buddhism and general systems theory.[2]

General systems theory was relatively obscure at the time. There had, however, been some recent books on the subject which allowed Joanna to see its relevance to religion. Macy would pioneer a field of study linking these two important subjects. Her understanding of *paticca samuppada*[3], the Buddhist doctrine of dependent origination, and its interface with general systems theory would become the philosophical cornerstone of her social activism in years to come.

In 1976 Joanna Macy embarked on a four-month pilgrimage to India and Sri Lanka. While in Sri Lanka, she encountered the Sarvodaya Movement for the first time.[4] Fascinated by the way A.T. Ariyaratne, the founder of Sarvodaya, and others had "taken Gandhi's ideas and recast them in a Buddhist mold," Joanna thought to herself, "This is what I would have invented if I hadn't

---

[2] General systems theory looks at how open systems (biological, cognitive, social, ecological) self-organize and interrelate. Systems are considered integrated wholes, the properties of which cannot be reduced to the sum of their parts. For example, the human brain is a complex open system, just as the cells and tissues which make up the brain are systems in themselves. Social systems, such as a human family or community, exhibit dynamics of self-regulating organization. Wilderness areas, viewed as systems, are composed of a highly complex web of life, each plant, animal, or insect species dependent on subtle relationships with the others. All open systems can also be seen as the parts of a greater system, the living planet. For further discussion of general systems theory, see "The Systems View of Life," in *The Turning Point*, by Fritjof Capra.

[3] *Paticca samuppada*, Pali, "Dependent Co-Arising," refers to the conditioned factors of life, death, and rebirth in a detailed, twelve-point description attributed to the Buddha.

[4] For a description of the Sarvodaya Movement and its founder, A.T. Ariyaratne, see pages 126-128.

found it." The Movement combined the "psychology and mysticism of compassionate action" with pragmatism.

Back at home in Washington after her introduction to Sarvodaya, Joanna became interested in environmental issues, particularly the problems of nuclear power. Her son Jack had written a paper during his first year in college on thermal pollution from nuclear reactors, which had a "formative influence" on Joanna. She soon found herself shoulder-to-shoulder with Jack and thousands of others occupying Seabrook Nuclear Reactor in New Hampshire.

More activism and more study of the nuclear and environmental problems made Joanna acutely aware of the perilous position which humankind occupies, and a terrible despair overcame her heart. She felt that there was no one to turn to in her grief, even though she had loving friends and family. "What is there to say? Do I want them to feel this horror, too?" she asked herself.

She also recognized that to feel despair in our cultural setting brings on a sense of isolation. "The distance between our inklings of apocalypse and the tenor of business-as-usual is so great that, while we may respect our own cognitive reading of the signs, our response is frequently the conclusion that it is we, not society, who are insane," she wrote in 1979.

This distress would lead directly to what Joanna calls "despair work." She began to regard her personal pain "as a healthy pain, like the kind felt as circulation is restored to a limb that has gone 'to sleep.'" She developed meditation techniques to enhance this awakening and to deal with the despair, and she wrote about her experience in an article which appeared in *New Age Journal* in 1979, shortly before she left the country to work for the Sarvodaya Movement in Sri Lanka. Joanna regarded the article as a completion of her own despair work. She could not have known at the time that the article would generate mail from hundreds of people and would launch her into leading "Despair and Empowerment" workshops around the world.

The Sarvodaya experience set a framework for the workshops, lectures, and activism to come. In June 1979, Joanna Macy returned to Sri Lanka on a Ford Foundation grant to work for one year as a volunteer for Sarvodaya. Her aim was to "learn how religious beliefs and aspirations are reflected in the goals of the Movement, how they serve to engage the people's trust and energy, and how they are conveyed and put to work through language, behavior, and organizing techniques." She discovered that the Dharma permeated the Movement at every level. She believes that because the Movement's ideals—loving-kindness, compassionate action, altruistic joy, equanimity, generosity, kind speech, constructive work, and equality—are universal, "the experience of Sarvodaya can have meaning for the rest of the world in these troubled times."

After returning to the U.S., the avalanche of interest in the Despair and Empowerment Work claimed Macy's time for the next few years. She also began work in the area of Deep Ecology, the subject expounded in her book *Thinking Like a Mountain: Toward a Council of All Beings* (co-authored with Seed, Naess, and Fleming). "Deep Ecology Work is designed to expand our sense of self-interest to include the planet and other life forms," she writes.

In 1988, Joanna Macy began to organize "councils" of people to discuss her Guardian Sites idea for sacredly guarding the nuclear missile and power plant areas. There are now Guardian Sites groups in Berkeley, Boulder, and New Mexico (which, along with Nevada, faces governmental preparations for huge nuclear waste burial sites).

All of this has led Joanna Macy to think a great deal about the subject of time. "I have come to suspect that our culture is in a denial of time," Macy explained. "In addition to the problems of time speeding up—with the nanosecond measurement used in computers, and so on—there is a fear and loathing of time and, seemingly, a need to conquer it which, I suggest, comes from a patriarchal mindset that has the same view toward matter.

As this mindset wants to escape from matter into a realm of pure spirit, so it wants to escape from time into a realm of eternity. The challenge which I find myself pondering over is how to re-inhabit time."

Macy's dedication to re-inhabit time enfolds her concern for future generations of humans and non-humans. As physicist Brian Swimme said in introducing Joanna Macy at a Berkeley meeting, "She has a lot of friends. Most of them aren't born yet."

The following interview took place in Joanna's meditation room in her home in Berkeley, where Joanna and Fran now live. For ten years or more I have seen Joanna Macy in Buddhist meditation retreats in various locales. Most of these meetings have been in silence. Nevertheless, we have also had several conversations over the years, and I have attended some of her lectures. I have found these encounters to be inspiring and provocative due to Joanna's original thinking which she weaves with ancient wisdom grounded in the doctrine of *paticca samuppada*, the interdependence of phenomena.

I have also found her to be a genuinely compassionate person. Some months after the interview, we had a phone conversation which began, customarily enough, with Joanna asking how I was. I told her truthfully that I was having a hard time. When she asked what the problem was, I felt entirely safe in describing my sadness to her, trusting that she would understand. "Let my heart rest under yours," she said quietly. "It can be a support until yours is strong again."

Interview with Joanna Macy

February 10, 1989 • Berkeley, California

Catherine Ingram: In looking at what we are facing on this planet, how do you feel about people bringing children into the world today? You probably weren't facing the threats to existence which we now face when you had your three children some twenty years ago. How can people feel that they are doing a responsible act by bringing in more beings to this ailing and overpopulated planet with its life support systems taxed to the limit?

Joanna Macy: I feel this question so deeply, and it breaks my heart. When people ask about this, I must acknowledge that any answer I could give risks being trivial and even obscene.

When I gave birth to my children, it was with unmitigated joy. It hurts me to see young couples now wondering if they should feel guilty about having a baby or wondering if they are indulging themselves to do this most elemental and beautiful act of our biological and spiritual nature. When young friends of mine make the choice and bring forth life now, I feel doubly grateful, because I know that they do it in a context which is so problematic. It would be so easy for them to say, "No, the prudent, the wise, even the compassionate thing to do is to hold back. No, I won't tax the planetary system anymore," or "I will adopt a child from a suffering or underprivileged family." And I have no quarrel with those options. But when I see young men and women choosing to bring in life, I'm very moved in the way I'm moved by certain deep organ tones saying, "AHHHH, we're not lost yet, AHHHH." This is an act of faith, it's an act of commitment to our time. The song will go on. It's the way I'm moved by John Hershey's play, *The Wall*, about the Warsaw ghetto. It's a triumph of our race that in any situation we'll know how to dance or sing or make love.

In the act of parenting in this time, there's something special going on that perhaps couldn't happen for our planet in any other context. There's something being brought into awareness when you hold that child, when you raise that child, when you're with that child as it's getting its bearings in this insane world. There is something in the posture and playing out of parenting that weaves a particularly needed thread into the pattern of our time. In comparison to this, it seems that parenting under cloudless skies was so simple as to be almost half-witted. Parenting now brings with it some heartbreaking dimensions that are also triumphs for the human spirit. It's not just the child who needs it, we all need it. We could say that we need this more than ever.

CI: To affirm life, to commit to it.

JM: Yes. My daughter got married three weeks ago, and there's that womb to womb to womb connection that is so elemental. I pass this on to her. And I cannot begin to imagine what the sufferings may be for her or the children of her womb...

I feel like Demeter searching for Persephone, raging around the world, "*Where* is she? *Who* took her and made our world so desecrated and withered? It's turning into a wasteland because someone took her; she's been raped, she's been abducted, and I will rage until she is returned." There's this Whoooom, and this comes from here [both hands reaching out from her womb]. This must not be denied, because what is going to save us? Do you think our smarts are going to save us? Our smarts have gotten us *into* this!

CI: I really struggle with this. I find myself grieving over the children that I won't have out of my love for them. Or sometimes I think that I will have children after all and be willing to bring them in with the burdensome knowledge of what they may face.

JM: Well, maybe you want to ask them if they want to be born. Maybe they have some voice in this.

CI: Maybe...

JM: In considering this question and going through that pain, that anguish, into the commonality of our story, what I've experienced again and again is an eruption of release and joy and hilarity.

CI: Which we just had for a moment, actually. We unmasked the devil for a moment and felt that release.

JM: Yes, we did.

CI: Joanna, I would like to talk with you about Gandhi. You often refer to Gandhi in your talks and writings.

JM: I'm so glad to be alive in a time that came after Gandhi. I couldn't imagine otherwise. He revealed the enormous leverage of the human heart when you take it seriously. He also trusted people. People would find themselves capable of enormous, stalwart steadfastness and personal sacrifice. Just amazing.

CI: Yes, I've read that he brought out the best in people because that was all he would see in them. He would inspire ordinary people to be willing to be arrested, to be beaten, even to die, many of them.

JM: That is true in our society as well.

CI: You mean that if you can speak to the heart, you can raise that kind of dedication?

JM: Yes. People are capable of much more than most politicians realize. Politicians continually underestimate people.

CI: So many of Gandhi's acts were very simple, but they had so much power to speak to the heart that they would ripple through the entire culture. This one man fasting in jail could stop all the civil riots in India.

JM: Yes, Gandhi's sense of being at rest while in action represents to me a mystical element, although he was not a mystic. There is a quotation from him that I wrote in my journal years back about how the drop of water is at rest in the ocean, but the ocean is active. In our own actions, when we know the activity is coming from beyond ourselves, we can have that notion of rest and being embraced. That has tremendous appeal to me in times of great stress and burn-out. Even the most nobly motivated among us wear ourselves silly rushing to this appointment, to that convention, to this civil disobedience, or what have you. Gandhi seemed, both in his words and in his life, to personify resting in action.

CI: I hadn't thought of it that way, but it's true. He led a very full community life and, in addition, spun cloth all those years as well, perhaps more than many weavers who had nothing else to do but spin. And he took care of the goats and looked after the sick people in his ashram. He midwifed an independent India within the rhythms of a rural life.

JM: Yes, I think we all need a functional equivalent to the spinning wheel to steady our busy minds.

CI: Do you think that the Sarvodayan principles of villages helping villages can in some way be applied to communities within our country, such as the homeless, or people with AIDS—communities which cry out for our help and are not getting nearly enough? Have you thought about this—how to apply Sarvodaya Shramadana to Western life?

JM: Yes. I think that there are strong lessons from Sarvodaya that we can discover and apply in our society or rediscover in our own setting. Most particularly, in the Sarvodaya movement, they really trust the intelligence of the people.

CI: So people say what they need, and they are heard.

JM: That's right. It means not coming in with blueprints or ready-made solutions, but rather listening to people, helping them to evolve frameworks through which they can hear themselves and each other. It means to offer frameworks in which they can enact physical projects, time-limited and measurable, which they can enjoy doing and in which they can take pride. All of this is a notion of one's own self-esteem within a context of global diversity. It's been a great teaching for me, and it holds great hope for all of us, that we don't need to fragment into sparring camps in order to honor our distinctive origins. Whether we're Muslim, Sikh, or what-have-you, we can honor our origins in an interactive, pluralistic context. This is fed by the teachings of the Buddha— honoring and recruiting and enrolling the disenfranchised as healers and organizers. The dropouts, the old people. In the case of Sri Lanka, the women, the unschooled, the landless, the kids. Yes, I've thought about it a lot. Once, after coming back from organizing a work camp, I imagined a Sarvodaya U.S.A., or a Sarvodaya International. But the lessons I harvested from my experience there got carried out in different ways.

CI: Still, it makes sense for us just to talk with the homeless or the people with AIDS and try to enlist them in coming up with solutions.

JM: There's a lot of goodwill and concern about what to do. But we're culturally caught in the notion that if we're going to do something, we have to know what it is before we begin. If there is a problem, we have to know first what the solution is. So we don't do anything until we already have a mental blueprint or the grand solution or some kind of panacea. Or we say, "Well, I don't know what to do. I won't do anything, because there's nothing I can do about it," instead of saying, "Hey guys, let's get together and find out what's working and what's not. Let's figure it out."

And I suppose that in a classic Sarvodaya way, it would be inviting the homeless together—or AIDS victims, school dropouts, cocaine addicts, inner-city teenage mothers, or what-have-you—and saying, "Talk about your lives. What works and what doesn't work?" Not even having the arrogance of coming in and saying, "What do you need most? How should we design the programs?" but rather, "What do you have to say? You're the experts. And if you can hear your own experience together, then you can probably make this system work for you. And we'll be here to help you make it work for you, because we know some things about the system. What is it that is coming down for you now in your life? What is your truth?"

That's what Parsifal asked when he went into the wasteland in the legend of the Grail. He was on his way to King Arthur's court to become a knight, and he found himself going through a land which had lost all powers of regeneration. The fields were lying swamped and infertile, the grain fields, just stubble. Even the rulers were impotent. Parsifal found himself in the capital in the castle of the fisher-king. Instead of people running around ringing alarms and being frantic at the state of things, everybody was just fine, just fine. Just moving, like robots. All the courtiers, everybody was just fine. They were under a spell, you see. And Parsifal had been told that he could awaken them from this spell. Not by having the answers, because he wasn't very smart, he was just a fool, and not by being brave or strong, but by asking questions. Well, he was too embarrassed to ask questions the first time, so he left and nothing changed. And he didn't get to King Arthur's castle. He had to circle around through immense suffering and find himself again in the wasteland, again at the castle of the fisher-king. The people were still under the spell, but this time he remembered to ask the questions, and they woke up.

CI: What questions did he ask?

JM: He asked, "What aileth thee? What's the matter? How is it for thee? Tell me how it is." Inviting people to just speak the truth of their experience. And that woke them up.

CI: Gandhi said, "I must warn you against the impression that mine is the final word on nonviolence." Joanna, I know that you have written about "cross-fertilization" of Gandhi's thoughts. Do you see any evolution of the concepts that Gandhi espoused in his understanding of nonviolence? Are there any improvements? Gandhi seemed very willing to have there be other ways of seeing nonviolence emerge in history beyond his time.

JM: He said that nonviolence was not for the weak but for the strong. He would rather have had somebody engaging in violence out of conviction than engaging in nonviolence out of cowardice. That comment seems to me to say something about the dilemma that many pacifists or believers in nonviolence confront when looking at the Central American scene, for instance. Many of us feel it's inappropriate to pass judgment on the use of arms and violence against those who are invading, killing, blockading, and destroying. For us as members of this Empire to sit by and say, "Oh, but the response should be nonviolent and it's wrong to take up arms..." Well, I simply cannot bring myself to do that.

CI: You are referring to the people of Central America who are being oppressed and tortured; you cannot ask them to remain nonviolent.

JM: Yes. I think this is an issue for a lot of people who want to be serious about nonviolence.

CI: Do you think there's a way to take up arms and somehow maintain the principles of nonviolence?

JM: No, I don't know how you do that. But I think that fearlessness is important for nonviolence. Nonviolence is really important for making that journey into the heart of things where change must happen. Nonviolence is essential for being able to go where your brother or your sister is, because no healing can take place without touching. And we can't touch each other with guns pointed at our chests. I don't know how you can get to a point of fearlessness if you're relying on arms. I think the true Fearless One is naked. But I speak these things untested, Catherine.

CI: What is the role you see of bearing witness?

JM: I know from standing outside gates of weapons plants in the rain with a silly-looking placard with cars rushing by and hardly seeing me, spraying me with puddles, I have felt, "What could be more impotent?" And knowing at a deeper level that this is my part of this whole picture. I'll just bear witness. And I do believe it changes the whole ecology. If there weren't those sorry-looking figures there standing in the rain with their placards, we'd be more doomed than we are.

CI: You have said that when you are working on saving the whales, you are also working on saving the rain forest, because there is a law of interconnectedness of all things. Issues such as the nuclear threat or the disposal of nuclear waste, the greenhouse effect—these are things that may affect the security and the abundance that some of us might enjoy in the future, but for a lot of the world's poor, the threats are more immediate. "Will we have enough food tomorrow?" "Will my child die from disease today?" "Will she die from contaminated water?" Some people say that the great environmental issues are the rich people's worry and that the poor are working on just getting fed and keeping a host of diseases at bay. I'm sure you're familiar with this criticism. Will you address this point?

JM: Well, I think it's true that to be able to look at longer-term trends and recognize the enormity of the danger they represent requires some leisure. It requires some education. It requires having the time and peace of mind to be able to sit down and read the newspaper. It requires that you are a little bit free from the unrelenting scramble for the next meal. So I think it is true that you can make certain generalizations about the class and educational background of the environmentalists.

CI: But the point is that since they do have the leisure and education to look at some of the problems, why not address the situation from the poor people's perspective and make sure that no one is hungry before we deal with the long-term problems?

JM: Well, this relates to the interdependence of all phenomena. Such a charge suggests that these issues are separable, that by working on one you're not affecting the other. It's an ignorance of the facts to think that global warming or the oil spill over Antarctica or the poisoning of our seas is unrelated to hunger. In the last years, there has been much more data showing the inseparable connection between militarism and the decimation of the biosphere and the exploitation of the land and people of the Third World. You can see this whether you're looking at Aswan in Egypt, at the foothills of the Himalayas, or at the terrible erosion in the Andes. These are no longer separate issues. It's not a question of "Shall I work on the environment or shall I work for human justice?"

Charging the environmentalists with not being concerned about human poverty and oppression is an example of the kind of thinking we're trying to overcome. We're trying to grow out of saying it's either that or this. We are deeply embedded in our world. Everything we do reflects on our natural environment.

CI: Your Buddhist scholarship has centered to a great degree on the doctrine of *paticca samuppada*, or the interdependence of phenomena. Your understanding of this doctrine is linked with the interdependence of spirituality and social activism. Will you speak about your understanding and experience of "dependent co-arising" in this vein?

JM: I came to the Dharma out of a full set of life experiences that centered around service. Growing up in the Christian church, I was very motivated by teachings such as: "Go ye forth unto all nations..." and, "Inasmuch as you have done it unto the least of these, my brethren, you have done it unto me." That grabbed me very much as a child and as a teenager. I had also been very strongly affected by phrases such as the one from St. Paul: "We are surrounded by a cloud of witnesses."

CI: The witnesses being...

JM: Our fellow beings of all times, and all of us being part of a much bigger story than could be encompassed in a curriculum vitae.

It was after doing things such as relief work following World War II, and working with Americans for Democratic Action, and then involvement in the civil rights movement that I encountered the Buddha-dharma in the sixties. It was in the context of working with the Peace Corps in a Tibetan community in India where I was living with my husband and my small children. My first real take on it gave a kick to my heart that was twofold. One part was beholding these Tibetan laypeople's and lamas' way of being human. And the other was the doctrine of *anatta*.[5] To understand their way of being human, I picked up some writings on the Buddhist path. There was a moment, on an overnight train on my way to Kangra Valley where this Tibetan community lived, that I experienced sort of a jolt, or a mini-*satori*:[6] *anatta* meant that I could be free of the self. In the Christian tradition, there's always a question of what to do with this "self." You can try to improve it, or you can crucify it. You can sacrifice it, you can mortify it, you can punish it, you can extol it, you can make it feel good, and so on. I noticed that Christians would get into a kind of cycle where you would act and feel good about it, but you're supposed to feel humble, and then feeling humble, you degrade yourself. Even humility, if that's the path you take for the self, can get you in a trap because then you can feel good about being humble. And so the first major insight I had about the Buddhist teach-

---

[5] *Anatta*, Pali, is defined by Buddhist scholar Nancy Wilson Ross as, "Absence of a permanent unchanging self or soul."
[6] See note 3 on page 91.

ings came in the realization: "I don't need to do anything with that 'self,' neither punish it nor make it noble and good, because it's just a convention, it's a fiction.
Whew! Oooh, that feels good." And then instantly there
followed, "Oh, we can be released into action." So from
the outset, the Dharma presented itself to me in terms of
that liberation into action.

CI: That's interesting, because that release into action is
not an extrapolation made by everyone who comes to realize *anatta*. Yet it was so immediate for you.

JM: Yes, it was. Although at the very beginning, when I
knew that I was going to leave India, I wanted to ask for
teachings, and I had the audacity to say to myself, "All
right, now I'm going to go up to Kangra, and I'm not going to do economic planning for the craft center in order
for them to build economic self-sufficiency and I'm not
going to work on the cooperative marketing scheme. I'm
going to ask for teachings." This I did with the naive as-
sumption that I would get some teachings which I could
take in my hands, and then oooh! I would have them.
Instead I was set down to watch my mind and empty
myself. So instead of being given anything, I was asked
to let go of what I had! And that was *vipassana* [insight
meditation], which I've always returned to as my central
path. But it was in the teachings of *paticca samuppada*
that I managed to see the absolutely breakthrough nature of the Buddha's thought, which was non-linear
causality. This was something that stood in contradis-
tinction both to the Vedic[7] thought of his time and to
contemporary mainstream Western thought.

CI: In that...?

_____

[7] *Vedic*, Sanskrit, of the *Vedas*, which are the oldest texts of Indian
Hindu literature, dating back to approximately 1500 B.C. *Veda* means
"knowledge, or sacred teaching."

JM: In that causality is not one way. It's mutual or re-ciprocal. It's only with general systems theory coming in through science in the last two generations of our culture that we have the conceptual language and constructs for being able to think about this. That is why I teach systems theory.

CI: So in other words, rather than there being a first cause and then a progression of effect, cause, effect, cause...

JM: That's right. Rather than a linear chain of events so that you can either think forward to what's going to happen by extrapolating, or you can trace the etiology by going backwards in time in an infinite regression toward the Prime Mover and beyond—instead there is this intricate, elegant, and, in some weird way, obvious recognition of our profound complicity with everything that's happening. We interact as phenomenal beings to, in a way, create each other in ongoing self-organizing systems. That says a lot about our power. We can break through what we've constructed because it is interdependently sustained in relationships. We can break through by altering the relationships or altering what seems to be a given at any point. We all live this, but our minds aren't used to thinking this way.

CI: Let me try to understand this. You're saying that rather than untying from the first cause, we can just jump into the system at any point and affect the entirety of the system.

JM: That's right. On an emotional or spiritual level—I must confess I don't like the word "spiritual"—maybe on a mystical level, this attracted me very much by the image it presents of our interactive presence to each other as beings—not pawns, not victims—engaged in a dance. We often perpetuate the patterns of a particular dance, but we're also able to alter the figure at any point when we can allow ourselves to become aware of how we, with our assumptions or projections, feed into a particular pattern. We see that "Oh, I am not doomed to continue forever this game of oppression, or injustice, or denial, or rat-race. As an interdependent co-creator of it, I can move over here." Freedom may certainly be somewhat limited by these patterns, but with awareness, the possibility of another choice always comes up.

I found that the texts which had been gathered and translated into the anthologies of Buddhist thinking by nineteenth century Western scholars had been done by people who had already decided that Buddhism was world-rejecting and passive. The Europeans who did the first scholarly studies—whether German or French or English or Russian—were in reaction against a kind of hyperactive social gospel they saw in Western society. They were in a society where the mystical dimension of religion had been lost, where the introspective had been dishonored, where it was all focused on the external. Seeking to right that balance, they looked to India and projected that interiority, the mystical that they sought, whether it was Vedic or Buddhist. In the process, they neglected two things. They neglected that there is an interior mystical dimension in Christianity itself, which is now coming forward strongly, and they neglected that in the Eastern traditions there was this strongly extroverted emphasis on social action.

CI: So they just split it off entirely for their own purposes and in reaction to the conditioning of their own time.

JM: Well, not *knowing* they were doing that. You know, you're never conscious of what you're projecting. As I read into the *sutras*, I was startled again and again by the very clear focus on "This we see in order that it make a difference in our lives and the world." As the Buddha said, I teach *paticca samuppada* because I believe that it is true. And whether or not it's true—now I'm paraphrasing—I teach it because it gives reason for doing one thing and not doing another, for the implica-

tions it has for the way we live in the world. That was
very clear, both in terms of the *sangha*[8] that he organized and the physical context of his teachings. He lived
and practiced not in the deep woods but on the periphery
of the big cities, with courtiers, with businessmen, with
members of the royal family. And he often spoke to issues of state which they would bring to him, issues
which we now call social justice, or political participation, or social and economic equality. These didn't
eclipse the issues of attaining to *nibbana*,[9] but they were
right up there.

I was also excited to see what was being taught and
experimented with around economic sharing. In the
sangha, there was no private ownership. In some of the
teachings, crimes of theft, lying, and murder were traced
to private ownership. What the Buddha was experimenting with in the constitution of the *sangha* totally fit
into, and was illumined by, the teaching of interdependence.

CI: So that spoke directly to you in organizing your own
work.

JM: Yes, this said to me that reality is so organized that
it requires that we live in certain ways or else suffer ter-
ribly. Now this is radically different from the belief system in which I'd grown up where you live certain ways
because a Big Daddy God tells you to, or because this is
the commandment of some immutable supernatural
essence. In the West, ethics have been derived from a
moral absolute. In Buddhism I found a set of quite
strong, pungent social teachings that came out of a view
of relativity—of radical relativity of all phenomena. We
don't need to posit a supernatural divinity to give sanc-

---

[8] *Sangha*, Pali, is the Buddhist order of monks and nuns. *Sangha* also
refers to a community of spiritual seekers or friends.

[9] *Nibbana*, Pali, (*nirvana*, Sanskrit) is the goal of spiritual endeavor in
traditional Buddhism. *Nibbana* refers to an unconditioned state of existence, or the cessation of suffering. It requires complete transformation of the three unwholesome mind states: greed, hatred, and delusion.

tion to these commandments. They're written in the heart already by our interdependently co-arising nature, or, to put it in systems terms, as self-organizing open systems. If that's what we are, dynamically interactive, then we have to live in certain ways.

CI: And the feedback loop is that one just pays attention and sees the effects of one's actions.

JM: Yes, you see the feedback, but it also helps if you've got somebody to point it out. That's why people flocked to hear the Buddha and recite what he said, and eventually to write it down, because that saved them...

CI: ...from a lot of trial and error.

I loved what you said in your interview with the *Inquiring Mind*—that practice was not for perfection but for wholeness.[10] We could also say that it's not for escaping from the world, but for participating in it fully.

JM: Yes, but they are different, and that's a good thing to bring out. It is so wonderful, Catherine, that in all the traditions of Buddhist practice which have come to the West, this is happening. The striving for purity and perfection, while understandable and laudable in its own right, can sever us from our world and be a terrible burden.

CI: The poet James Broughton says, "It is harder to love the world than to denounce it, harder to embrace existence than to renounce it."

Let's talk about some of the work you're well-known for. For years, you've helped people face their despair about the threat of nuclear holocaust or the destruction of the environment. Again, you've connected this work with Buddhist teachings, specifically the Buddha's Four Noble Truths in terms of recognizing how *anicca* [Pali:

---

10 The *Inquiring Mind* is a biannual Buddhist journal published in Berkeley, California.

impermanence] and *dukkha* [Pali: unsatisfactoriness or suffering] play a role in facing the fact of suffering, and learning to, as you put it, "sustain the gaze." Why are people so resistant to looking at what is happening to our world and to facing the despair? I know the simple answer is that it's painful.

Our entire media colludes in this hysteria of: "We're great, we're wonderful, let's wave the flag and pledge allegiance. We may have some problems, but this is still the greatest country in the world, rah rah." The Buddha used an analogy for this kind of attitude: children playing with their toys in a house that's burning. The house is burning on many levels, as you well know. And yet there are so many people still in denial about it. What is beneath this tremendous denial?

JM: I think it has to do with the notion of the self that our culture has conditioned us to believe through its emphasis on individualism. That view and the way it is conveyed puts a tremendous burden on a person in terms of holding himself together, in terms of competition, in terms of defendedness. I think that Robert Bellah in his book, *Habits of the Heart*, portrays this very well.

"Self" is always a metaphoric construct or hypothetical piece of turf around which you construct your strategies for survival and draw the boundaries of your self-interest. Then when you see your world falling apart, what do you do? How do you look at something like this? It's overwhelming. We're in the process of destroying our physical basis for life. And in *many* systems it may be beyond the point of return. How do you look at that? You think, "Well, I can't take it. It will be too painful, too overwhelming, and, in some sense, it's not my business." So that concept of self has been conducive to impotence.

CI: "There's nothing I can do about it..."

JM: Right. That phrase, "I don't think about it because there's nothing I can do about it," has fascinated me—

and the "it" can be a substitute for "acid rain" or "the nuclear arms race" or "the ozone layer" or what-have-you. I've really thought a lot about what is being said there. What's being said is sort of a double victimization, being so powerless that not only do I assume I can't do anything about it, but also I can't even think about it—which is a *non sequitur*, but very telling. So what's drawing me more and more is to work directly on that notion of the self and provide people with experiences and illustrations that can help them shed that old notion of self, like an unwanted, outmoded, too tight skin—and then help them move into a more capacious sense of self. In doing this I find that moralizing is totally ineffective and inappropriate. People aren't going to be scolded into looking at what's happening, which is still the tack that most activists are taking. But rather they want to be invited to come home to the way of participation in this world, knowing they are part of the web of life, which in our heart of hearts is what we want most.

CI: What are some of the ways you would have someone experience their being part of the web of life?

JM: The despair work is very strong in this regard because it allows people their own responses of anguish to what is happening to their world. These responses, of course, have been kept at bay, and the denial has, in turn, produced psychic numbing. It's a kind of spiral—the more we deny, the more we are numbed. I do this work not only because when we are open to our responses it frees energy, as any cathartic process will do, since it takes enormous energy to keep denying—denial is very expensive—but I do it so that people can honor these responses. Not just vent them like blowing off steam, but see them and treasure them. They can see that their true nature is *karuna*, compassion, which is a suffering *with* our world—whether they're experiencing fear, anger, guilt, or sorrow underlying it all. It cannot be reduced to a question of personal survival, even though most psychotherapists have been caught in a reductionist pattern of trying to tell their clients that this is just a question of personal maladjustment or private pathology.

CI: Yes, I read that you yourself had that experience in therapy.

JM: That's right. So it's been interesting, because some of the people who have been doing despair work would attempt to stay in a cathartic mode—"What we need to do is let people beat their breasts and tear their hair, and then they can act"—and then they realize, "Oh, it's beyond catharsis." It's in honoring the depths of our responses to what is going on in the world that we experience that the pain comes from caring, and that caring springs from interconnectedness. In other words, our responses are a direct doorway into, or proof of, interdependence. Realizing this can pop us out of that narrow prison of the separate ego.

CI: So you're saying that the numbing and the tremendous expense of denial is actually based on the heart's wanting to, as Ram Dass put it, "give away the store."

JM: Yes. And it's also based on a false notion of the self—that idea of a self which is so fragile that it needs to be protected, that it could break or get mired in despair.

CI: Do you have hope about our future? Is there hope?

JM: Frankly, I tend to be allergic to the term. Hope has been used as a dodge. Hope is like waiting for something else. Hope is like looking for the Lone Ranger to come galloping around the mountainside...

CI: Someone else to save us...

JM: Right. And, in a time that is as chancy as this, when we're going around a narrow and gravelly cliff face which slopes outward, to say "Oh, I'm hopeful" is a little dim-witted. It's not skillful. You can't waste any energy being hopeful or being hopeless. You just have to pay tremendous attention right now. And then you aren't asking, "Will I make it, will I not make it?"

As T. S. Eliot said, "I said to my soul: be still, and wait without hope/For hope would be hope of the wrong thing." Anything we hope for would be in terms of our old outmoded mental constructs. Does the caterpillar, when it dissolves in its cocoon, say, "Am I going to make it to a butterfly?"

I think that the possibilities right now are tremendous, because *if* we manage not to blow ourselves up or cook ourselves, if we manage not to completely lay waste our world—and we'll know about that pretty fast because the desertification and deforestation and the rest are growing exponentially, then that means we will have come to our senses. That's incredible, see. We're in a time when we either go right off the cliff like lemmings, or we stop, turn around, look at each other, and wake up. Either way, there's no excuse to be bored.

CI: Much as we might wish to be.

JM: As the Chinese proverb has it, "May you live in interesting times."

Ram Dass

Upon receipt of a telegram from his family in the summer of 1985, Ram Dass once again faced a major crossroads in his life: whether to continue his intensive meditation practice or to serve in the world. He was in the sixth week of a retreat at a monastery on the outskirts of Rangoon, Burma. Arrangements for this interlude had been made well in advance, as visas for a long-term stay in that exotic country are difficult to procure. He had adjusted to the rigorous monastic schedule: up at 3:00 a.m., the last meal of the day served at 10:00 a.m., with hour-long sitting and walking periods the rest of the time until 11:00 at night.

Ram Dass had come to this monastery to train with Sayadaw U Pandita, one of the most renowned teachers of vipassana (insight) meditation in the world. The training, as originally taught by the Buddha, is the practice of mindfulness—a systematic technique of noticing mental and bodily experience moment to moment, such that the teacher might ask the student: "On which breath did you fall asleep last night, the in-breath or the out-breath?" This microscopic observation provides an understanding of how greed, anger, and delusion arise in the mind and produce suffering and how non-attachment, love, and clarity foster mental peace.

Ram Dass had been making great effort and would daily report his meditation experience to U Pandita, when one day he received a telegram which said that his step-mother was about to undergo surgery for cancer. Ram Dass showed the telegram to U Pandita and said, "I've got to go home."

U Pandita considered the situation. He had lived for over fifty years in monasteries, practicing and teaching insight meditation. During that time he had seen tens of thousands of students come and go. He had taught throughout the Japanese occupation and American bombing of his country in World War II. Over the years, many of his close friends and students, all of his teachers, his parents, and eight of his nine siblings had passed away.

"You've made so much good progress, and you're at a critical point," U Pandita said to Ram Dass. "You should stay."

Ram Dass said simply, "I can't." He looked into the old man's eyes. "We both saw the poignancy of my karmic predicament," Ram Dass later explained. "That's what I saw it as anyway—not as right, but as poignant."

* * *

Ram Dass is best known for his transformation from Harvard psychology professor to psychedelic mind explorer to spiritual guide and friend, a journey he chronicled in *Be Here Now*. The book, which has sold nearly a million copies, was perhaps the single most influential catalyst for a generation of spiritual seekers in the seventies, and the phrase itself has become a mainstream cultural expression.

These days, Ram Dass gets high on service. He is an active board member and fundraiser for Seva Foundation which has projects ranging from providing cataract operations to restore sight for the blind in Nepal, to providing goats for widows in Guatemala.[1]

Ram Dass also maintains a regular meditation practice, periodically taking time for intensive retreats. It is this blend of doing and non-doing which has finally provided him with a sense of peace with his life. It had been a long search.

Ram Dass was born Richard Alpert on April 6, 1931 in Boston, the third son of upper middle-class Jewish parents. He grew up in the wealthy suburb of Newton, Massachusetts. When he was eight years old his parents bought a farm in New Hampshire where the family

---

[1] Seva Foundation was founded in 1979 by a group of people who had helped in the worldwide eradication of smallpox. *Seva* is the Sanskrit word for "service."

would spend summers. Here, young Richard developed a love of the country—swimming in the lake, playing tennis, and fooling around with the printing presses that were on the property.

His father, a successful lawyer, became prominent in the Boston community for raising money for the United Jewish Appeal, helping to found Einstein Medical School, and co-founding Brandeis University. He later became president of the New Haven Railroad. Young Richard watched his father's success with the proper respect befitting a man of such accomplishments, but his heart belonged to his mother, the great love of his early life. Nevertheless, his father's example and the cultural conditioning to achieve would influence many of his next years.

After prep school and high school, Richard Alpert received his B.A. from Tufts College in 1952, his Masters from Wesleyan College in 1953, and his Ph.D. from Stanford in 1957 where he taught for one year. In 1961, he moved on to Harvard where he held appointments in four departments. He also had research contracts at Yale and Stanford.

So Richard Alpert, Ph.D., entered the sixties as one "who had made it." He had all the right accoutrements for that status—degrees, position, possessions, books and articles he had authored, the "inner circle" of friends and acquaintances. He was, however, miserable. Inside, he couldn't help but feel that something was wrong. He knew that his teachings were the ideas of others and that even these "weren't getting to the crux of the matter." He developed physical symptoms before every lecture—nervous tension and diarrhea. He looked around at his colleagues in psychology and saw that their lives were not fulfilled either. Gradually he became aware that he didn't know whatever it was that would have it all make sense. "There was a slight panic in me that I was going to spend the next forty years not knowing, and that apparently that was par for the course," he later wrote. "The whole thing was too empty." Nevertheless, he raced along in his thriving career, driven by anxiety and ambition.

Down the hall from Dr. Alpert's busy, successful research center was a small office which had been converted from a closet for a new professor, Timothy Leary. Leary had been discovered bicycling around Italy by the Head of Harvard's Department of Psychology. He and Alpert quickly became drinking pals and in time began to experiment with psychedelics. During a trip to Mexico, Leary had ingested Tionanactyl mushrooms and proclaimed that he had learned more in the six or seven hours of that experience than he had in all his years as a psychologist.

The two friends began consciousness research using psychedelics on themselves and eventually on hundreds of "subjects." Along with colleagues Alan Watts, Aldous Huxley, and Ralph Metzner, Leary and Alpert stimulated a generation of hippies in the tumultuous sixties to explore their minds and to question all conventional reality, with a motto of "Turn on, tune in, and drop out."

The conventional institutions to which Leary and Alpert belonged, however, were definitely not inspired by the research, and Alpert was summarily thrown out of Harvard. He watched his own fall from academic grace with a curious detachment, wondering if he had really gone over the edge of sanity now, "...because craziness is when everybody agrees about something—except you!" Yet, somehow he had never felt saner. The psychedelics had given him a glimpse into a reality where one's essence "existed independent of social and physical identity...beyond Life and Death."

The problem, he found, was that no matter how "high" he got, he always came down. After six years and approximately 300 psychedelic trips, Richard Alpert felt a gnawing frustration: what he knew from all of those experiences *still* wasn't enough. A "gentle depression" set in.

He decided to go to India with a vague idea of meeting "holy men" and somehow discovering the "missing clue." After several months of wandering around India and Nepal, Alpert's despair became acute. He had made no spiritual discoveries, yet he had no reason to return home to the States. In his deepest depression and at a point when he had become almost infantile, he met his guru, Neem Karoli Baba, also known as Maharaji.

In some ways, Maharaji was just an old man wearing a blanket and being fed by devotees while lying around in his temple. When Richard Alpert first arrived at the temple he was suspicious of everyone there, especially Maharaji, who had promptly asked for the Land Rover in which Alpert was traveling. In a short time, Alpert came to see that Maharaji had no interest in the Land Rover or any other worldly possession, and if he had, Alpert would happily have given it to him. For it was in this old man's presence that Richard Alpert first experienced unconditional love. He felt that Maharaji knew his every thought, his every secret, and yet loved him for what he was "behind all that."

Maharaji didn't give formal teachings. His was more a manifestation of the Way rather than a map. However, he did consistently say two things: "Love everybody" and "Serve everybody." In keeping with this teaching, he gave Richard Alpert the name "Ram Dass," servant of God. One day, Maharaji called Ram Dass to his side and said, "You make many people laugh in America?" Ram Dass answered, "Yes, I like to do that." Maharaji said, "Good...You like to feed children?" Again, Ram Dass answered, "Yes, sure." Maharaji asked a few more questions and then, smiling, he reached forward and tapped the puzzled Westerner on the head three times. Deeply moved by the encounter, although not understanding it, Ram Dass left the room in tears.

When he returned to the West, Ram Dass began speaking about his experiences in India and soon many Westerners followed in his wake, looking for Maharaji in Himalayan villages. *Be Here Now* was published in 1971 and changed thousands of people's lives. Maharaji passed away in 1973. In that year Ram Dass founded the Hanuman Foundation, dedicated to service projects such as the Prison/Ashram Project to aid prisoners in developing a spiritual practice and the Living/Dying Center to help people move consciously through the dying process.

Ram Dass's talks continued to inspire thousands of people throughout the seventies. With the opening of Naropa Institute[2] in the summer of 1974, a huge gathering of spiritual seekers found delight in the playful bantering of Ram Dass, the converted Hindu, and Trungpa Rinpoche, the Westernized Tibetan Buddhist, as they spiritually battled for the hearts and minds of the crowd, alternating lectures every other night.

Ram Dass has long had an interest in Buddhism and, over the years, he has studied with many Buddhist meditation teachers, primarily in the *vipassana* tradition. Yet he has never forgotten the words of his guru, and he makes an ongoing effort to "Serve everybody."

Seva Foundation provides a vehicle for Ram Dass's service as well as his talent as a speaker and master of ceremonies, such as when he hosted a sold-out benefit for the homeless of New York at St. John the Divine Cathedral in December 1988. The principles of Seva's "compassionate service" are told in stories in Ram Dass's and Paul Gorman's book *How Can I Help?* Donating his lecture fees to Seva, Ram Dass is one of their primary sources of funding. However, he lives modestly in a cottage on the estate of friends in San Anselmo, California. He is new to the householder life after so many years on the road and is happily throwing himself into decisions concerning washer/dryers and kitchen appliances.

I met Ram Dass at Naropa Institute in 1974, having previously read *Be Here Now* and embarking on a spiritual quest as a result. Over the years I have traveled in coinciding circles with him; in 1977, along with a group of friends, we toured monasteries in Thailand. What makes this man special is not only that he is a con-

---

2 Naropa Institute was founded by Chögyam Trungpa Rinpoche and modeled after the ancient Indian Buddhist University of Nalanda. It was named after the great Indian scholar, Naropa, who had once been head of Nalanda University.

summate storyteller, but that he is truly a seeker before he is a teacher, a peer who is willing to share his mistakes and vulnerabilities publicly and without censorship and to invite people to laugh with him in his foibles. Over the years I have observed a strengthening in his desire to serve, a one-pointedness in his spiritual practice, and a calming in his heart. He is a powerful teacher despite "the egg on [his] beard."

The following conversation took place at my home in Larkspur, California, where Ram Dass and I spent nearly four hours talking. We had a wonderful time together, drinking tea and letting our minds roll and frolic into the late afternoon, the San Francisco Bay twinkling in the distance. As he was leaving I thanked him for *Be Here Now.* Somehow in all the years, I had never said those words to him. I watched him walk down the hill as I reflected on the love and insight that the sharing of his journey has inspired in so many others, and I felt waves of gratitude for having known him.

Interview with Ram Dass

June 17, 1988 • Larkspur, California

Catherine Ingram: We live in a time in which we have unprecedented exposure through the mass media to the world's suffering. We can find out that thousands of people just died in some horrible accident this morning halfway around the world. I sometimes wonder about the balances of this kind of knowledge. How much can one take in and still be effective and not overwhelmed?

Ram Dass: Most everybody is overwhelmed. And they respond with various defense mechanisms. Denial, isolation, increased greed ("I'll get it while I can"), righteousness ("It's their own fault"). There are a whole set of mechanisms that people use to keep from being open, because the quality of the human heart uncontrolled by the mind is that it will give away everything.

It's the mind which is constantly saying, "You can't afford; be careful; you'll lose too much." So the suffering makes us increasingly afraid of our own compassion. It increases our own fear that we will give away the store. We have to find ways to exercise the compassion of our hearts, and at the same moment learn how to know what the limits are and be able to say no without guilt.

CI: Martin Luther King talks about having the "strength to love."

RD: Exactly.

CI: But I sometimes feel that my heart is breaking.

RD: There are many levels of heart. And the human heart will break because it empathizes. The deeper heart—the *hridayam*[3], the *jivatma*[4], or the *hsin hsin* in Chinese—that heart is the one that looks at the universe, just as it is, in a non-reactive way and says, "Ah so," "Yes." And it includes your own human heart which is breaking, but your identity isn't only with your human heart. Your identity is with a deeper, intuitive heart wisdom, which is different. You don't deny the pain, but you don't get reactive to it.

CI: Someone reading these lines might say, "That's the classic cop-out for so-called spiritual people." Are we able to respond in appropriate ways to effect change from that state of equipoise and acceptance, or do we become complacent?

RD: Well, the history of wars and human interaction around disequilibriums, such as the haves and have-nots, is full of reactivity. Reactivity has been shown to be extremely short-sighted. I don't really mind being

---

[3] *Hridayam*, Sanskrit, "heart."

[4] *Jivatma*, Sanskrit, "individual soul."

criticized for saying what I'm saying. As a student of Aikido and Eastern martial arts, I know that quietness of mind is master of the deed. The quieter you are, the more clearly you hear how it all is and what part you can play in it. There's a difference between the emptiness that is fullness and the emptiness that is avoidance.

CI: There is a new class of homeless in America. I've just read Jonathan Kozol's book, *Rachel and Her Children*, in which he strongly indicts U.S. government policy for the homeless problem. I wonder if you have any thoughts on the causes of homelessness in America and who these new homeless are?

RD: I am very aware that there are political root issues of this problem that have to do with developers and real estate interests. For example, New York City is holding something like 70,000 units empty, buildings they have reclaimed or taken over. Economic self-interest is a lot of the root cause.

I think the problem also has to do with downward spirals that happen because of economic instabilities. People start to lose control of the game. They build up to a certain blue-collar level of having a house, a car, and all that, and then they get laid off, and they can't ever get back to their former level again. They just keep losing ground. What I'm impressed with is that a lot of the homeless I meet on the streets are middle class. These are not people who are used to living below poverty or outside the society, although it's mainly the minorities who get the real rough end of the deal. And they're perplexed. I can feel their perplexedness. When I work in a soup kitchen, I can also feel their dignity, and their dignity is bruised.

I've just done a slide show about suffering and how we deal with suffering. It starts out with the American dream, with what we all bought into, what everybody thought the dream was, and how well the dream would work. Then when the dream didn't fulfill you enough, you bought into the models that were presented by the Johnny Carsons and the Dynastys and Dallases—that more is better—that the dream *includes* the more-ness. So the bigger the car, the happier you'll be.

Then if you chance to look down, you see that between the cracks have fallen people who also wanted to be part of the dream, but not only are they not getting more, they aren't getting enough. You begin to see the rents in the fabric of the dream structure, and that leads you into defensive mechanisms in order to hold onto the dream. What are the alternatives to trying to hold onto a dream? What are the ways to live without the dream?

The slides then show social action with Gandhi and Mother Teresa and others. Then it takes us through all the leaders saying we want peace alongside all the war and violence and cruelty, Auschwitz and Dachau and all that. We say everybody should have shelter, and the slides show bigger and bigger houses. Then it shows the homeless. We say there should be enough food, and it shows fatter and fatter people and more and more supermarkets. Then it shows the hungry, such as a woman with an empty breast, holding a baby.

CI: Although for years you have been involved in social activism and service through Seva Foundation, lately you seem to have become more politically active. You recently sat at the Nevada Test Site with Dan Ellsberg, and you spoke on the steps of Congress about U.S. policy in Central America. What has prompted this new interest in political activism?

RD: Being in Guatemala mobilized me. We [Seva] were providing goats, seed, and yarn for weaving and selling the crafts and tool bags to villagers who had been decimated. And the cause of the decimation was United States policy in Guatemala. Here we were building an organization in this Guatemalan community, and I felt concerned that the military would see us as a threat and then hurt these people. And then a fellow who worked for one of the Guatemalan aid projects told me, "We just help the people learn how to pick themselves up so that next time it will be easier." It was such a humble aspiration.

I was so deeply ashamed in Guatemala for the United States role there (and I realized that since I was a United States citizen, it was *my* role there), that I was reactive, and being reactive is not the mode from which to do social action, as Gandhi and others have said.

CI: How do you see your role as a tax-paying citizen?

RD: I saw that as a U.S. citizen I had two roles. One was to directly help these human beings, and the other was to speak out. The minute I started to do that, it opened like a huge avenue and I realized that I've got to be more conscious, I've got to be very careful in how I do this. Let me explain what I mean by that.

In the early years, from the sixties into the mid-seventies, I was on the government lists of undesirables. I'd go to England, for example, and they wouldn't let me into the country. They'd deport me to Amsterdam because of my drug history. Finally I got off the list around the mid-seventies, and since then I've been an irrelevant weirdo. [laughing] And I realize that here in one little move I could put myself back into that arena of being somebody that the government is concerned about, which does make you have to start living your life much tighter.

CI: You get audited and...

RD: Everything. And I didn't really know if that was the optimum way to play the game. Requests started coming to me to talk about my Guatemala experience, and I thought, "Before I do this, let me just know what I'm doing. I don't want to jeopardize Seva, so I'm listening to hear how to play. I'm very new at the game."

CI: Do you feel that there is a place for outrage, if you will, in witnessing some of the unspeakable horrors that are going on? I know that the Christic Institute[5] and others must struggle with this—a feeling of outrage. Yet people often feel motivated by their outrage to act.

RD: I think there is a place for outrage, but it always has to be tempered with the equanimity that comes out of an appreciation of the way the universe is—why violence is done, and how it comes from fear and greed and holding on. So you're outraged as a human heart, and at the same time you're appreciative of why it is the way it is and how it happened. I feel that being led by my outrage isn't the place for social action. It would just polarize more in the long run, as the anti-Vietnam war movement did in the late sixties.

CI: Let's get back to Guatemala. I'm reminded that Stephen Gaskin's people went down there after the earthquake in 1976 and began getting involved in local farming cooperatives.[6] Once they saw the impoverished condition in which the whole country was living, they began helping out in other ways, putting in soybean crops, and so on. Gaskin said that slowly but surely, various Guatemalans who had been aligned with them would be "disappeared."[7] The Gaskin folks finally left Guatemala because they were putting their friends there in too much danger by having contact with them.

RD: We work through Guatemalan agencies that are very sensitive and know they are at risk. They tell us exactly what we can do and what we can't do. They are very sophisticated about how we can be used as leverage to help them...how we can also hurt them. It's delicate.

---

[5] The Christic Institute is an investigative organization which is most well-known for its work on the Contragate Project. Based in Washington, D.C., it was founded in 1980 by the legal team who had won the Karen Silkwood case.

[6] The earthquake which occurred on February 4, 1976 in Guatemala measured 7.5 on the Richter scale and killed 22,778 people.

[7] Used in this context, "disappeared" refers to the abductions of people in Central America.

CI: I recently heard you tell stories about the widows you worked with there, extraordinary accounts of sorrow.

RD: Oh, I would say that a good two-thirds of the people that I met in the villages had had a member of their family murdered or disappeared. In the worst cases, they had been forced to watch their relatives be tortured and die slowly over time. I mean, watching a younger brother have rocks forced into his eyes, his feet flayed on the bottom and then being forced to walk. Watching a mother be tortured to death and her relatives can't touch the body. She's in the middle of the village square and the soldiers are urinating into her mouth as she's dying. The worst imaginable stuff. And the horror of it is that the soldiers are Mayan Indians as well. They have just been brainwashed into thinking that this is a communist conspiracy when it's basically an economic question, as you have pointed out in your writings.

CI: It's been an economic question since the fifties for Guatemala.

RD: It's always been one. It seems to me that this is an interesting window of opportunity for a shift in policy in Central America. That's why I'm tempted to leap into the action. I just want the wisdom of my spiritual elders to guide me. I don't mind going to prison if that's what I'm supposed to do, but I need to make sure that that's the best way to use my gift and my grace.

CI: You spoke about the collusion of our life here, the responsibility that you feel as an American citizen. We are becoming more and more aware that we are living in this incredibly rich society which is dependent on the labor and oppression of the world's poor.

RD: But it doesn't necessarily have to be that way. It's in that beautiful line of Gandhi's—that civilization is the art of voluntary renunciation. We haven't yet understood the joy of letting go of a little of our largess, which, in fact, we would hardly miss. I mean, it's like the difference between a Mercedes and a Dodge. Our small renunciation would allow other people to live and have a better standard of life. It wouldn't wipe out our affluence at all to feed and clothe and house everybody in the world, and it would take such pressure off all of us, because the ugliness we have to live with, not just as the ugly American, but as part of all the affluent countries—Japan, Germany, France—the psychic cost of all that is actually more than we can bear.

That's part of what our addictive patterns are about, part of what the neurosis in the culture is about. There is a lack of well-being with all of our affluence. That's partly because we are looking away from suffering so much in order to try to find happiness. Again a line from Gandhi, "Think of the poorest person you've ever seen and ask whether your next act will be of any use to that person." Now, can you find happiness with that in mind? If you can't, you're schizophrenic. You have these little compartments of, "Now I'll spend so many hours writing checks for the poor; then I'll put that away and I'll go have fun." The deeper thing is to keep your heart open in hell and find joy right in the midst of all of it.

CI: Let's talk about AIDS. What is the message of this disease? What is this saying to us historically?

RD: Well, one of the things it's saying is that the sexual freedom movement that started in the sixties, when carried to its ultimate, is lethal. But interpreting that in terms of good and evil is a whole other issue, and I don't think that's really the message. It's mind-boggling that the people who have mostly been hit by the disease, thus far, are needle users and gays, both of which are minority groups in a society which considers them expendable or a weakness of the culture. Therefore the dragging of the feet of the government is motivated by seeing these people as second-rate citizens, so that from within the gay community, which is very familiar to me, the way in which the disease is heaped upon the prejudice is exponentially horrible. A fellow will get AIDS, and when he tells his parents, they're too ashamed to acknowledge it to their friends. They don't want to deal with him, so he's ostracized by his family because of the social pressure on the parents. This happens again and again.

Another level of the message is the intimacy between self-gratification and death. Sex and death have always been linked, but needle-using is another form of gratification and sharing the needle can be linked with intimacy, and so on.

It is time to remember Gandhi's statement: "There is enough for everybody's need but not enough for everybody's greed." We've gotten very greedy in wanting more—more sex, more rushes from drugs, more, more, more. And what more leads to is death. More power leads to more heart attacks and more violence. More rich food leads to cholesterol. More is risky.

So that's part of the message that's coming out of the AIDS scene. It's taken what was often a very superficial, manipulative, rather cruel subculture—the gay community—and brought out qualities of compassion in it that are so beautiful that many of them hardly know themselves at all.

CI: You say it was a "cruel subculture."

RD: It was so based on physical and sexual attractiveness. Narcissism. And it was cruel in the exaggerated way it did that. It identified with the most bitchy components of the women's culture—looks, and so on—but it was worse.

CI: And has AIDS transformed the gay community in those ways?

RD: Oh, absolutely transformed it. It's deepened them as human beings because they're suddenly dealing with death. Death from AIDS is one of the most terrible ways to die because opportunistic diseases are so unpre-

dictable. It's not like cancer where there's a kind of linear progression. With AIDS you go and treat one problem
and maybe you get better, and then something else comes
along, so it keeps beating your will down. From a spiritual point of view, it's an incredible disease because it
takes away your control. Those are windows of opportunity for spiritual awakening if it's handled just right.
For most people, their evolution hasn't prepared them
for that way of seeing it. Part of my work is to introduce
that kind of perspective without seeming Polyanna-ish
or callous.

CI: How can you counsel someone in any way other than
to accept death in the face of having AIDS?

RD: There's no other way. But the denial is very strong,
often in the belief that some treatment is going to work.
The thing is to counsel them to continue to make an effort to heal themselves and yet to expect death. My constant saying is, "The probability is you're gonna die.
Now let's start from there and talk." But I don't go to
people without their asking. They've got to seek me out. I
don't lay it on people because I don't have a moral right
to do that. If somebody wants to live through denial until their death, it's up to them. From my years of working with the dying, that's too clear.

CI: What has it meant to you personally to be working
with AIDS patients?

RD: Most of the dying people I have worked with over the
last fifteen or twenty years have been older people, but
these AIDS patients are very young, so there's a whole
new way of time and death that I'm dealing with.

The second thing is that, at least within the gay community, these people contracted AIDS from sexual practices that have been part of my own history. So there but
for whatever go I.

And still another part of it is that there's so much of
it now. I'm dealing with death, or people facing death or

fear of death probably three to four times a week. These are very intense processes, and I am blown away by how much the spiritual work, the practices I've done, are paying off. I never realized what a gift it was until I saw the way the gift worked.

I recently went to visit the "Coming Home" hospice in the Castro in San Francisco to speak to the staff. I was supposed to speak for thirty minutes and then they were going to show me through the place. They said, "Oh, by the way, there are eight patients who have asked to see you." So I had three minutes with each patient. I'd walk into a room, and there would be somebody with one eye closed with Kaposi's Sarcoma, his face all swollen. He's gonna die within maybe two weeks. Or there would be an old black needle user. It was just one after another. And I had three minutes to get in, go through my own reactivity, get quiet, make contact, be available to the person, get up, disengage, go and do the next one. I went into a place in myself like the place you do *dokusan* from.[8] You set yourself aside.

CI: What do you say to somebody in three minutes who is lying there dying of AIDS?

RD: It has nothing to do with what you say. It's where you are in yourself. Gandhi's line fits perfectly: "My life is my message." You offer your presence, you offer the way you feel about death, the way you feel about their symptoms, and you do it all just in your presence. It's not the words, it's the quality of the way you say them. It's where you say them from. You can say something that keeps the game going, or you can speak in a way that leaves the door open so that they can come out of it if they want to. You don't force them to come out of it.

CI: What do you feel about facing your own death?

---

8 *Dokusan*, Japanese, literally "go alone to a high one;" this generally refers to the formal meeting of a Zen student with his or her teacher.

RD: I can't tell how I will deal with my own death or the suffering prior to death, my own dying. There are two issues—one is dying, and the other is death. The Eastern image of "dropping the body" is one that really appeals to me. I also identify with an awareness that has no dimension of time and space or birth and death. I'm watching my aging body with a certain kind of compassion and interest. I identify and pull back, identify and pull back, but there's a deep root of identification with something that isn't the body.

CI: I recently heard Jesse Jackson, Jr. speak in Los Angeles at a fundraiser for his father about the crack cocaine problem. He said that we need to address the social ills which foster the use of drugs. People often use drugs to change their mind state in order to relieve their hopelessness even for a little while.

RD: Exactly, because their options are very narrow. I can understand why somebody in an inner city ghetto will take drugs. And no middle-class honky is gonna come along and say "Just say no," as she holds up her glass of wine or her cocktail at night. But the answer to the drug problem is neither in armies nor in legalizing drugs. The root cause of the problem is the fallacy of the American dream, and how do you change that one?

CI: What about the new research which paints our society as addictive in general?

RD: That's quite interesting to me. Addiction to money, power, sex, drugs. To think of addiction as only to drugs is too narrow. Our society has an addictive structure. Addiction is rooted in feelings of inadequacy in the presence of conditions that seem overwhelming. I wouldn't be surprised if a major contributing factor is the long-term effect of living with the bomb, or the economic volatility of the interdependent economic structures of the world now. Nobody can quite control it.

CI: We're living under tremendous tension from a variety of threats.

RD: But the tension is created by our mind's way of dealing with uncertainty. So if you go back to that root cause, and teach how to deal with uncertainty, then you make warriors for living with *anicca* [Pali: impermanence]. *Anicca* warriors—or peaciers, as I'd rather call them.

CI: Many people have taken a spiritual path and, after some time, find themselves saying, "Now what?" They often turn outward to the world at this point to share with others or to help out in some way. The rolling-up-the-sleeves stage. Do you see this as a natural progression of understanding—spirituality leading into social action?

RD: Empirical evidence would not seem to bear out that that's a natural sequence. There are a lot of spiritual people who just keep going deeper and deeper into their own process. They see the way in which the most subtle impurities get magnified and create suffering by their action, and they really feel that they have to get enlightened first.

Because I have a karma yoga[9] orientation, I see my non-participation *is* participation. My guru said, "Feed people and serve people." However, teachers such as Sayadaw U Pandita would say, "Don't go back into the world now because you can do so much more if you complete this next phase."

It is my intention to use my experiences in the world in the same way Gandhi did, as experiments in truth, as a vehicle for coming to God. I realize that a lot of that is rationalization, in me as it was in Gandhi, and that I

---

[9] Karma yoga, Sanskrit; this is one of the four main types of yogas. Karma means action. Yoga means union; in this case, it refers to union with God. Karma yoga represents selfless action whereby one dedicates the action and its results to God.

just can't handle not responding to the pressures of the world. I don't have the inner conviction. But I can honor somebody who does choose the path of renunciation.

Even though I know very little about my guru Maharaji's practice, I know that for years he sat in a lake, and then he sat surrounded by fires for many years, and he lived in the jungle and he didn't even come out till he was about forty-five. Nobody even saw him until then, from the time he was about eight or ten years old. He was just somebody in the jungle doing his thing. And then he comes out and you can feel that his thought forms are so powerful, so rooted in Dharma, that one thought can change a major game!

CI: So we're talking about efficacy here. The inner work creates so much clarity and strength that whatever thought or action comes from that has real power.

RD: Exactly. I remember a time with him when Indira Gandhi was going by with her jeeps and elephants and army generals and all that. Maharaji was lying on his table with his blanket falling off, and he was giggling. He was saying, "Look at all that, and it's just a worldly king." He made it sound so trivial to me that I perceived a mind state where you could see a Reagan or a Bush as a sort of bumptious teenager. It's a certain spaciousness of mind that doesn't get lost in the fray at all. It sees the cycles of incarnation in a time perspective as vast as the kalpas[10] and yugas[11] of the *Bhagavad Gita* or the *Ma-*

---

[10] *Kalpa*, Sanskrit, a world cycle. In the Vedic scriptures, a *kalpa* comprises four cosmic ages, or *yugas*, and lasts approximately 4,320,000 years.

[11] *Yuga*, Sanskrit, refers to one of the revolving four ages of the world: *Krita*, the golden age in which there is no hate, envy, or fear; *Treta*, the age in which such righteousness declines by one quarter; *Dvapara*, in which righteousness has dwindled to one half; and the *Kali Yuga*, in which righteousness is reduced to one quarter of the time of the golden age. The *Kali Yuga* is believed to have begun in 3102 B.C. and is still underway. In this period of time, "disease, fatigue, anger, hunger, fear, and despair gain ground; humanity has no goal."—from *The Encyclopedia of Eastern Philosophy and Religion.*

habharata.[12] Sure the bomb is gonna fall. We've done that before, and here we go again. I can't really say why people who are in those realms of spiritual attainment should involve themselves in the rather trivial market-place that seems to preoccupy us so much.

That's what is bugging me, see, because I'm really good in this marketplace game, in the political, social, educational game. I'm a master. But it's copping out at some level, because if I would just pull back and empty for maybe five years, I might have something to offer.

CI: Do you know when you're out of balance, or not living up to what you say?

RD; Oh boy. The horror of it. It's too ghastly to live with. There's that great story of the mother bringing her kid to Gandhi and saying, "Please tell my son to give up sugar." Gandhi said, "Come back in a week." The mother left perplexed. A week later, she came back and Gandhi said to the kid, "Give up sugar." The mother said to Gandhi, "Couldn't you have told him that last week?" Gandhi replied, "No, because *I* hadn't given up sugar last week."

CI: Gandhi's simple lifestyle was also part of his message. How do you relate to that?

RD: Well, Gandhi really set standards that hit on my middle-classness with the issues of money, property, and so on. I have a credit card, I have a car, I have money in the bank which will last me until December before I have to work again. I mean my faith isn't deep enough yet to go without entirely. Partly I can say that I'm liv-

---

[12]The *Mahabharata* is one of the two major Sanskrit epics of India, the other being the *Ramayana*. The *Mahabharata*, compiled between approximately 200 B.C. and 200 A.D., is a complex story of the political maneuverings of rival cousins which culminated in a great war. The *Bhagavad Gita* is the most famous section of the *Mahabharata*, and is the climactic moment in the story of the war. It consists of dialogues between Krishna and Prince Arjuna in which Arjuna comes to realize that Krishna is God in a human form.

ing in a different culture. It's inefficient for me not to use my credit card, not to be able to take planes and rent cars because that's what's necessary for the role I'm playing. But I don't really trust that, because I am too middle-class in the way I see it. Krishnamurti, for example, never touched money for years, but he had Seville suits and other people paying. I don't think having a bag man is the same as not touching money in the way Gandhi didn't deal with money.

There is a simplicity in Gandhi that I crave. My life *is* getting simpler. It appears very complex, but inside it's getting to be very simple. Simplicity is the result of stopping the identification with so many desires. Maharaji said to me, "Give up money and sex and you'll know God." Giving up the identification with lust is what I hear in that statement, and that's also giving up the identification with lust regarding money. I feel that I am much less preoccupied about money than I was even five years ago. I can feel it falling away very, very fast. As for sexuality, it's not as compulsive and obsessive as it was for thirty-five years. Part of that is my age!

CI: That must be a real relief.

RD: [Laughing] Yes, and there's so much time in the day now. I don't know what to do with all of it. Have to meditate.

CI: You've often spoken of your difficulties in working with lust in the past.

RD: Well, that's certainly something I've had to work with—seeing the way in which lust is divisive, the way it creates objects out of people. Gandhi had a kind of blanket repudiation of gratification in a way that is a little too purist for me. It's like Ramana Maharshi saying that the only time you should have sex is to procreate. I'm not in tune with that yet. But I can feel that if to have sex requires that you see somebody as an object, then it costs more than it's worth in the long run because it increases paranoia, isolation, and separateness.

CI: What is the relationship between your work on yourself and how you serve others?

RD: [Pause] Gandhi said that everything he was doing was in order to get *moksha*, liberation. That's the real karma yogi. People say he was such a caring human being, but he said, "I'm only doing this for myself." That's the way I feel. Now society doesn't want to hear that, because it sounds selfish. But it really isn't. It has to do with the real root causes of suffering.

CI: You mean belief in self?

RD: Yes. Belief in self and attachments of mind create suffering for you and everybody. So you're driven to work on yourself as an act of compassion.

CI: In the past you've spoken of having to deal with a lot of projection about being a wise or a holy man. Over the years you've become well-known to thousands of people as a spiritual teacher. Is it more comfortable for you now in dealing with their projections?

RD: Well, it's great because it burns you out faster. Fame is a tremendous gift because it gives you so much power in people's lives that it's really obvious when you misuse it.

CI: The effects of misusing that power must be overwhelming.

RD: Oh boy, ten or fifteen years later I am still dealing with the karma of that flicker in my eye, answering someone's projection, and what that sucked them into between us.

You know, there is another teaching from Gandhi which has served me well because it has given me the courage to admit that I have made errors, and that is when he talked of the relationship between consistency and truth. As a human I still know only relative truth, and my understanding of truth changes from day to day. Gandhi said, "My commitment is to truth, not to consistency." That line stands alongside Aurobindo's line that the spiritual path is one of falling on your face. You get up and brush yourself off, turn and look sheepishly at God and then you take the next step, you get on with it. These two lines give me the courage to be inconsistent, and to be publicly inconsistent. The egg on my beard is very obvious.

CI: So even though you might revise your understanding of truth, you don't feel you've taken a detour from your path.

RD: No. People often come to me and say, "I've fallen off the path." I say, "That's impossible because people who have fallen off the path don't say, 'I've fallen off the path.'" Somehow I have faith in the universe—I'm not sure where it comes from—even with all the horror and the torture and so on. This is hard to say because it's morally reprehensible to even think that the people who died in the Holocaust are, from a soul point of view, on an evolutionary path in which that experience was functional. That sounds too horrible to consider. But that's the part that isn't humanistic about the spiritual path. I have such a deep conviction about that, and it's part of what allows me to be in the presence of suffering. If somebody is suffering, even though I will do my best to relieve them, there's another part of me that trusts that the suffering is in the greater good and if I could see, I could understand. But, I can't see, so I can't understand.

CI: Given that you feel that way, my question is about Gandhi's way of nonviolence. Do you see nonviolence as an ultimate truth or do you see it as specific to his time and circumstances? In other words, if we were going to do any kind of action, would nonviolence always be the way?

RD: I think so. It's tricky because the *Gita*, you see, doesn't advocate that. That's where Gandhi waffled in the way he rewrote the *Gita*. He couldn't handle the part about killing as a Dharma. I think that when you are talking about people who are not enlightened, then *ahimsa* is the only legitimate path for not creating karma. But I think an enlightened being can kill because they are, by definition, free of desire. So if you can kill without any desire, go to it.

CI: Yet people may delude themselves about their level of enlightenment and then act outside the realm of conventional moral codes.

RD: Yes, while I am aware that different levels of teaching are for different people, the level of teaching which is beyond conventional morality is tricky. When acting in that way, the main question then becomes, "Will this do good?" So that whatever you would do would bring things into harmony, into unity, into the Tao. In the Hindu tradition, Vishnu and Shiva are both enlightened forms, and they have very different functions—one being to preserve and the other to destroy. One moves things toward unity, and the other disrupts them. Yet, they're both part of Dharma.

That leads you to the Coyote figure, or to that rascal quality of Hanuman.[13] It was interesting to me that when Maharaji was alive, he would tell each person around him a different thing. To one he would say, "Smoke dope." To the other he'd say, "Don't smoke dope. Dope's the worst thing for spiritual development." Because everybody had a relationship with him, everybody

---

13 Hanuman, Sanskrit, literally, "the one with big jaws," refers to the monkey king-god of the *Ramayana*. As a devoted servant to Ram, hero of the *Ramayana* epic, Hanuman leapt from India to Ceylon, pulled trees from their roots, and moved the Himalayas. He is known in Hindu lore for his devotion.

had the feeling that their *sadhana* was the *sadhana* that Maharaji was acknowledging.[14] Then once he left his body, and there wasn't that continuous validation, we were left with each other, and the tension was incredible. Each person felt they had the direct line, and the lines were often contradictory.

CI: Whose finger was pointing at the real moon?...

RD: Right.

CI: I know the Hindus say that we're in the Kali Yuga, the age of destruction, and it appears to be the case. Do you see light prevailing? And if you don't, how do you muster the energy to keep going, and how would you recommend others keep going? Is it necessary to be fixed to a goal in order to do the work? What if it's all going into hopeless ruin? Maybe we should just go meditate somewhere.

RD: I hear the question. The way I've answered that question in the past still feels pretty valid. People come up to me and say, "Are we facing Armageddon, or is this the Aquarian Age?" I decided that I should have an opinion, so I thought about it and came up with this: If it's Armageddon, we're gonna die, it's gonna end, and the best way for me to prepare for that is to quiet my mind and to open my heart. That's the way to go into death. And if it's the New Age coming, the best way for me to prepare for that is to quiet my mind and to open my heart. So it doesn't matter, because I still have to do the same thing today—quiet my mind, open my heart, and relieve the suffering that I see around me.

In a way that's been my plan. I'm not future-oriented about my life because I'm aware of how quickly circumstances can change. While certain things are not reversible—like what we're doing to the forests and species

---

[14] *Sadhana*, Sanskrit, derives from *sadh*, "to arrive at the goal," and refers to practice leading to spiritual attainment.

which will disappear—there can be a critical mass of horror that shifts consciousness. What we're seeing is an exacerbation of the symptoms that provokes a response that can continue to exacerbate the symptoms or not. It's not a clear prediction as to which way it will go.

If I'm to be an instrument of healing, my attachment to how it comes out has to be zilch. Absolutely nil. A part of me has to keep its territory of equanimity. And yet, because I am a human incarnate, I have to work full time to make it better.

As I read the Club of Rome reports, as I look at the ecological errors we're making, I feel my blood chill. As I see the intractable nature of the human personality and the way it engages in wars, it horrifies me. But then I watch how the economic pressures in the Soviet Union force a change in philosophy so that a Gorbachev can exist, which forces a change in Reagan's seeing them as the Evil Empire, which forces a cutting out of medium-range ballistic missiles, and suddenly everything that we in the anti-nuclear movement were fighting for is starting to happen. What I've said at a lot of the anti-nuclear rallies is that you folks don't realize that you have already won. The game is over. You did what you set out to do. But the people in that movement are often busy feeling fragmented or feeling a lack of power because they didn't have the opponent at their knees. As Gandhi said, the English had to leave but he wanted them to leave as friends. If there is a winner, nobody wins. Everybody loses.

CI: Do you have any predictions about our future, apart from whether or not it's Armageddon or the New Age?

RD: Yes, I think there are a lot of things down the road. For instance, the power of the have-nots will ultimately be a motivation to reduce the vast economic disparities. That will change everything, but it may take a long time. Jerry Brown once said to me, "The ship of state turns slowly."

We tend to see symptoms and scream, but if you just keep working at them slowly, slowly, the process keeps changing. I still have a strong sense of the power of love over worldly powers or the power of might.

CI: I am seeing ways in which I really deluded myself in the beginning of my spiritual training into thinking that somehow I was becoming quite a refined being. As I get older and more familiar with my very conditioned human impulses, it becomes rather humbling. The teaching for me now is about life in the human form.

RD: Right. You finally realize that the human impulses are around and they're *supposed* to be around. They're not an error and not a weakness. In a way I don't feel that Gandhi fully acknowledged his humanness. He saw his humanness as weakness.

CI: Which a lot of spiritual people do.

RD: I think that's the misunderstanding of renunciation. It's a lower level of renunciation which is very predominant in the Hindu culture. It's the idea that we've fallen by taking a human birth. That's the same as original sin—the apple in the Garden of Eden.

CI: Sometimes I wonder if from our evolutionary point of view we're breaking ground in new spiritual understandings beyond what has been written or taught, by having access to various traditions, especially here in America, from Gandhi and the Buddha, to Christ and the Sufis, and all kinds of obscure esoteric ones as well. Perhaps out of this conglomeration, we have actually developed a new way of understanding our humanness, of being able to play with it and at the same time cultivate detachment from it.

RD: I hear what you're saying and part of me espouses it. The other part feels it's too much *chutzpa.* When I look at people whom I revere as wise persons who have been steeped in a tradition, I think that the things we think we are finding anew are really pretty old news, and that we just don't hear them well enough yet. Trungpa Rinpoche and I were on a television show once, and I was kidding him about attachment. I said, "You know, you're attached. You won't give up your lineage." And he said, "I'd give up anything else, but not my lineage." And I said, "Better luck next life." But I could see in the way he looked at me that I was a real neophyte, and that I just didn't understand.

It scares me to see the subtlety of attachments of mind by which we temper the wisdom according to the cultural context in which we live in order to defuse the power of the spiritual aspects. That's why I don't want to throw it out too fast. I was so eager to throw it out for so many years, and now I'm less and less eager. When I look at somebody like U Pandita, in a lot of ways I figure he's really just a hung-up guy; but he's also an exquisite computer printout of a technique of liberation. There's a tendency, when we get near a teacher who's really demanding, to build a defense in our minds against the teaching because we feel like such dismal beginners next to someone such as U Pandita. So we want to somehow reduce him. I've done that with many people. But by rejecting the carrier, I may lose the method and its power to help me. I've done it again and again.

CI: Me too. I can always find the fatal flaw.

RD: Right. We become connoisseurs of the clay feet of all of our teachers.

CI: Do you have any myth about yourself, about what has happened for you in this life?

RD: No. I really have absolutely no idea who I am. I don't know whether at this moment I am an anachronism from another period who is waiting for the flame to go out, or I'm just at the beginning of something that is so vast that it is frightening even to think about.

Nothing my mind can create about what's happening to me is as interesting as the process that is actually happening. The process is the product. It's not going anywhere. There's nothing I want anymore. If I get involved in television, it's not because I *want* to do television. It's just functionally something different, a more effective way to play the same game.

I don't think it would help to have a myth. It would be entrapping because it would lead me to reject certain things that I find part of the richness of the moment.

The other day I was interviewed by the *Boston Globe*. The caption under the picture they ran of me was, "Supremely at ease with himself, 25 years after being dismissed from Harvard." The reporter had said to me, "You're not married?" And I said, "No." And he said, "Do you think you'll ever marry?" And I said, "I have no idea." I could see he assumed that if I am not married at this point I must have a model—either I'm gay or I don't believe in marriage, or I'm celibate. But I don't have any model. I have no idea whether or not I'm about to marry and have children. It all seems as interesting to me as any other option.

CI: Do you believe in enlightenment? Do you have an idea of what that might be?

RD: That's a funny way of asking the question. Yes, I believe in enlightenment. I guess I would say that. I believe that it is possible to be free. Free of holding, free of models, free of expectations, free of attachment and clinging of mind.

The closest I ever got to that state was being around Maharaji. It was confusing because there was nowhere I could find him. There wasn't a "him" to find. I kept wanting to nail it down so I would have a being to be with, and he wasn't a being to be with. That was the closest sense of the reality of the concept of enlightenment I got.

At certain moments I have a flickering experience of what that is like. Then it passes like a firefly in the night, not necessarily to be followed by another firefly in the foreseeable future. But, as the Third Zen Patriarch of China said, "Even to be attached to the idea of enlightenment is to go astray."

One of the things that my own development of wisdom has given me is the patience to stop counting, How many more births? or How close am I? or When will it happen? It doesn't make any difference because it doesn't make it go any faster. In fact, the preoccupation is just another attachment which slows it down. So I just float along and do what I do because there's nothing else to do. You can't act in denial of your own wisdom.

CI: Does that mean you think you're going along at the perfectly ordained pace, which is "cooking you," to borrow one of your expressions, at just the right speed?

RD: Well I do wonder if at some moment I'll wake up and say, "What a fool you've been. You had this chance and you haven't pushed hard enough." This issue of free will is a big one. The Buddhists really hold the idea that there's a choice to work for enlightenment or not, and I think that's absolutely off the wall. We are just beautifully articulated lawful entities, like trees and leaves and cats. Our mind is just as much a part of the law as anything else. Our desire for enlightenment is part of the law and our practice or resistance is part of the law. And the law just spews you out enlightened at the other end sooner or later, irrevocably.

CI: As time goes on one is tempted to surrender to the mystery of it all.

RD: There is joy in the surrendering to the mystery.

Diane Nash

"There's Diane Nash. She's the one to get."

The crowd of mostly young white men had surrounded the department store entrance in Nashville, Tennessee, where the lunch counter sit-in was occurring. The year was 1960. Diane Nash, the coordinator of the Nashville sit-ins, made her way through the shouting, angry mob. She had been trained in nonviolent strategy and had emerged as one of the top student leaders of the movement. Her picture had appeared in the local papers several times; she therefore understood the danger of her position. Despite this knowledge, she became paralyzed with fear upon hearing the young men's remarks. As she explained, "In that crowd, someone could slip out a knife, stab me, quickly move away, and no one would know who did it."

She pressed on and managed to reach the lunch counter where her colleagues, also trained in nonviolent civil disobedience, were enduring the swarming crowd of whites around them. She sat down at the counter, thinking that if this gripping fear did not leave her she would have to call off the sit-in and return to the church from which the group had started out. "I gave myself a short period, ten or fifteen minutes, to make a decision. Either I would resign as chairperson, because I could not be effective if I was paralyzed with fear, or I would overcome the fear and get my mind back on my work." At the end of the allotted period, Diane Nash, twenty-one years old at the time, had found calm. Although fear still danced on her mind's periphery, it no longer overwhelmed her. She resolved to be careful and observant, but to continue the sit-ins. All the while, the crowd raged on around her.

* * *

Diane Nash, born on May 15, 1938, grew up in a middle-class neighborhood in Chicago with her mother and stepfather. She took pleasure in reading, and as a young girl in a Catholic elementary school, Diane spent much of her time alone. Overt racial discrimination was practically unknown to her, although segregation in housing and schools was a way of life.

Diane adored her maternal grandmother, who cared for her while her mother worked. They would play a game in which the grandmother would explain to the girl that she was the most precious thing in the world. "More precious than diamonds?" Diane would ask. "Oh yes, much more precious than all the diamonds in the world," her grandmother would answer. "More precious than a hundred dollars?" Diane would ask. And on it would go until young Diane was more precious than all the money, jewels, and riches of all the universe. Years later when asked what had given her confidence to go up against the system of segregation, Diane recounted her "game" with her grandmother. "I guess I believed her," she laughed.

By the time Diane reached public high school, she had become a raving beauty. Light-skinned with green eyes and brown hair, she was runner-up in one of Chicago's "Miss America" contests.

It was not until she moved to the South that Diane's life would take a dramatic turn away from conventional success. She entered Fisk University in Nashville in the fall of 1959. Although considered progressive, Nashville typified a southern town in that it carefully segregated blacks from whites—in rest rooms, movie theaters, public transportation, and so on. Although blacks were welcome to spend their money in the downtown department stores, they were not allowed to eat at the lunch counters in those same stores. In addition, the general atmosphere of white supremacy was, for Diane Nash, stifling. "To take a break from the pressures of campus I would have liked to go downtown with a girlfriend and treat ourselves to lunch," Diane explained. "In Nashville, I couldn't do that, and I began to feel very hemmed in."

Although she had known about segregation, she had never before "experienced it emotionally." Nash asked around campus if anyone was doing anything about it, and eventually she heard of a group which met at a nearby Methodist church one night a week and was led by James Lawson, a graduate student in Divinity School at Vanderbilt University. Lawson had been to India and while there had immersed himself in the study of Gandhi's methods. He had also been imprisoned as a conscientious objector for refusing to fight in the Korean War.

Diane Nash faithfully attended James Lawson's workshops and received "an excellent training" in the techniques of nonviolence. Lawson explained to the students both the philosophy and the tactical strategies of nonviolence, noting that some people consider nonviolence a way of life while others use the tactics primarily for social change. Although Nash had not yet accepted nonviolence as a way of life, there were certain principles which she considered to be true. "People are not the enemy; segregation is the enemy, racism is the enemy, sexism is the enemy, oppressive economic systems are the enemy," she explained. "The idea of fighting fire with fire is unscientific. I just didn't see how killing people or hating people was a solution to human problems." She also accepted the tenets of Truth and Love which were the fundamental basis of the trainings. "The idea that the truth will set you free made sense to me."

Nash, however, did not believe that nonviolent techniques could actually work against segregation. But she continued to attend the workshops "because it was the only game in town."

In February 1960 lunch counter sit-ins began in Greensboro, North Carolina, and James Lawson's workshop group, inspired by the Greensboro sit-ins, planned its first action—sitting in at the lunch counters in Nashville. Diane Nash was elected chairperson of the Student Central Committee which would provide the leadership for the lunch counter sit-in movement. The Nashville students had previously tested several lunch counters by sitting down, being refused service, asking to speak with the manager, and then leaving peacefully, but now they began their civil disobedience phase by sitting down at lunch counters and refusing to leave. Huge crowds gathered, and sometimes the students were beaten by people in the crowd or arrested and "roughed up" by the police. As chairperson, Diane Nash moved from store to store checking on events. She remembers one occasion when "the waitresses must have dropped $2,000 worth of dishes because they were so nervous."

The sit-ins in Nashville drew national attention, largely due to the nonviolent practices of the students. The press and sometimes television cameras captured the specter of black students peacefully sitting on counter stools being dragged off by angry white men beating them about the face and head and burning them with lit cigarettes.

The sit-ins were too much for the city to bear. On the steps of city hall, Diane Nash, having just been released from jail on a sit-in charge, stopped Mayor Ben West as a crowd of marchers looked and listened. Nash asked the Mayor several direct questions about his views on racial discrimination and on the desegregation of lunch counters. In what has now become a famous exchange, Mayor West told Nash that he would recommend desegregation of lunch counters in Nashville. The crowd went wild. Nashville was the first southern city to desegregate lunch counters, and the leaders, the Student Central Committee of Nashville, became legendary within the civil rights movement. Through working on the Central Committee, Diane Nash met her husband-to-be, James Bevel, a seminary student also involved in the Movement.

The Nashville group and others from southern cities attended a meeting at Shaw University in Raleigh, North Carolina, sponsored by the Southern Christian Leadership Conference (SCLC), whose president was Martin Luther King, Jr. To set up an information clearing house for sit-ins occurring around the country, the students formed a new national organization, the Student Nonviolent Coordinating Committee, (SNCC) or "Snick" as it came to be called. Diana Nash was a founding member of the new organization. Over the years of the civil rights movement, SNCC would prove again and again to be the pacesetter for activism and innovation.

A year after the formation of SNCC, the Congress of Racial Equality (CORE) began the revolutionary Freedom Rides across the South. In an effort to desegregate interstate travel, an interracial group would ride in a bus through the south, whites in the back of the bus, blacks in front. When the bus would stop, whites would use the "colored" restrooms, blacks would use the "whites only" restrooms. Southern violence exploded against them. In just a short time, the small group of CORE volunteers had been badly beaten, their bus burned, and their members worn out. They decided to give up the Freedom Rides.

Diane Nash called CORE president James Farmer and asked if he minded if the students in SNCC took up the Freedom Rides where CORE had left off. "I felt that it was important that the Rides not stop just after all that violence had been inflicted on them," Diane Nash explained. "Because then the message would have been that if you wanted to stop the Movement, you just had to inflict a lot of violence, and it would have cost us a lot of lives to convince them otherwise."

Diane Nash was elected to coordinate the people of Nashville who went on the Freedom Rides. She had read Gandhi's words "about not expecting anyone who worked with him to do anything that he would not be willing to do." Inspired by Gandhi, she realized that she could not accept the position of coordinator unless she were willing to go on a Freedom Ride herself. After meditating for a period of time, she felt ready to do that, and she accepted the job. Although she never went on a Freedom Ride, she worked closely with the Riders, training them in nonviolent techniques. These included ways to protect their heads while being beaten and what to do in jail to keep from being demoralized: "set up a daily schedule, exercise, sing, write, talk to the jailers about freedom, justice, and the cause." Often, people about to go on a Freedom Ride would give Diane Nash sealed letters to be opened by loved ones in the event of their death.

Over the next few years Diane Nash incurred half a dozen jail sentences, ranging from three to thirty days. One internment was particularly difficult. At age twenty-four she had received a sentence of two and a half years for encouraging minors to desegregate buses. She appealed the conviction. While in a courtroom awaiting a hearing on the appeal, a bailiff asked her to move to the back of the room; the front rows were reserved for whites. Diane Nash refused to move and was sentenced to ten days for contempt of court. She was six months pregnant with her first child at the time. The Mississippi jail in which she found herself "had insects so large that at night you could hear them walking across the floor." She would lie awake in order to dodge the cockroaches which had the unpleasant habit of falling from the ceiling onto her bed. The few possessions she had brought with her, a hairbrush, toothbrush, and change of underwear, had been taken from her. Most importantly, vitamins and medicine for her pregnancy had also been confiscated. Yet her training held her in good stead. She set up a schedule for herself and passed the ten days in relatively good spirits. Upon her release, the judge refused to call up the charge which carried the long sentence, even though Diane assured him she would continue to encourage minors to ride the buses.

Diane Nash and James Bevel next turned to voter registration campaigns. After the Birmingham church bombing in 1963 which killed four black schoolgirls, Nash and Bevel felt that the only way to protect their families was for blacks to get the right to vote. Diane Nash presented a plan to Martin Luther King, Jr. to create a nonviolent brigade which would surround the government of Alabama Governor George Wallace. This army would "[sever] communication from the state capitol, close down the power company, and [block] the railroads, runways, and bus driveways." Dr. King initially reacted to the plan with little enthusiasm. He had just come from the Birmingham funeral of the four girls, and he was drained of energy and vision. A disappointed Diane Nash continued to advocate for action in redressing the bombings and obtaining the right to vote. Within the next two years, her efforts became the inspiration for the Selma Voting Campaign which won voting rights for blacks, one of the greatest victories of the civil rights movement. Martin Luther King, Jr. presented Diane Nash and James Bevel with the Rosa Parks Award, the highest honor given by the Southern Christian Leadership Conference.

Soon thereafter, Diane Nash, now a mother of two, noticed a photograph in a magazine of a Vietnamese woman holding a badly burned child. The look on the woman's face began to haunt Nash, and she decided that she would to go to Vietnam if ever the chance presented itself. In December 1966 she had her chance. Along with three other American women, she toured North Vietnam as a member of the Movement to End the War in Vietnam.

As the seventies got underway, the "black power" and "black pride" forces appealed to Diane Nash's sense of self-esteem. For the first time she understood what "black is beautiful" meant. Being proud of her black heritage lifted a tremendous burden from her. "It was a period of real liberation for me," she later explained. She began to feel alienated from whites. Futhermore, she no longer believed in nonviolence ("It seemed a powerless way of doing things"). For the next couple of years, however, she noticed that groups who advocated violence seemed ineffective. "While they may have had just causes—some aspired to goals that I also shared—it was impossible to persuade large numbers of people to join them." Nash came full circle back to a commitment to social change based on love, not on separation.

Long since divorced from James Bevel, Diane Nash raised her children on her own. During the children's school years, Nash worked as President of Black Women for Decent Housing, and she also assisted people who had been on public aid. While organizing a group of ten-

ants to cooperatively buy the building in which they
lived, Diane noticed that the tenants began to "put obstacles in their own way." Nash decided that if she were
to be effective in helping these people, she would need to
understand their mental habits, needs, and fears. The
study of psychology proved to be her next step, and in
1987, at the age of forty-nine, Diane Nash entered
Chicago State University to obtain a degree.

Her dream is to create an urban as well as a rural
community where unemployed youths can learn trades
such as carpentry and plumbing. They would also be
trained in what Diane calls "agapic energy" (a term
which she explains in the following interview) in order
to effect social change. "The possibilities are endless because there's so much work to be done," Diane explained.
"We could build a nonviolent army and put these kids to
work."

I met with Diane for two and a half hours on the 80th
floor of the Sears Tower Building in a plush conference
room loaned for our use. Although we looked out over
the city of Chicago in the last summer of the eighties, we
were soon time-and-space traveling to the steamy, tumultuous sixties and into Mississippi, Alabama, Geor-
gia, and Tennessee. With calm, direct eyes and soft voice,
Diane Nash recounted her life in the civil rights movement, careful to remember the details, wanting me to
understand how it was.

I had grown up in the South, and painful memories
flickered through my mind as we spoke. I pictured life
for a black person in those days, remembering how separate we were in that time, seeing in my mind's eye the
dilapidated shacks in the part of town where our maids
lived, looking out from the car window at the produce
and tobacco fields where black men labored in the hot
Virginia sun. The black people I knew lived in another
world within our midst. A young white girl could have
accepted such existence for blacks as a normal way of
life and never have noticed their pain. Hearing Diane
Nash, I felt tremendously grateful that she had won her
battles. They were won for all of us. In the words of

Martin Luther King, Jr., "Injustice anywhere is a threat to justice everywhere. We are caught in an inescapable network of mutuality, tied in a single garment of destiny."

Interview with Diane Nash
August 11, 1989 • Chicago, Illinois

Catherine Ingram: What did the civil rights movement achieve, and where did it fall short?

Diane Nash: I think we were very efficient at setting up goals and achieving them. We had the goal of desegregating lunch counters, and we did that. We wanted to desegregate interstate bus travel, and we did that. We desegregated movies and more restaurants. We wanted the right to vote, and we got it. One very important thing that we did not do was to set up frameworks in which young people could direct their energies toward social change, frameworks similar to the workshops that Jim Lawson conducted. You know, during the period of time when I was looking for a group, if Jim Lawson hadn't been doing those workshops, I probably would have had to make some kind of adjustment to the situation as it was. I probably wouldn't have done anything on my own, and would likely have led a different kind of life. And I like the life that I have lived. For many people younger than me who may have the same interest in looking for ways to effect change, the opportunity has not been there. Setting up frameworks is something that we didn't do in the Movement. This is the work which interests me now.

As far as what the civil rights movement did not accomplish, I hear people say, "Well, yes, the Movement in the sixties desegregated public facilities and got the right to vote, but it didn't deal with economic issues." I think that no one movement can be expected to do everything for all time. Every generation and every individual has the responsibility to accomplish certain things. It was true that we didn't deal with the economic issues, but that gives people now the opportunity to do that. They have as much responsibility as anybody.

CI: There is a new report by the National Research Council called "A Common Destiny: Blacks and American Society" [1989] which states, "Since the early seventies, the economic status of blacks relative to whites has, on average, stagnated or deteriorated." In addition to a growing economic disparity and joblessness, there are other problems in the black community. We hear reports about the disrupted black families; we hear that the fathers are not staying with the families. Some people say that this is the central problem in the black community, the ridgepole of the other problems, such as the rise of drug use, crime, and homelessness.

DN: Strong families are central to the well-being of any culture or group. But, I don't feel particularly inclined to discuss the problems and situations of black families except in a forum where I am mainly speaking to black people, because I think it's going to have to be black men and women who solve the problems of the black family. Many of the problems that black people now face are problems that are equally great for white people, such as the poisoning of our air, land, and water, and the nuclear threat. White Americans face such big problems now that I think it's important for them to deal with their own problems. They have enough to do.

CI: If we were to break it down that way, it becomes rather segregationist.

DN: No, no. I think that you have to change yourself. You can't change anybody but yourself. And once you change yourself, then the rest of society has to fit up against you. The problems that we now face threaten both blacks and whites—environmental pollution, the hole in the ozone layer. These are not racial issues.

CI: Those are threats which we all share, I agree. But a black man has a five times greater chance of being murdered than a white man, and it is most often at the hands of another black man. This is more likely at this time than that he will die in a nuclear holocaust or from environmental pollution. I don't want to make you uncomfortable with this question. I just feel that you, as a leader who has witnessed so much positive social change and now a decline in the quality of life for black people, might have an assessment of what is happening and where to go from here.

DN: One of the things which is paramount right now is that there needs to be a change in the attitude of the American people towards democracy. If there is not, we are not going to have democracy for very much longer, and it will become very clear that we don't have it. We are not taking an appropriate share of responsibility for the society. Many people feel that just voting is enough, that those remarkable three minutes that they spend in the voting booth every couple of years is all they owe in terms of deciding what happens in the society, and that's just not true.

As we remember from civics lessons, in a democracy it is the people who are in control. People look to their elected officials or to somebody other than themselves to accomplish things, yet it's clear that our elected officials are not going to get done the things which need to be done. The people as a whole need to see themselves in charge of the elected official and take matters into their own hands.

Not long ago there was some deadly nuclear waste that was being transported on an expressway through Chicago. An article buried in the newspaper mentioned that if these trucks had an accident, it could be disastrous for the city of Chicago. I happened to be in a classroom with some people who read this, and they kind of shook their heads and said, "Isn't that awful?" After a few minutes, the teacher came into the class and the people went on with life as usual. That really struck me.

It is kind of crazy that we read about businesses dumping so much waste into the lakes and waterways and yet we go about life as usual. It would be as if you were waiting for a meal and I came in and told you that the person in the next room who is cooking the meal is putting poison in your soup and you said, "Yeah, isn't that awful?" And they bring in the soup and you don't say anything, you don't do anything, you just eat it. Clearly you'd be crazy. And that's kind of what we are doing. If we were to read something such as that news story and then take off from work the next day, find the president of the company which is dumping this stuff, and make a citizen's arrest, or get our friends together and do whatever we could, whether we were successful or not, I'd say that at least we would be behaving more rationally and in a healthier way. But for millions of us to just turn away is really nuts.

CI: Sometimes we become inured to threats and injustices by growing slowly accustomed to them, so that there is no longer a shock value. For instance, in your own case, when you went to college in the South after having lived in the North, the discrimination against blacks had a profound effect due to the contrast with what you were used to. Were the students who were from more liberal places more outraged by the segregation than the people who had experienced it as a way of life?

DN: It didn't work out that way. I have thought seriously about this question, and I have discussed it with others. People from the North often had one kind of motivation—that was the kind I had—they hadn't experienced that kind of discrimination before and it was shocking when they did. On the other hand there were a number of people from the deep South on the Central Committee who repeatedly put their lives in danger, and who were motivated because they were so sick of the situation.

CI: The malaise of today seems of a more ephemeral nature; racial injustices are a bit more subtle. Do you think this contributes to the apathy which we now see? You spoke of cautioning people about thinking they were fulfilling social duty by spending those few minutes in the voting booth, yet most people don't even vote.

DN: Well, I'm not really of the opinion which has been promoted by the mass media that young people today are not interested in the things that the young people of the sixties were interested in, namely promoting a better world and caring about fellow human beings. They call this generation the "me" generation. But, you know, when I was asking around on the Fisk campus in the late fifties to see if anyone knew of an organization which was trying to do something about segregation, I became convinced that the students were apathetic. They didn't seem to be interested in doing anything, and some of them even wondered why I was interested in doing anything. They told me that the white man had always run things and would continue to have his way.

As the Movement got under way and a program of action developed that people could do, such as showing up at a particular lunch counter at a particular time, more students joined. Later on, as the Movement gathered momentum, there were thousands of students ready to go to jail. And many of these were the same students that I had thought were apathetic! The problem had been that they didn't have a vision of what could be done, and they didn't know how they could fit into a solution. Once those things were supplied, then those same students that I had thought were apathetic were ready to participate in the Movement. Again, one of the problems today is that there have not been frameworks in which young people can learn and organize.

CI: Martin Luther King, Jr. said, "I have chosen the path of love. Hate is too great a burden to bear." You in the Movement certainly experienced tremendous hatred directed toward you. Dr. King's statement seems a very practical choice. To hold the burden of hate is too great a stress on the heart. Does that speak to your experience?

DN: Yes. Hating white people didn't seem to make sense, because to decide to hate a group of people that you did not even know as individuals was just clearly stupid.

CI: The very thing you were fighting against.

DN: That's right. In our workshops I remember Jim Lawson saying that in order to hate people and do violence to them, it's necessary to dehumanize them. He was talking about how southern whites had to do that to blacks, that in their minds they had to reduce blacks from being human to being niggers and inferior and whatever else they dreamed up. They said these things and people believed them.

CI: Was nonviolence a way to show those people who would see you as less than human that you had a great moral force and dignity?

DN: Well, I would like to say something here. I found that when I began teaching people about what is generally called nonviolence, the word "nonviolence" became an obstacle. The reason for that is that "nonviolence" means "the absence of violence," and that's not all we're talking about here. We're talking about a wider definition—the philosophy, the strategy, which includes nonviolence and the absence of violence, but also means much more. As social discoveries are made, just as in natural sciences when inventions are developed, we need new words in order to be able to talk about them. For example, before electricity was discovered, we didn't need words such as watts, volts, amperes, etcetera. After electricity was discovered, we needed those words to communicate about it.

I realized that I didn't know of a word in the English language that really described what we were talking about when we said nonviolence so I got an etymological dictionary and came up with another term: agapic energy. The way I arrived at that was through examining the three words for love in Greek. There was filial love, the love between parent and child. There was eros, or romantic love. And there was agape, which meant brotherly love or love of mankind; those are sexist terms, but we could say "love of humankind" or "brotherly and sisterly love." Now the adjective for agape would be agapic. Then we add to that the notion of energy, which can be likened to that of natural gas energy, and also has the meaning of power or force. So agapic energy is the power of love of humankind, or the force of brotherly and sisterly love.

Love generates energy. You can think of the extra energy that a mother needs when she stays up all night with a sick child. Or we hear stories of people who have lifted incredible amounts of weight if an object falls on someone they love. There is an energy that is generated by love.

Agapic energy also includes a whole process that you take a community through, and that process consists of five stages: research, education, negotiation, demonstration, and resistance. All of this is included in agapic energy, with truth and love as the basis. It's a much wider concept than just the absence of violence.

CI: Your spiritual understanding and practice is a self-regulatory process versus something being imposed from without. You are more inclined to let your conscience be your guide. Will you speak about that?

DN: Yes, I think self-regulation is really the best kind of spiritual practice. I had a girlfriend in high school who made a statement which I wasn't able to relate to at the time, but which I understand now. She said that human beings do not need organized religions in order to tell them what is right to do. She said that everyone in his or her heart knows that you shouldn't kill, you shouldn't steal, you shouldn't lie, and so on. And I have found this to be true. Yet, I look at the way we raise children; we teach them to obey their parents, obey their teachers, obey the law, obey their ministers. There are all these external things we teach children to obey, but we never tell them, "I have confidence in you, you are a good person, you will do the right thing." We don't say, "Look in your conscience, obey your conscience." As a result, children lose touch with their self-regulation. Then when they're grown, even if they are able to make contact with their self-regulation mechanisms, they have no confidence in them because parents and society have always told them to obey some external law. So we now have a society where, when something goes wrong, our reflex is to pass a new law. The problem with this is that the people who are acting in an anti-social manner aren't going to respond to that new law. Their response is to figure out how to do what they want and get away with it. This kind of thinking is what we encourage children to do when we set up laws and punishments rather than nurture their abilities to self-regulate.

CI: Once someone is older and has been conditioned in a certain way, is there a specific practice to do to nurture the conscience or to encourage agapic energy? Is there a particular undertaking that you personally do?

DN: I have so many years now of following my inner direction that I do it almost automatically, although it's still not easy for me. Very frequently it's like swimming upstream. You have to decide that what other people think of you and what you've been taught is not important and that you are going to evaluate things for yourself and see if they make sense. Deciding to do that has led me to give up many of the things that I was raised to do, and to adopt my own way of doing things. This applies to religion, to feminism, to ways of rearing children, to nonviolence.

CI: After the bombing of the church in Birmingham when the four schoolgirls were killed, you and your husband considered, as one of the options of response to the attack, finding the people responsible for the bombing and having them killed. Instead, you chose to work for the right to vote to redress this kind of attack on blacks. Your willingness to even consider violence seemed to mark a departure from your commitment to nonviolent strategy.

DN: You know, a commitment to nonviolence has never been just an automatic response in me. I think it's human to feel an inclination for violence, to have it at least occur as a thought. It certainly did occur to me, anyway. I haven't come to the point where it doesn't enter my mind. But I think the important thing is to be able to process the situation until you don't just respond on your reflex. I look at my options and then choose. And that's what we did in that case.

CI: What is your new thinking with regard to religion at this point?

DN: Well, I grew up Catholic, and when I was in my mid-twenties I decided to examine my childhood religion and see how much of it I believed in or did not believe in. It took me about two years to do that, and at the end of that time I did not believe very much of it. I went into a period of being an atheist, and then for several years I was an agnostic. Now I consider myself a deeply religious, spiritual person, but it's my own religion.

I believe in the force that brings the sun up every morning, the force that keeps our organs functioning and our hearts beating without our thinking about it, the force that turns a seed into a carrot or into a stalk of corn. I now have a very active spiritual life. When I was part of an organized religion, the beliefs actually interfered with my relationship to the creative force, which some might call God.

CI: Do you know of the discussion by Alexis de Tocqueville on equality versus equal opportunity? He suggests that we cannot legislate equality, but we can legislate equal opportunity. If we were to look at these concepts in terms of political systems we would see that in a capitalist society, the attitude of "May the best person win" would be considered equal opportunity. In socialist and communist societies, they would be more inclined to try to make everybody equal. From the perspective of the Movement, which of these did you want?

DN: Well, I don't like to get into "isms," because I have found that life is more dynamic. I'm not a capitalist; that's clear because I don't have any capital. [laughing] And I'm not a communist or a socialist. I can't think of any "ism" that I affiliate with. I think that things should be done that best benefit people and serve their best interests at a given point in time. At a particular location at a particular time, one thing will need to be done. In a different location in a different time, an entirely different thing will be needed.

We were given a wonderful planet to live on, but the political, economic, and social conditions we've inflicted on ourselves have made it, to varying degrees, an oppressive, exploitative, kind of place. And so what I'm doing is removing obstacles to human well-being, because I think that if those obstacles are removed then people can choose to be what they are supposed to be.

CI: Those obstacles being?

DN: Some of the political and economic systems that we have—racism, sexism, government and economic policies that leave people homeless. I'd like to see people have the opportunity to learn things that they need to learn, develop themselves, grow and achieve the greatest potential that they can.

CI: Stokely Carmichael[1] allegedly said that the only position for a woman in SNCC was prone. I wonder what

---

[1] Stokely Carmichael was one of the early leaders of the Student Non-violent Coordinating Committee. He was particularly instrumental in launching the "black power" movement in the late sixties and early seventies.

the women inside the Movement felt about this kind of sexism.

DN: Well, three or four years ago I asked Stokely about that and he said he made that statement as a joke. I confirmed what he said with another woman who was there, a feminist, who said that the remark had occurred during a joking session. So at this point it seems that it was a joke.

CI: Nevertheless, there did seem to be rampant sexism in the Movement, and many feminists felt that the men in the Movement hogged the limelight while the women, who were often marching on the front lines and staying up working all night, were seldom mentioned in the media.

DN: Well, you know I played into that myself, because when there was work to be done, I would do the work. But when there were TV cameras around or someone to be quoted, I was very content to let some of the guys who were interested in the TV cameras say what they had to say. I wouldn't do it that way again for a number of reasons. I used to think that there was virtue in not stepping up to be quoted. But what I saw was that often the people who were interested in the publicity more than in the work and going to jail and doing the hard stuff had the public forum to speak whereas I didn't, and that was too bad. It was too bad for me because I was frustrated, and I think it was too bad for society as a whole, because the people who really did the work and had the work as their central interest saw things differently and had different things to say than the people whose central interest was promoting themselves. When the society heard what these people had to say, they assumed that it was from the Movement, and they didn't always get an accurate picture. If I had it to do again, I'd be concerned about doing the work, and I'd also be a spokesperson for the work that I did.

With my own personal family, this was also the case. I was very content to work hard and let my husband get the credit for both of our work. Well, he was a very competent individual, but he really got credit for both of us. That meant that after a few years, his earning power was about three times what mine was. When we divorced, and I had two children to support, my earning power did not reflect the investment I had made in my husband.

CI: You have said that although there were egotistical characters in the Movement whose motivations you questioned, you never felt this about Martin Luther King, Jr. You felt that he was completely sincere in his motivations. Yet I know that you had disagreements with him. Tell me about working with him.

DN: I personally respected Martin a great deal. I appreciated and loved him deeply. As I said, it was clear to me that his motives and commitment were sincere. He was also incredibly competent. I was always impressed with the amount of work that he could produce, and I used to marvel sometimes at how he could write a speech at the same time he was doing a thousand other things. He seemed tireless. But mostly, I was struck by how regular and how human he was. He used to enjoy shooting pool and playing ping-pong and joking. He was always cracking jokes and laughing. Oh, I thought he was eloquent. You know, I'd be working with him, and I'd then attend a rally and hear him speak and I'd come out re-energized.

CI: Did he ever make those kinds of speeches when you were in informal situations?

DN: Not a great deal. His public speeches were the most inspiring for me. He and I argued a lot, particularly over strategy.

CI: SNCC had a more radical approach, and Dr. King's, through the Southern Christian Leadership Conference,

SCLC, was more an attempt to appeal to a lot of different factions.

DN: Yes, see, the people who were trained in agapic energy in SNCC were roughly ten years younger than he was. And SNCC was really the vanguard of the Movement. A great deal of Martin's and SCLC's success was due to SNCC, which would be positioned out in front, while SCLC would be more conservative. So because of SNCC, SCLC was much more palatable to whites, and was seen as much more moderate than it would have been seen had SNCC not been out in front. But the people in SNCC and even many of us in the field staff of SCLC were frequently frustrated with Martin and others in SCLC because we thought they were moving too slowly.

CI: In retrospect, do you still think that SCLC moved too slowly?

DN: Well, you know I think we all played the part we were supposed to play. In retrospect I'll tell you what I do think. I've been amazed and upset with the way the media and history have portrayed the Movement as though it was Martin Luther King's movement. It was not. It was truly a people's movement. Martin was not the leader of the Movement, he was the spokesman, and a very competent, eloquent spokesman. He was a great man. What I'm saying doesn't take anything away from Martin.

It's so important to portray it as a people's movement because, firstly, that is the truth, and in nonviolence the truth is to be taken seriously. And secondly, if people see it as Martin's movement and they think of him as superhuman or a saint, then when something needs to be changed they are tempted to say, "I wish we had a leader like Martin Luther King today." People need to know that it was just people like themselves who thought up the strategies and managed the Movement. It was thousands of people. It was the dentist in Nashville who put so much time into being treasurer of the Nashville Christian Leadership Conference. It was the people who managed the rallies and got on the phone with their friends and said, "Let's boycott downtown until they let our kids out of jail."

People are surprised when I tell them that the Freedom Rides, the sit-ins at lunch counters, the Montgomery Bus boycott, the march on Washington, the Selma Campaign—those major elements of the Movement—were not things which Martin thought up and suggested we do. It's important that people realize that. Charismatic leadership has not freed us and it never will, because freedom is, by definition, people realizing that they are their own leaders. I don't care how great the man is, and up to now charismatic leaders have been mostly men—that should have clued us that something was wrong!—but no matter how great the person is, there is no one person who can or should free the many.

Gary Snyder

*That old Zen lunatic Han Shan, whose Cold Mountain po-
ems tell of his hermit life in ancient China, asked, "Who
can leap the world's ties/ And sit with me among the white
clouds?" Some 1,300 years later, in the mid-1950s, Gary
Snyder translated Han Shan's words from the Chinese and
inspired comparisons to the old hermit himself. Jack
Kerouac portrayed Snyder as Japhy Rider in his classic
book,* The Dharma Bums, *in which the Kerouac character
(Ray Smith) and the one based on Allen Ginsberg (Alvah
Goldbook) discussed their friend Japhy:*

*[Goldbook:] "I wonder what will happen to him in the
end."*

*[Smith:] "I think he'll end up like Han Shan living alone
in the mountains and writing poems on the walls of cliffs,
or chanting them to crowds outside his cave."*

*It is over thirty years since Kerouac wrote those words.
So far Gary Snyder has ended up in his homestead in the
high Sierras in California, living on a parcel of land with a
community of family and friends and fulfilling his dedication to "a sense of place." Since 1971 he has worked this
land, built his home there, raised a family, and, along with
friends, constructed a Zen retreat center. He has also
managed to write Pulitzer Prize-winning poetry, give lectures around the world, and continue his work as an eco-
warrior protecting the "wild."*

*Snyder has a sophisticated understanding of what he
calls "the wisdom of the wild," the fundamental intelligence
of the eco-system in its natural state and the way it balances itself over time. He is respectful of its mysteries, although his knowledge and perception of living organisms
and their interaction with each other is vast. There are few
who can articulate this better than Gary Snyder. Even
when he writes of being in New York City, as in his poem,
"Walking the New York Bedrock, Alive in the Sea of Infor-*

*mation," we can visualize sprigs of maple and oak stirring
beneath the cement.*

*Gary Snyder is also a student of the mind. His interest
in philosophy goes back to childhood; by the time he was in
his twenties he was learning Chinese and translating texts.
He began formally studying Zen in 1956 and to this day
continues a regular meditation practice with periodic
sesshin[1] throughout the year.*

*It is this far-reaching combination of interests which
makes it difficult to describe Gary Snyder and which
makes him one of the great Renaissance men of our time.
Here is a backwoodsman with knowledge of all that runs
in the streams and creeks of his "bio-region"; a man who
is comfortable hiking and camping alone in the mountains
for months on end; a man who chops wood, plants trees,
changes diapers, dances, and sings—a sensitive macho-
man; and here is a scholar/poet bent over centuries-old
Chinese texts, pondering the words "One the Way and one
its Power." Here also is a man trained for more than thirty
years in zazen. As the "10,000 things"[2] come and go, he is
able to sit quietly and do nothing. A lot like old Han Shan.*

* * *

Gary Snyder was born on May 8, 1930, in San Francisco and grew up in the Pacific Northwest in Washington and Oregon among stands of Douglas fir and western
red cedar. According to Snyder, growing up in the woods
"made me what I am." Even as a child he was aware of
the destruction of the forests by massive logging—an
awareness which would intensify in years to come. The
son of socialist parents, Snyder helped his family
homestead their land, where they kept cows and planted
orchards and gardens. He learned carpentry and raised
his own chickens; in summers, he worked in logging

---

[1] *Sesshin*, Japanese, literally "collecting the heart-mind." *Sesshin* refers
to intervals of time spent in the intensive practice of Zen meditation.
[2] The Chinese used the character for "10,000" to mean myriad, or a
quantity large enough to encompass all of creation.

camps and forests. Although the depression years were rough on the family, Gary has fond memories of his mother reading poetry to him at night. She had wanted to be a writer herself and always encouraged her son in that direction.

When he was nine years old, Snyder discovered Chinese landscape paintings in the Seattle Art Museum and felt an immediate affinity, thinking that the images on the scrolls looked just like the mountains he knew in the Northwest. This began a deep respect for Oriental culture. By the time Snyder was in his teens he had also fallen in love with mountaineering and had climbed the great peaks of the Northwest—Mount St. Helens, Mount Hood, Mount Adams, Mount Baker, and Mount Rainier. Snyder considers his mountain experiences "an initiation by all the great gods of the land here." He began writing poetry at the age of fifteen in order to express his feelings about these experiences.

After high school in Portland, Oregon, Snyder became a sort of handyman, working odd jobs in galleys on ships and writing poetry in his spare time. He was offered a scholarship at Reed College in 1947 when a professor at the school read some of his poems. At Reed, Snyder quickly developed a reputation for brilliance in poetry and anthropology, particularly in his studies of Northwest Coast Indian myths and folktales. After graduating from Reed in 1951, he went on to Indiana University for further study in linguistics and primitive oral traditions but left after one semester. Snyder then moved to San Francisco where, through his friendship with Philip Whalen, he became interested in Zen meditation. Along with friends Allen Ginsberg, Kenneth Rexroth, and Jack Kerouac, he became part of the Beat poets scene in the city's famous North Beach. Spending summers working as a fire lookout in California and Washington and winters studying Oriental languages at the University of California in Berkeley, Snyder was intellectually and perhaps spiritually preparing himself for the next major phase of his life, his study of Zen in

Japan. He would later describe studying Zen as "a continuation of mountaineering on another plane."

In 1956 Snyder left for Kyoto to study at the First Zen Institute of America. He spent most of the next six years practicing Zen in Kyoto until the death of his teacher, Oda Sesso Roshi. Shortly afterward, Gary met his wife-to-be, Masa Uehara. They were married on the rim of an active volcano on an island off the coast of Japan, the ceremony conducted by the renowned wandering Japanese poet, Nanao Sakaki. The couple had their first child, Kai, while still in Japan, but immediately returned to America in 1968. After several years in San Francisco, during which time Masa gave birth to their second son, Gen, the Snyders left the city for rural life on the San Juan Ridge in the Sierra Nevadas in California. It has been home ever since.

Since then Snyder has become one of the most listened-to poets of our time. His collection *Turtle Island* won the Pulitzer Prize for poetry in 1974.[3] Snyder's poems tug at our memories of times when we were in harmony with the wild, when there was no separation between who we were and where we lived. This was the way of life through most of history. For example, until recently, the Athabaskan Indians of Alaska had no concepts or word for the "wild" in their language, so integrated were their lives with nature.

Snyder is determined to "write about a pine tree as a pine tree would want to be written about, from inside." As a "spokesman for the nonhuman" Snyder uses meditation to open his mind "to the point that it's empty enough that other things can walk into it, so that a rabbit can walk in your mind, so that trees or rocks become part of your mind."

Being a voice which calls on us to remember where we come from, where we live, where our water comes from, who our human and nonhuman neighbors are, and what the local history has been, demands the art of story-

---

[3] Turtle Island is the American Indian name for the North American continent, based on the myth that man rides on the great turtle's back.

telling. On a six-week visit to China in 1984-85, Gary Snyder and Allen Ginsberg often spoke to the Chinese of the plight of the American Indians and the loss of their lands in the takeover by the Europeans who colonized North America. When they saw the Chinese audience nodding their heads in sympathy, they would then compare the American Indian situation to that of the Tibetans facing the loss of their homeland to the Chinese.

Whether exploring new wilderness regions with native peoples in Alaska or sacred "dreaming spots" with Aborigines in Australia, whether reading at a benefit to save the Okinawan coral reefs off Japan, or mediating the local land use disputes in Grass Valley, Snyder nonviolently advocates for what is "good, wild, and sacred."

His sons are now grown. After twenty years of marriage, Gary and Masa Snyder have divorced. Snyder is now engaged to marry Carole Koda. His next work is a collection of prose pieces on love, wilderness, and Zen community called *The Practice of the Wild.*

This is my third interview with Gary Snyder since 1984. On a hot day in July 1988, I drove up to his place in Grass Valley, California, a pilgrimage I had wanted to make for years. Gary's son Gen served me a cold drink while we talked and waited for his father to return from chores in town. Soon Gary arrived and took me on a tour of his rustic homestead known as Kitkitdizze, the Wintun Indian word for a local aromatic plant. The land, which according to Snyder was "barely good," has over the years "showed us a little of its power." Next Gary showed me the beautiful Ring Of Bone Zendo which serves the community's meditation and meeting needs.[4]

Snyder was working in Allen Ginsberg's little cabin at the end of a meadow (Ginsberg is part owner of the property although he seldom resides there), and it was here that we had lunch and talked for the next couple of hours, stopping only once to silently observe a wild turkey which Gary had spotted through the window.

---

[4] *Ring of Bone* is the title of a collection of poems by the San Francisco Beat poet Lew Welch, who disappeared in 1971.

Interview with Gary Snyder
July 14, 1988 • Grass Valley, California

Catherine Ingram: You are considered an advocate for nature, for the wilderness. What is your ongoing activism in this field?

Gary Snyder: Well, I haven't been much of an activist in the field for a few years because I'm working on a book right now, and I'm staying here at Kitkitdizze to do that, but it is a book about these very issues—reinhabitation, bioregionalism, deep ecology, the nature of the wild, what human consciousness and human culture bear in relationship to the wild, and the balance between discipline and freedom with regard to the wild. Those issues have been keeping me pretty close to home.

But even here I do keep involved to a certain extent with local forestry work—the locally based Forest Issues Task Force—and a larger ongoing effort to understand and critique the logging industry and U.S. Forest Service's management of public lands, particularly forests, in the United States. It involves a huge area of land that belongs to all of us, although most people don't think of it as their own land. But it is.

And that's just the tip of the larger iceberg, which is worldwide deforestation. So through my involvement on the local level, I'm working on and involved in issues that go all the way to the tropical rain forests. That's the way ecological activism works, since everything is connected. What you learn from working on, say, a soil or water or forest or wildlife or pollution issue in any one spot on the globe is very informative about what's going on everywhere and how it works everywhere.

CI: In many cases today, we are seeing irreversible eco-logical damage. What do you think should be our top ecological priorities?

GS: Well, on a planetary scale, I think there are two or three top priority issues. One is, as I just mentioned, worldwide deforestation. There's been a lot of informa-tion and a lot of concern over the tropical rain forest is-sues lately. An area of land roughly the size of Indiana is being clear-cut annually in the tropics. Those ques-tions are not limited just to the wild forest systems but involve the life of inhabitory people who live where a logging cut is scheduled, and who are treated as though they don't even live there. So human rights issues are very much involved also.

The planetary scale of the concern has to do with things like the contribution of the tropical forests, and all forests, to the world's oxygen supply. Another con-cern is the significant loss of soils that follows massive clear-cutting, which is linked to the whole question of world soil loss and soil fertility deterioration. A third concern is loss of species through destruction of habitat. The extinction of species. As you said there is irre-versible ecological damage and this is the worst sort. Loss of species is pretty much irreversible, and loss of soils *is* irreversible. Destruction of forest habitat, espe-cially in certain parts of the world, results in a kind of erosion or baking away of the soil that means that it's going to be very difficult to ever get the same kind of forest back again.

It turns out that every one of these habitats and species is literally a community—a certain group of trees and creatures that all travel together through time. When that community is broken up, you can't easily re-establish it.

On the level of air, water, and soil, deforestation is of profound concern to everyone, even though we might not see it as important to us right off. The effects of acid rain tie into that also. I think a lot of people who are working with ecological issues right now agree that worldwide deforestation and its concomitant effects, worldwide habitat destruction, are some of the most serious ecological problems.

CI: Do you tie this in with the pollution of the air, the greenhouse effect, the pollution of our water supplies, and so on?

GS: Well, it definitely connects with water; to what degree it connects with air, I'm not sure. You see, algae are also oxygen providers to the atmosphere. But then we have to look at the pollution of the ocean and atmosphere problems going all the way up to the ozone layer, and the ozone hole. There's not any one thing that's not connected anymore. That's proposing it on the simple level of human self-interest. You might think practical people would take that seriously, let alone those of us who would be as concerned even if human beings were "okay" and it was simply in the interest of other forms of life. But human beings aren't even okay in this.

So you asked me what some of the issues I'm concerned about are. I see that as a lifelong set of issues or complex of problems that won't go away. What can we do about it? At one end are dear friends in Earth First! who actually do nonviolent direct action protest by climbing up trees, blocking bulldozers and, rightly or wrongly, sometimes spiking trees.[5] Who would have thought a bunch of young people would risk their lives for the sake of old trees? It's beautiful. Old growth stands of Douglas fir or redwood or spruce or cedar. A number of people are

---

[5] Founded in 1980, Earth First! is an environmental organization of about 10,000 members, many of whom consider themselves "rednecks for wilderness." The organization's controversial practice of "ecotage," the sabotage of equipment used by loggers and anyone thought to be destroying the wilderness, puts them in the forefront of radical environmental activism. Tree-spiking, driving a nail into a tree and then camouflaging it, does not injure the tree but renders it useless for lumber as it would destroy the blades of the saws at the mill. Critics say that the spikes pose a danger to mill workers who may be injured by flying shrapnel when the saw blades shatter. Earth Firsters say that automation "has placed most workers in control booths, out of danger."

out there in the field doing that. That's the direct action level.

All the way to the other extreme, in a sense, are people who are lobbying the World Bank to re-think its investment policies and to get them to be conscious of the need to include ecological health in their predictions or strategies when they start underwriting projects in Third World countries. Actually the World Bank has recently been showing a change of heart. They've asked Herman Daly, who wrote a book called *Steady State Economics*, to come in as an advisor and to bring long-range sustainable economic policy concerns into what they're doing.

CI: Is this the result of public pressure?

GS: I don't think so. The World Bank is pretty well insulated from direct pressure. I think it's based on common sense. I think they're smart enough to be the World Bank, so maybe they're also smart enough to realize that human self-interest is involved. But I wouldn't say that they're a bunch of deep ecologists or anything.

CI: You know, we are so dependent on trees for so many things, such as paper, to name one of our favorites. In our modern society we are terrible abusers of paper, with lots of waste, even the most conscious of us. This is just one example. It seems that there will have to be a gigantic change of our entire way of life—to stop using fossil fuels, to stop cutting down the trees—quite radical and touching every aspect of how we live. Does any part of your work, or work that you know of, offer viable alternatives, a whole different way of life?

GS: Well, you know, for some years now, certain Occidental thinkers have been playing around with the idea of alternative ways of life. That's what gives us socialism. That's what gave us the Communist revolution. That's what gives us a number of other social experiments. People deliberately— intellectually, almost—trying to come up with alternatives that look or feel better than this way or that way. I'm one of the people who has looked at what a saner society would look like, and what models we might draw upon, looking back in history or sidewise into other kinds of cultures—agrarian, pre-agrarian, primitive, prehistoric. I don't think that those are wasted exercises. We have to remind ourselves that no society is ever totally free of domination, exploitation, and injustice, in one form or another. But that doesn't mean that we can't learn a little bit here and a little bit there. By studying history and anthropology, I think that we are made aware that there is not just one irreducible, hopeless human nature that makes us automatically warlike, automatically greedy, automatically competitive. It's not quite as simple as saying that human nature is bound to end up with something like K-Mart.

CI: It's not genetic, in other words.

GS: Well, some of it is. What's interesting is to see that there's a certain amount of human drive that works in certain ways, but different societies have different ways of softening it or of encouraging it. One society encourages people to be greedy and competitive and says "Go for it. You owe yourself everything you can get." Another society may also have people who have those tendencies, but they soften it and say, "Have good manners, be generous, share, don't be stingy."

CI: Such as some of the more enlightened Oriental societies.

GS: God knows if they're more enlightened or not.

CI: I mean in times of history when there was peace and a flourishing of Dharma and of poetry, such as Emperor Ashoka's time in India about 2,000 years ago...

GS: Well, you know, the more I look into that, the more every one of those cases has its dark side. Still, it's true, Japan had almost 400 years of relative peace in the Heian Period.[6] They didn't even have capital punishment for about 350 years. There have also been some fairly long, stable periods of time in China. But even so, it wasn't all that easy. The Chinese have always had a gruesome penal code and, as they say, "Internal contradictions were grinding away." That brought the end of the peaceful dynasties. The taxation and interest rates, the inequalities by steadily widening the gap between the rich and the poor which put the peasants in worse and worse conditions, finally ruined China. Ultimately, they didn't have good economic and social policies. But they could never get their hands on what it was. So there are no enlightened societies, ultimately, but some were more fun than others.

CI: Should we try to live like those "more fun" societies?

GS: Well, we can't really live like them. We have to work with what we've got. And the potentiality of what we've got isn't bad. Rationalism, participatory democracy, a tradition of egalitarianism, a concern for human rights—much of the inheritance of the European Enlightenment is our working base.

CI: Isn't that a very mechanistic way of approaching it?

GS: Yes, but that's what we've got.

CI: But it seems that, well, white folks have been particularly destructive and particularly at odds with nature. Do you see from an historical point of view how we evolved this way? Is it simply that we were in the colder climates and had to conquer nature to exist, or what?

---

[6] The Heian Period in Japan began around 794 A.D. and lasted for the next few centuries. Heian was the capitol city at the time. It later came to be known as Kyoto.

GS: Well, it is true, Western European metropolitan culture launched itself out into worldwide exploration and exploitation with an energy unlike anyone else in history. I don't think it's because Western culture is inherently more destructive. I think it's just a combination of factors that let it loose. And some of it would have been quite unpredictable.

You can't make a blanket statement about all of Western culture, because Western culture has so many odds and ends of corners. It's actually very diverse. "There's an enormous gulf between Denmark and Sweden," people laughingly say, for instance. Not to mention, between Finland and Italy. There are subcultures of all sorts in Europe which have never been interested in going out and traveling around the world. The line of development is the upper-class, metropolitan trading economy which evolves into mercantilism. Then proto-capitalism and capitalism evolve, launching high-risk, high-profit ventures which become a game that some people can engage in. The royal families of England, for example, were some of the first investors in traveling corporations, such as the Hudson Bay Company. So it's institutions, if you really wanted to pinpoint it. Certain institutions in Western culture allowed certain groups of people to start doing those things. The rest of the people couldn't afford it, and they didn't really want to go on long trips anyway.

CI: What about the great dynasties of China, Japan, and India. They didn't get into the exploration/exploitation frenzy quite as much.

GS: No, they just ruined their own landscapes. India became deforested over the centuries. Most of the people became impoverished. The Indian economy has gone downhill for the last 2,000 years. The quality of life for the average Indian peasant was much higher 2,000 years ago than it is now.

CI: Maybe it was kind of clever of us to go other places and muck up *their* areas.

GS: Yes, that was our discovery. Yet I wouldn't say "our" really, because I don't consider that my membership. My place is on this continent.

The same thing happened in China as in India. China and India gradually reduced forests and habitat and wildlife species, and the human population went up. They ground themselves down to a point of being really miserable by the nineteenth century, and, being vulnerable because of their misery, they were taken over by imperialist powers. And yet the dynamics were their own. If you want to look at the nature of the problem, you probably would look at the nature of civilization itself, East and West.

CI: We're talking about the nature of the mind.

GS: Well, right at this moment we're talking about the nature of civilization, which includes hierarchies of class, of power, and of money. Specialization. With civilization comes the oppression of women, slave-owning classes, accumulation of wealth and power in certain hands in certain places, like in big cities; and the building of pyramids. Is that what we want? We are told that this is so great that we should suffer just to have these monuments. But for the average person who had to put in the time so that somebody could have a palace, it probably wasn't worth it.

I'm looking at another way of seeing the world which would be to say our monuments would be our *wild areas*. Leaving behind wilderness for the future would be the monument of our civilization. Dick Nelson talks about this in relation to the Athabaskan people, the indigenous people of central Alaska.[7] He says that if you travel

---

[7] Anthropologist Richard Nelson spent twenty years studying the ways of life of Eskimos and Athabaskan Indians. His book *The Island Within*

over central Alaska, there is virtually no trace of human habitation. Yet there have been people living there for 8,000 years. He says one way to look at it—the way nineteenth century people would have looked at it—was to say these people had absolutely nothing going for themselves. They haven't even left a trace. From another standpoint, which we might also say is a spiritual standpoint, the fact that they could live there for 8,000 years and have a very complex and rich intellectual and spiritual culture and yet leave not a trace is a considerable monument.

CI: Do you know that Chuang Tzu poem called "When Life was Full There Was No History"?

GS: Exactly, yes. Same kind of thing. So Chuang Tzu and Lao Tzu are talking about the way primitive people have lived here on the planet. They've lived here actually tens of thousands of years, leaving very little trace. We have to re-think what that means. Does that mean that they were dummies, or does that mean that they had a way of living that was quite interesting and that we should have regard for?

You asked if we can learn anything from other societies. Yes, we can learn a lot. We can learn that there are other ways to do things, and that human nature is not an absolute given as some people think, that there's a lot of flexibility in it. Then, the other side of it, asking why do things like this happen, is just asking fundamental questions about the human ego, taking human nature on as a question.

I feel the correctness of the fundamental assessment by Shakyamuni Buddha that most of our problems are caused by the human reluctance to accept death, impermanence, ephemerality, and the efforts that people make to build an illusion of permanence around themselves, which also becomes an illusion of separateness. If people

---

(North Point Press) is taken from the journals he kept while living in the Pacific Northwest.

can acknowledge their membership in the fabric of the whole, acknowledge that they are part of the habitat, part of the network, part of the web, and feel that the welfare of the web is their welfare, and their welfare is the welfare of the web—in other words, not be mindlessly but mindfully one with the whole—that is an extraordinary spiritual and political step right there, and it dumps the cartridges out of the weapons. It makes people approach things in a different way. So that's why we practice meditation—to get at those kinds of things in ourselves.

CI: I struggle every day with how gently or heavily I am stepping on the planet. I'm sure you're familiar with Jerry Mander's feelings about technologies and the question of whether or not they are "neutral."[8] We love our computers and yet they are a tool which reflects a society hell-bent on speeding up and exploiting as fast as possible, because computers are used in satellites and airplanes to track down natural resources, for example. Of course, we all fly in airplanes, drive cars, and do

---

[8] Jerry Mander makes the case in *Four Arguments for the Elimination of Television* that many of the problems with technology are *inherent* in the technology and cannot be reformed. "If you accept the existence of automobiles," says Mander, "you also accept the existence of roads laid upon the landscape, oil to run the cars, huge institutions to find oil and distribute it, and a general speeding up of life.

"And so it is with television. It doesn't matter whether enlightened people or unenlightened people get at the controls; television wires together hundreds of millions of people all over the planet and can speak into their brains with very powerful imagery all at the same time, homogenizing thought and culture. That is a political fact; it is the one speaking to the many. To speak of television as 'neutral' and therefore subject to change is as absurd as speaking of the reform of a technology such as guns."

With regard to computers, Mander asserts: "Computers are of greater benefit to large institutions—multi-national corporations, government, and military—than to environmentalists and progressive organizations. The large institutions achieve via computers an ability to operate on a global scale and at a speed which would be impossible without them. They have more computers, better ones, bigger ones, with more outlets; this facilitates such endeavors as the instantaneous transfer of funds to finance development and the mapping and acquisition of resources. So it is not a question of who benefits, but rather who benefits most? For the environmentalists, the existence of computers in the world has produced a net loss."

many things that participate in the costliness of this way of life. What are your own internal contradictions on these questions? Sometimes I feel I'm not really walking my talk.

GS: Well, there are several different strategies by which to live in the world. One is to withdraw from the world and to choose purity. To do that you could live in an ashram or a monastery or a nunnery or a utopian community. Or you need your own household, and you can rigorously try to eliminate from your life and from your economy all of the things that you think share in or contribute to what you identify as wicked in the world. I know a number of people who do that in different ways. Pure, hearty Quakers who make their children eat nothing but oatmeal. Hindu vegetarians who won't let their kids eat cheese unless it is rennet-free. Although I'm sort of making fun of them, I admire people who choose that way. It's essentially the monastic choice. And it has been a choice that people have had available to them for thousands of years. Does the monastic choice make any difference or not? It's a question I wouldn't even try arguing. Are you simply escaping from the world and being irresponsible, or are you in some magical way making the world better? You hear both arguments.

In my case, my choice is what you might call from the Buddhist standpoint, the lay choice, the bodhisattva choice, the choice of engaging in it as it is—living in it as other people have to live in it, eating the same poisons and running the same karmic risks. By running the same karmic risks, if I have a good idea, at least I have it in the context of what other people have to do. Also by running the same karmic risks and by living the same life, I am committed to using the same tools they use. If I lived in a monastery, I wouldn't need a car and I wouldn't need a computer. Since I've decided to be an activist, so to speak, and a layperson, I need to drive my children to school and I need to do my shopping and pick up materials, and I have no apologies for that.

In the same way, if "our sacred enemy" is using computers to guide missiles and to manage unimaginably fast heaps of information, am I going to puritanically keep myself at a disadvantage and write with paper and pencil, or not use the telephone while they're running messages by satellite all over the globe? I would not be much of an enemy. [laughing] Actually I don't buy the point of view that says if you use your enemy's tools and if you live your enemy's life in some way, that you inevitably become like your enemy. I don't think that's true. I think that I can pick up the same tool and use it in a different way. It makes a huge difference in who's handling the tool. As the Chinese saying has it, "Two men are running down the street. They look identical, but one is a thief and one is a policeman."

So, at any rate, I have—and many of my comrades have—opted to use our own sense of selectivity about it. And if it gives more clout to our work to use a CB radio or a telephone, and if it puts us in the better position to talk back, we'll do it.

You know what you can do with a computer? This is what some friends of mine did in the Forest Issues Task Force. Because the law requires that certain information be available to you, they were able to take a computer down to the county courthouse and download from the county computer all of the names and addresses of every registered voter in the county. In twenty minutes they had the complete address file of the county in their little 20-megabyte hard disk. They can now program that to selectively print address labels by any demographic set of criteria they choose. They are doing that to fight back on the Forest Issues Task Force front.

CI: Critics would say that the dangers in having these technologies used in the wrong hands outweigh the benefits used in the right hands.

GS: Well, I don't think that the answer is that simple. It's like drinking and smoking; it's like sex; it's like driving. You go into it with your eyes wide open. You know it's dangerous. But if you choose to do it, there's a way to do it. If you choose not to do it, fine. Actually I like living dangerously. And I like living in this century at this point right now.

CI: You said something once about how contradictions really don't bother you.

GS: Well, I really do think that this is part of what engaged Buddhism means, what the bodhisattva spirit means. It means that you don't back off from taking things on, or getting your hands a little dirty, or quaffing a little poison, or running risks. And it's not the only way to go. I have great admiration for my peer Quaker and my peer Amish and my peer monastic Buddhist friends, but I wouldn't say that the way that I and some of my comrades have chosen is necessarily inferior to that either. I'd say there are two paths that we shall allow to be equal and see what happens. We need both.

CI: You spoke at one time in your essay, "Buddhist Anarchism," about gentle violence being an acceptable response to stopping what is wrong. Then you modified that in a later interview to "You set yourself against something rather than flow with it," and you spoke at that time about having to "karmically dirty" our hands to live in this world. How might people today say no to a wrong in a contemporary issue? How would you "set yourself against it"?

GS: Well, it depends on the nature of the wrong and it also depends on how close it is to you. Things that are dumped in your lap, things that come up to your front door, you are really karmically obligated to deal with, I do believe. Poverty, oppression, rank injustice right in front of you is yours. It's been given to you to take care of. The old Quaker concept of bearing witness and putting yourself out in front by civil and disobedient means is probably the best you can do. Although, politically speaking, if you really want it to work, call the newspapers too. In other words, a civil disobedient or bearing witness move is personally and morally satisfying if you simply do it, and it may do some good. But to make it really effective, we involve the rest of the society and let them know what we're doing, what's happening, and make it into an issue. If we go farther than that, we're into terrorism.

On the other side of that, you move into all the many ways you can work within the system of a participatory democracy, some of which are pretty good. It involves being there fast and having the equipment, like getting 10,000 letters off instead of just 500. And sometimes some of those things work.

Underneath it all is the essential requirement to be constantly involved, at least for a few people, in understanding what the structural causes are. The structural causes might be said to be of two sorts. This goes back to something I said earlier—the structural causes as they are in history and the structural causes as they are in the spirit.

The structural causes as they are in history are class structure, institutions, the nature of civilization itself— the concerns that Western Marxists, the Frankfurt school, post-Glasnost theoreticians, enlightened post-capitalist theoreticians are still wrestling with. How do we understand history? How do we get control of our institutions? Is it possible to have sane governments? Is it possible to restructure our society on a deep level and make it work? Those are what I mean by structural analyses. As the Marxists say, if you only correct things on an electoral level, you are constantly applying band-aids, but you haven't stopped the disease. And so we are still engaged in trying to understand the nature of the illness on a social and historical level.

And then, on the other level, is that concern that we know from the world of spiritual philosophy and practice—the question of how we drop the ego, how we get out of our own way. How do we as individuals liberate ourselves from greed and hatred and ignorance, and is there any way that that can be done on a larger scale than just the individual? Is it possible that three or four of us might do it together?

So if you talk about amelioration to environmental or political questions, there's always going to be some uppity Marxist who says, "Well, it's really the fault of capitalism," or somebody else who says, "It's really the fault of patriarchy." Well, yes, those things are true, but we still have to take care of things in the here and now, and we still have to get at the deeper level of things.

CI: Do you see some progress on any fronts?

GS: Yes. Two of the greatest changes of heart that are under way right now in Western culture are the relationships of men and women and the relationship to the natural world. The women's movement is profoundly unsettling to the institutions of the past, and the ecological movement is profoundly unsettling.

CI: Do you feel these two areas are connected?

GS: Oh, I've got baskets full of material that people are sending me from all over on women and feminism and the ecological issues, with arguments flying back and forth. It's a very hot set of interesting questions. I think that there are really deep cultural issues involved there, spiritual issues. Wisdom—whether social, political, or cultural—is wherever you find it.

CI: Do you think nonviolence is always the way?

GS: Yes. Nonviolence is always the way, but you can't always do it. This is the compassionate and practical paradox of the first precept, the precept of nonviolence. In an ultimate sense, there is no evasion of the precept.

CI: What do you mean by that?

GS: That there are no excuses, there are no justifying circumstances for violence. However, in our contingent and organic being in this karmic realm, the very law of impermanence is a law that is often enacted by processes that are violent. And we sometimes have clear choices before us that are of a very paradoxical nature which throw us between responding with violence or choosing that violence be done to ourselves or to someone else. So with no further ado, we respond. The response of the being who chooses not to be a victim is a fair response, and in some of these contexts it's hard to know who is being violent to whom.

Furthermore, the whole question of eating and the dynamics of the food chain stand in a scary and sensitive territory that is beyond the reach of any literal application of the precept of non-harming, because each being acts out its own ultimate, essential nature. The hawk cannot but be a hawk, the rabbit cannot but be a rabbit. However, when we look at it in the human realm, perhaps our range of choices is broader. When I make the choice to kill a chicken and eat it, I don't excuse myself for doing that. On the other hand, I don't apologize. It's the choice I make.

CI: How do you hold it in your mind, this act of violence?

GS; I hold it in my mind by acknowledging it, by not making any excuses or any justifications, by not saying, "I had to do this," but by saying "I *chose* to do this." It's the acknowledgment and the gesture of acknowledgment. Actually, it's the moment of stopping to say "Thank you," that makes a huge difference.

CI: Do you feel that through meditation practice you become more sensitive to certain choices that you used to make that you can no longer bear to live with? Do you find a lessening of violence in your life?

GS: Oh, to the contrary. I came into this as a young man with an *extreme* nonviolent sensibility, a real revulsion against the nature of a universe that required suffering and death. Through practice, and this is true of many of us, I came to understand how it's possible to accept the universe as it is, to understand the play of the process, to know that I can make my own choices without self-justification and without apology, and to accept the karma that comes with that. This is exactly what you have to do in every case. You're not an adult until you accept the karma that you make. Then you can *choose* to make karma.

CI: But, if you're aware that you're making karma, by say, being violent or causing harm in some way, it seems the mere knowing that you're going to have to pay for this somewhere along the line, now or later, would make one disinclined to continue to do those things.

GS: Well, one of the things that you learn from practice is that you don't mind paying. As they say in prison, "Don't mess with crime if you can't do time."

But what I've just said is kind of tough-sounding. In actual fact, I almost never kill anything. When I eat venison it's because I find a road-kill on the highway, and I've learned how to salvage road-kills. When I used to keep chickens we did eat our surplus roosters sometimes, but you do it with a kind of sadness, not with pleasure. The people I have known who hunt, the serious hunters and the subsistence hunters like the Athabaskan Indians in Alaska, go about their hunting and fishing in a very low-key way, very modest, with a trace of sadness. They sense that quality of tragedy, because they understand that they are taking life. It's not with a victorious and conquering spirit at all, but with a very modest spirit that they approach killing.

CI: How did Gandhi influence you?

GS: I was very influenced by Gandhi in my early twenties. I read *The Story of My Experiments with Truth*, and I was deeply moved by that. Like so many people of my generation, I wanted to, in some way, make Gandhi my role model, both in a commitment to absolute nonviolence and in a simple way of life. And I've honored that commitment, but I remember reading that Gandhi's great supporter, the Indian industrialist Tata, once said, "It cost me a fortune to keep Gandhi simple." Tata was the one who underwrote the ashrams, you know.

So I came to understand that simplicity and nonattachment are truly a matter of attitude and not necessarily a matter of externals. I've known people who have lived simply but who are attached to their simplicity and desperately engaged with their little pair of sandals and their little pair of eyeglasses, whereas other people who have more are sometimes freer, more liberated.

Practice to me has been liberating in the direction of understanding complexity and tolerance of what, when I was younger, might have appeared to be the failings of others. But as you grow older you understand how difficult it is for everybody to be pure, or for *anybody* to be pure. And you also realize that the truth of things lies in the appreciation of complexity and of paradox...and in a whole lot of forgiveness.

Brother David Steindl-Rast

As a lad growing up in Nazi-occupied Austria, David Steindl-Rast lived with daily air raids. Ordinarily, warning sirens alerted the populace to find an air raid shelter before the bombs fell. One day, however, the sirens' blare occurred at the same time as the bombs began raining down on the beautiful city of Vienna. Young David rushed into the closest building, a church, and hid under a pew with his face in his hands. The sky outside flashed terror and the ground shook, shattering glass and scattering debris all around him. He peeked at the vaulted ceiling of the church above him and hoped that it would hold through the bombing. Nearly an hour later, a long siren tone signalled that the bombing was over.

David emerged from the church into a beautiful May morning, feeling overwhelming wonder and joy to be alive. Although many of the buildings which had stood a short time ago were now in smoking ruins, David's eyes fell on a few square feet of green lawn in the midst of the rubble. "It was as if a friend had offered me an emerald in the hollow of his hand," Steindl-Rast has written. "Never before or after have I seen grass so surprisingly green."

* * *

David Steindl-Rast was born on July 12, 1926 in Vienna, Austria and grew up nearby in a small village in the Alps. His parents were divorced when he was very young, and David lived with his mother and two younger brothers while receiving his primary education in the two-classroom village school. Winters were for skiing in the Alps.

David's memories of growing up in the Austrian countryside include splendid visions of religious customs. Because the local population were mostly devout

Catholics, they seemed to live "from one religious feast to the next." Religion was so woven into the fabric of the community that, according to Steindl-Rast, "the sacred, the cultural, and nature were all of one piece."

For his secondary education, David moved to a progressive Catholic boarding school in Vienna for two years. When the Nazis came in 1938, Steindl-Rast's mother, concerned with the Nazis' interference with and disapproval of the school, moved to Vienna to be with her son, bringing her other two boys with her. The school became a teenage hotbed of opposition to the Nazi occupation, even if the only acts of defiance were those dreamed up by boys, such as congregating in groups of more than two and going off on forbidden camping trips together. The young men also rebelled against the Nazi establishment by becoming deeply religious at an age when they might have normally rebelled against their religion. David's mother encouraged her son's underground activities and, in doing so, incurred the suspicions of the Gestapo, who questioned her on more than one occasion. Despite the war, despite the Nazi occupation and undercurrent of fear, David had a "wonderful time" in his early teens, explaining that at that age "kids don't think about being frightened." As the war years went on, however, David began to realize that the older boys, many of them friends who had taken him under their wings, were being sent off to war and killed on the front lines. "After only half a year, half of them were dead," Steindl-Rast explained. David and his friends began to accept the idea of an early death as inevitable: "We had no expectation of living beyond the age of twenty."

Steindl-Rast was drafted to serve in the Nazi army but "had such a guardian angel that [he] was never sent to the front." After a year he took off his uniform and went underground. His mother hid him at home until the war was over and the Russians had marched into Vienna. By this time, there was almost no food in the city. Steindl-Rast remembers living on the ragweed which grew in springtime on the dirt ruins of the bombed houses and on the peas full of worms which the Russians provided. For a time, Steindl-Rast worked in setting up refugee camps and, later on, clearing rubble from the university. "You had to shovel debris for so many hours before you could register for school," he laughingly recalls.

It was in this period that a friend gave David the Rule of St. Benedict. Italy's Saint Benedict of the sixth century is considered the father of Western monasticism. In 520 A.D. he proposed a rule of life for monks and nuns which made monasticism a more gentle proposition than it had been previously. Saint Benedict emphasized humility, a constant striving to seek God and to abandon self-seeking, prayer, study, manual labor, and "stability in community," or what we would now call a dedication to a sense of place. David was fascinated with the ideas presented in the Rule. He imagined himself at the point of his death and thought that the monastic life as described by Saint Benedict is how he would have liked to have lived. But he dismissed this vision because he knew of no monasteries which lived purely according to the Rule any longer.

Instead, Steindl-Rast concentrated on his studies of painting and art restoration at the Vienna Academy of Fine Arts. He celebrated the end of the war years by attending Vienna's wondrous balls, operas, and festivals, bribing his way into such venues with cigarettes he procured from friendly American soldiers. But in his heart a longing for monastic life still flickered, and he secretly decided that he would take whichever came first, "the right girl or the right monastery."

As the war had destroyed many art pieces in Europe, David found fascinating work in art restoration over the next few years. He also became interested in children's art and its likeness to primitive art. This led him into child psychology, and he earned a Ph.D. at the University of Vienna, majoring in psychology and minoring in anthropology.

After finishing his studies, Steindl-Rast came to the United States. His maternal grandmother had lived in the U.S. for many years, and his mother had moved to

New York as well. Six months after his arrival in the U.S., Steindl-Rast heard from a friend about a group of Benedictine monks who had recently begun a monastery dedicated to living according to the original Rule of St. Benedict. Steindl-Rast set out to find the group based on the scant information provided by his friend. Within a couple days, he was in Elmira, New York at a little farm in the country with a group of monks still living in a barn and tents on the property and practicing the Rule in its pure form. Although it was a few months before he was able to live at Mt. Saviour, David Steindl-Rast knew he had found his home.

Steindl-Rast joined the Benedictine monks at Mt. Saviour Monastery in 1953 and there began his life as Brother David. For the next decade, he received training in philosophy and theology, and he rarely left the monastery's grounds. However, the dozen or so monks at Mt. Saviour enjoyed a rich intellectual life as many of the great thinkers of the time visited the monastery and would stay up late into the night in dialogue with them. The Prior at Mt. Saviour, Father Damasus Winzen, was well-known for his scholarship in liturgy and religious art, and this brought additional prestige to the small, avant-garde, country monastery.

During these years Brother David began to develop a planetary social consciousness through outside contacts with the monastery. Great social activists, such as Dorothy Day and the staff at the *Catholic Worker*, were in regular touch with the monks.[1] Daniel Berrigan, who was the first Roman Catholic priest in the history of the United States to receive and serve a federal sentence for peace agitation, was a regular visitor and would hold retreats for Protestant clergymen at Mt. Saviour.

---

[1] Dorothy Day (1897-1980) was a Roman Catholic social activist and author. She co-founded the Catholic Worker movement, a pacifist organization in New York City, which established "houses of hospitality" for the poor. She is most well-known as the co-founder of the *Catholic Worker*, a publication based on Christian ideals of voluntary poverty and charity and dedicated to social justice and nonviolent resistance to the "warfare state," first published in 1933.

Brother David also began to take a great interest in other monastic traditions, especially those of the East. He was amazed to read the work of D.T. Suzuki, the Japanese Zen scholar who was one of the early Buddhist influences on the intellectual community in England and the United States. "I began to see that this monastic calling was something that united us," Brother David explained.

Because Father Damasus was not able to oblige all the requests for lectures that he received, he often sent one of the monks in his place. Consequently, Brother David began to lecture on the subject of prayer, as well as social consciousness and an ecumenical understanding of religious traditions, sometimes to the surprise of his audience. "It was a favorable position," Brother David noted, "because rather than speaking to the converted, I would be speaking to people who had come to hear about prayer. So when I would talk about social issues, there was some impact."

His interest in Zen led Brother David to a meeting with Eido Roshi, then known as Tai-Shimano, a Zen monk who had recently come to New York from Japan. The two monks immediately felt a deep rapport. Soon after they met, Brother David received an invitation to participate in a teach-in at the University of Michigan against the war in Vietnam. Brother David invited Tai-Shimano to participate also. On risk of being deported from the U.S., Tai-Shimano attended the teach-in with Brother David, and the two monks shared a room for several days. "It was as though we had lived together a hundred years," Brother David said. "It convinced me in this understanding that monasticism builds a bridge across traditions."

Tai-Shimano invited Brother David to study at his zendo in New York City. Although it was considered highly irregular at the time, Brother David approached the monks at his monastery with a request for permission to study Zen. In considering the request, the Prior invited Tai-Shimano to visit Mt. Saviour, and the Zen monk came for a two day visit. In what Brother David remembers as an agonizing interchange, the Benedictine monks questioned Tai-Shimano about his understanding. "They asked him all kinds of theological questions and, as he was not familiar with Christian theology, he fell into all the traps," Brother David recalls. "I was mortified by the experience and thought that when he left, that would be the end of the story." The monks took Brother David aside and said that the Zen monk had made no sense to them whatsoever; however, they had watched him carefully. "The way he walks, the way he sits, the way he eats, convinced us that he is a true monk," they told a surprised Brother David. "You can go."

Thus began a Christian/Buddhist bond which pioneered a dialogue between these two great religions. Brother David became one of the first Christian monks to formally study Zen in America, although he had to enroll at Columbia University in Japanese studies "as a cover." At that time, the late sixties, "it wasn't quite acceptable for a Catholic monk to study Zen." Brother David practiced meditation at Tai-Shimano's zendo in New York City for the next three years. It was the beginning of his training in Zen, and he eventually studied with many of the great Zen masters who taught in the U.S., such as Suzuki Roshi, Yasutani Roshi, and Soen Roshi.

Meanwhile, Trappist monk Thomas Merton had also been examining the link between Christianity and Asian religious traditions, so when Father Damasus suggested that he and Brother David visit Merton, Steindl-Rast was delighted. "Merton had done so much reading that he was way ahead of me in understanding the relationship between Buddhism and Christianity," Brother David said. "So the practical aspects—the personal experiences—were very interesting to him, and I had experience there." The mutual exchange between the two Christian monks, theoretically-informed Merton and practice-oriented Steindl-Rast, formed an affinity which continued until Merton's accidental death in Bangkok in

1968. Merton once told Steindl-Rast, "We will need the courage to do the opposite of everybody else."

As the years passed, Brother David became a world-renowned lecturer and philosophical bridge-builder between East and West, between monks and householders, and even between peace workers and the military. In 1985, for example, I attended a talk Brother David gave to a group of U.S. Army Special Forces (Green Berets) in Massachusetts, who were being trained in a six-month program of Aikido, meditation, biofeedback, and psychology. Brother David began by remembering his own army service and eventually led the discussion around to peace. The Special Forces group found Brother David to be one of their favorite guest lecturers.

For two decades, Brother David has been a social activist. He has marched for peace. He has spoken about hunger and the need for the First World to address the needs of the Third and Fourth Worlds. And he has reminded us of the challenges and opportunities of our time as we face ecological crises. His lectures have taken him all over the world—speaking to starving students in Zaire, intellectuals in Germany, Papago Indians in Arizona. Yet he is a hermit at heart. Although he remains a member of Mt. Saviour Monastery in New York, he spends much of his time in solitary retreat in California.

It is Brother David's spiritual essence that is most memorable. His message is that of gratefulness. In his book *Gratefulness, the Heart of Prayer*, he writes: "If the fullness of gratitude which the word grate-ful-ness implies can ever be reached, it must be fullness of love and fullness of life." It is that fullness which Brother David suggests will provide us with a sense of belonging, because it is gratefulness which can facilitate our realization of interdependence. As Brother David once told me, "Gratefulness is the only appropriate response to that which is given—and this life is a given."

I have met Brother David on numerous occasions and first interviewed him in 1983 at the Weston Priory in Vermont. He is a man of profound depth, and, at the same time, delightful playfulness, laughing intermittently and phrasing his words with pun and wit. The following interview took place at the San Francisco Zen Center where Brother David was staying after an evening lecture the previous night to a crowd of 800, a dialogue with Buddhist meditation teacher Jack Kornfield, on "The Sure Heart's Release."

Interview with David Steindl-Rast
July 1, 1988 • San Francisco, California

Catherine Ingram: Years ago you wrote that "wastefulness, fearfulness, and indifference are undoing us fast. Time is running out." What do you feel now?

Brother David Steindl-Rast: I have not seen much improvement, although it is amazing how slow "fast" is. It is helpful for us to live always on this brink and, at the same time, to realize that it may go on and on. We have to do our thing regardless how long it all lasts. Paradoxically, we have to act as if we had all the time in the world, and as if we had no time at all. If we hold these two together, we have a chance of doing the right thing. Then the rest is not up to us.

CI: What are you doing in your own life with regard to "the right thing"?

DS: Well, I have discovered that only if we spend much of our time in one place will we take responsibility for that place. So I've made a concerted effort to travel less and to devote myself more to being in one place.

CI: Yet in our last interview you said that as a result of your travels you had developed concern for the Third and Fourth Worlds.

DS: Yes, and that remains a great concern to me. I still travel more than I like, and I also get feedback on what is happening in other parts of the world from people who have been in those places for a long time and are deeply rooted there. I think the situation in many places is getting worse and worse.

So one of my questions is "What is it that we need?" Before we can do something we have to know what is concretely needed. One answer that I have discovered since I last talked with you is that we need what I call for lack of a better term, "global heroes." We need to have the values for which we stand embodied in actual persons.

Now while it is true that the world has, in some respects, gotten smaller, for most people the world has gotten bigger. Little communities have been broken open so now they are able to see the whole world. Formerly they knew only their own village or a few nearby villages. For us in the developed countries, the world has become smaller. You can no longer do something in any part of the world that will not influence people in other parts of the world. However, we are not really a world community yet. Community comes about when a group of people have the same hero. If we can find our global heroes, they will turn the mass of humanity into a global community.

I think of these heroes as "daring people"—people who dared to live the values that we need to cultivate nowadays. They are daring also in the sense of daring *us*. They dare us to become the people that we *can* be, to become in some respects like them, not by imitating them, but by trying to put into practice deep human values. Some of us who are interested in this idea are attempting to publish the lives of such global heroes.

CI: Are these contemporary people?

DS: No, in this particular series we are not focusing on people who are still living, but rather on people who have died, usually, for their cause. I am also asking these days, "What common basis can we find for solving the many problems that confront us?" What is it that might express in our time what in former times was expressed by, say, "the Tao" or "the Logos"? Maybe the phrase "Common Sense," with a capital "C," capital "S." This is the closest English phrase I can find for that reality which Lao Tzu called "the Tao." In his time, "Tao" meant "path." He gave it a deeper meaning.

Heraclitus called it "the Logos." That meant "Word," or "Thought," and he also gave it a much deeper meaning, which we might call our "deepest consciousness." We can make sense of the world because we have within ourselves what makes the world sensible—the Logos— the principle that animates the world and gives order to it. So Heraclitus and all the Greek philosophers were very much geared toward intellectual understanding.

What Lao Tzu and the Taoists were interested in was the Path. They asked, "How do we live, and walk through life in harmony with the Force, with the Flow?" The Taoists, too, were concerned with how to make sense of this world but by more than a knowing sense; they asked not only, "How can we intellectually understand?" but "How can we make sense of life and of the world?" We can make sense only to the extent to which that sense is common. That is why the phrase, Common Sense, suggests itself. The wider we stretch the sense of "common," the more sense we will be able to make of the world.

We are talking here about Common Sense or a Community Spirit not only with people, but with animals, plants, the whole cosmos—as the Logos was and as the Tao was. What makes it so difficult to use this term is that it has been usurped by people who mean anything but Common Sense. They mean rather "conventionality" and "public opinion" which they call common sense.

CI: Voltaire, I think it was, said that common sense is not so common.

DS: Exactly. People say, "Isn't it common sense to be out for Number One in a world in which dog eats dog?" But this is the very opposite from genuine Common Sense. It springs not from community, but from alienation.

CI: People often fear going against the grain in society. When there is a widely held belief, such as looking out for Number One, anyone who differs with that will often be seen as an oddball, out of step and out of time.

DS: Yes, and coming back to the idea of "daring people"—what daring people dare to do is to break through this crust of conventionality in the strength of that deep Community Spirit that unites us with all. They get in trouble with the powers of the time because the ones in power are those who are polled conventionally through public opinion. Yet, with the authority of Common Sense, one can take a stand against public opinion. Anyone who has done that becomes a guiding star for our own time because that is exactly what we must do today—take our stand on the authority that unites us against the authorities that divide us. This is what I try to empower people to do when I teach, to live by the authority of Common Sense. In Biblical terms, that is the idea of the Kingdom of God.

CI: Will you say more about the Kingdom of God?

DS: In Biblical terms, it is by the Holy Spirit that we as humans are alive, by the very life-breath of God. That Spirit breaks through the crust of the law and the letter and the flesh and of all that stands for conventionality, separation, and division. The Kingdom means living by the power of the Spirit.

We can envisage today, it seems to me, a world in which the child in each of us comes alive. This child-spirit would unite the world. To liberate that child-spirit within us is an extremely important task. Some twenty years ago we began to see that liberating the woman in us was a primary task. And that was not restricted to women; many men saw clearly that the anima within us had to be liberated. And on the strength of that psycho-

logical insight, one could have forecast a major sociological event that would take place: women's liberation.
While women's liberation has sociological overtones, it
goes far beyond sociology. Its aim is to liberate all human beings by liberating the anima in us.

In a similar way many people today are beginning to
see how urgent it is to liberate the child in all of us. Our
survival depends on the child in us being liberated. We,
too, can make a forecast: one of the important sociological issues of our time will be the liberation of the child.

CI: Well, I think this could be seen from two vantage
points. Of course, most spiritual traditions talk about
that childlike wonder and freshness and curiosity, or
what is called in Zen, "Beginner's mind,"—a way of
spontaneously greeting the world without precon-
ceptions. But then again, there is sometimes a brattiness
about children, along with a greediness and immaturity
about what it is to suffer and to subsequently feel compassion or empathy. America is often likened to being a
kind of adolescent bully on the world stage, for instance.
So partly I love that notion of developing childlike
qualities, and partly I feel that we need to be a lot older
in our ways, more sagelike.

DS: Well, before children become bratty, if we catch
them before that, we sometimes get the impression that
they are very old, wise beings. And it is that which needs
to be cultivated. My intuition is that some of the brattiness is created by society; it is not the natural attitude of
the child. There is a misunderstanding of the child built
into our culture, a blindspot. We presuppose that the
child is rebellious to start with and that we must keep
the child in check. We assume that the child is born into
the family as a little "savage" and has to be "domesti-
cated," has to be "civilized," and kept under control. In
preschool this is already presupposed: children are
rebels until proven otherwise. And even later on in society we are again and again assumed to be by nature
"rebels" that have to be bent to bow to authority.

The fact is, when you check it out psychologically, human beings have an inordinate inclination to sell out to external authorities, to bow to authorities, because that is easier for us, far less costly than to live by the authority of our own deepest convictions. Therefore, all the authorities in our society conspire to make us more subservient to external authority. Yet, the rightful use of authority, the *only* rightful use of authority that I can see, is to strengthen those under authority so that they will stand on their own two feet and take responsibility. The books and study of Alice Miller support this understanding of authority.

CI: Such as her book *For Your Own Good?*

DS: Yes, also *Thou Shalt Not Be Aware: Society's Betrayal of the Child*. And there are also such studies as Stanley Milgram did at Yale.[2] He set himself the task to find out how the Holocaust was possible, how people who went home at night to play chamber music and read poetry with their families could put to death the Jews, the Gypsies, and the Poles during their work hours. Milgram wanted to see to what extent average people, not only in Germany, but in the world, would go to inflict excruciating pain on an innocent victim for no other reason than that an authority figure told them to do so. So he devised that highly controversial and very ingenious test...

---

[2]In the early sixties research psychologist Stanley Milgram (1933-1984) conducted a series of "obedience to authority" experiments at Yale University, the results of which were first published in 1963. The actual subject was recruited from newspaper ads and thought he (forty men participated) was part of a test to determine the effectiveness of punishment in learning tasks. Each man was required to administer what he thought were electric shocks to a "learner" in the next room whenever the learner made a mistake in a word test. Although the shocks were not real, the learner often simulated pain by banging on the wall and refusing to answer any more questions. Using a range of from 15 to 450 volts, sixty-five percent of the subjects, often prodded by the "authority figure" experimenter present in the room, pressed the 450 volt switch. That amount of voltage, marked only with "XXX" was two notches beyond what was marked "Danger: Severe Shock."

CI: Using actors who pretended to be getting electrically shocked.

DS: Right. It didn't receive the reception in the psychological and psychiatric world that it deserved because we don't like to believe to what extent we—the average people—are willing to sell out to external authorities.

CI: But it does seem perennial. I was just reading an article about the people who were driving the train which ran over Brian Willson.[3] Basically they said they were just following orders.

People are often willing to give away their own power in exchange for being told what to do next, because following one's own path can be hard—terrifying and lonely. They'd rather have a leader tell them what to do and what to think. You see, I think this is a danger with your idea of a global hero.

DS: Yes, and in Germany where we are right now working on this project, you cannot use this word "hero" at all. It is totally out. We haven't come up with another word. We are talking about using something like "guiding stars."

CI: Or perhaps to simply refer to the kind of inspiration that Jesus provided, a reminder to love and forgive.

DS: Yes, my understanding of the Jesus event is precisely that it is a Common Sense breakthrough in the deepest meaning of that word. For instance, in Paul's letter to the Corinthians, Paul understood what Jesus stood for and he put it into one verse—"In Christ there is neither

---

[3]On September 1, 1987, Vietnam veteran Brian Willson began a nonviolent vigil at the Concord Naval Weapons Station in California to protest the transportation of bombs and munitions to Central America. He had sent a letter informing the Weapons Station authorities that he and others would be fasting and sitting on the tracks. On the first day of the protest, a train with orders not to stop ran over Brian Willson, severing both of his legs.

Jew nor Gentile, in Christ there is neither male nor female, in Christ there is neither slave nor free person."

But it took decades until at least a small group of people understood what it meant that "In Christ there is neither Jew nor Gentile." Then it took 1700 or 1800 years to recognize that "In Christ there is neither free nor slave." And we are still grappling with male and female! That's just where the crack in this social conventionality is allowing a little bit of Common Sense to break through. And when this is exhausted there will be other issues.

CI: This sounds like a view of consciousness as being progressive.

DS: Yes, I suppose it does sound as if I were saying things are getting better and better. Well, there are, within the general unfolding of things, some aspects where things are getting better. But I'm not one of those who uphold the idea that on the whole everything's getting better— that we started out in the dumps and are working ourselves up. In some respects things are getting worse and worse. If you look at some of the primitive societies and communities, there was a great deal of Common Sense in them. In early myth and ritual and symbol, a great deal of this communality is expressed. On another level there is a great deal of fear in primitive societies, a great deal of narrowness and exclusiveness: "Anybody who is not one of us is not human"—ideas like that. So in that respect, there is room for improvement. But it's not an ascending line and it's not a clearly descending line. We are making some breakthroughs, and on the other hand it is getting more difficult.

CI: One thing that seems to be at issue is whether or not we will actually survive. We are living in a time which has become dangerous enough and bad enough to possibly awaken us, if only out of self-interest, to live more gently on this Earth, to co-exist with the life forms on this planet. Do you think we're going to make it?

DS: It's a good question, but I'm not sure it's a question that should be answered. I'm not sure that the answer one way or the other is going to help anybody. If we say, "Yes, we are surely going to make it,"—first of all it would be difficult to substantiate that claim—and, if the idea is really accepted, it could have damaging effects. We may just go on like before and not do anything to stop the destruction.

Now the opposite answer, "We're not going to make it," can also have enormously damaging effects because people would say, "If we're not going to make it anyway, why bother?" So neither of these two answers is going to help very much. We must put as much effort into everything we're doing as if whether or not we're going to make it depended upon it. And we must find a way of living in which even if we are not going to make it, in the last second you can say to yourself, "Well, what I did was worthwhile." But the worthwhileness must never depend on the success.

W.S. Merwin has a beautiful poem in which he says, "On the last day of the world, I would like to plant a tree."[4] He develops the idea that you are not only planting the tree for bearing fruit, and not only as a sign of hope, but just for the planting of the tree for the first time in this spot in which it may or may not live for a long time, and may or may not see the sun coming up and feel the cool of the evening or experience its first night. This tree, this little seedling, is something worthwhile in itself, not only in the view of eventually bearing fruit. That is to me a strong, convincing poetic image, much better than trying to answer, "Are we going to make it, or are we not going to make it?"

CI: It always seems to come back to living in the present moment and finding ways to practice doing that without

---

[4] From W.S. Merwin's poem, "Space."

attachment to goals, whether they be saving the planet or getting enlightened.

DS: Yes, I think so. For me, prayer or contemplation are a celebration of life, not means to an end. Celebration of life means celebration of aliveness which happens to have the side effect that it makes me *more* alive, just like poetry is an outcome of mindfulness that makes you more mindful. It's not life itself, it's poetry. Life is greater than poetry. Prayer and contemplation are not life; life is greater than that. Prayer is the poetry of your super-aliveness which is spirituality.

The more alive you are, the more you will see the needs of the time, and the more you will have energy and willingness to devote yourself to those things. *Spiritus* means "life-breath." So your spirituality is a special kind of aliveness that includes your social commitment. If it doesn't include that, there's something wrong. You're not quite alive. I cannot take these things apart; they are all of one piece.

Not long ago I had the great luxury of spending a week in a workshop which dealt with body and spirit. One of the tasks that was given to us was to visualize our body and make a picture of it. Then we were to visualize our soul and depict it somehow. And then we were asked to make a picture of our spirit. I was surprised when we shared the results. Most people had actually visualized these three realities far less superimposed than I had. I can only superimpose them; I cannot visualize them being other than dimensions of one and the same reality. In depicting the body, I just drew the outline of a body in brown. Then for the soul, for me that wasn't something that was somewhere inside this body, but it was a particular kind of aliveness, so I just drew little leaves. This brown body now had little leaves growing all over it; it was just like a tree with leaves. And then for the spirit, it was still that same body with leaves, but now I used a yellow pencil, and the spirit was just radiating everywhere. But it was always the same thing, and so when I speak about those different areas, spirituality and social action, to me, these are aspects of a person's aliveness. The degree of your aliveness will depend on the degree of your commitment, on the degree of your vision, of your inclusiveness. Does that make sense to you?

CI: Yes, it does. Do you think that this quality of aliveness and understanding will *automatically* include social action?

DS: Since we are talking about life, and in life nothing is automatic, the word "automatic" is not a word that I would use.

CI: Well, let's use the word "evolutionarily" instead.

DS: I would say yes. In other words, what is wrong with a faulty spirituality is that it is not yet as alive or as evolved as it should be. And if somebody gets stuck in meditation, not seeing how it relates to social responsibility, I would say it's because they are not spiritual, or alive, enough, not that they are not active enough. Aliveness itself will inevitably make you alert to the needs of others, will make you alert to your opportunities to serve. This, in turn, will make you more alive by giving you the energy that you need to serve.

CI: Of course, the other side would be the renunciate's view, that simply meditating is an action with positive benefits for the world.

DS: I can only see that on the level that one may say, "My lifetime is limited, my energies are limited, my opportunities are limited, so all I can do for the moment is devote myself to meditating and that will fill a lifetime." But there exists the possibility that this dedication to renunciation will lead you to renounce the *notion* of renunciation that you had when you started out, and will therefore lead you and commit you to things you never thought of, activities you thought you had renounced. If you exclude that possibility, there is something drastically wrong with your renunciation; it is life-denying rather than life-affirming.

CI: Let's talk a bit about the Church in Central America. Last time we were together you spoke about Archbishop Oscar Romero.[5] After he became the Archbishop, he rose in spirit to the position—in much the same way as in the story of Beckett. It reminds me of that Shakespeare quote, "Some are born great, some achieve greatness, some have greatness thrust upon them." Oscar Romero seemed to have greatness thrust upon him.

DS: Right. He did not have great stature before that.

CI: Are there many such examples of this kind of heroic courage in Central America now among the priests and nuns and other Christians who are working there? And what about the practice of nonviolence in the face of what are truly gross injustices that happen there daily? I'm sure that the Christians who are working there must be tempted in many cases to aid those who fight against this oppression.

DS: Yes, having recently been in Maryknoll community, I have fresh information on this.[6] There are thousands and thousands of people, particularly in El Salvador and Guatemala, who take a brave stance and who suffer and die for it. Most of them are not so conspicuous as Oscar Romero was, although there are a few in exposed positions with great visibility. It's wonderful to know that very simple people also take this Common Sense stance.

---

[5] Oscar Arnulfo Romero originally began clergy work in El Salvador as a conservative. In time he came to be regarded as the most outspoken archbishop in Latin America, denouncing the brutally repressive, U.S.-backed government of El Salvador and advocating social and land reforms for the poor. He was assassinated March 24, 1980 while conducting services in his chapel on the outskirts of San Salvador.

[6] Traditionally involved in human rights issues, Maryknoll missioners are especially active in Central America. In 1980, two Maryknoll sisters were among the four nuns who were shot in El Salvador, an event which drew world attention to the human rights violations and political corruption in that country.

And Common Sense tells us that force creates counter-force; pressure creates counterpressure. So even though at the moment it seems tempting to help this liberation with weapons, or with some other violence, in the long run that is not going to achieve peace and justice. The temptation to resort to violence must be enormous, and so I admire the people who resist that temptation enormously. And even those who do resort to violence, I admire their courage, although I do not think that they are as deeply rooted in Common Sense as those who remain nonviolent are. History will bear this out.

Jesus himself is not a success story; it is a great historical failure that he would be crucified and die in such a way. But the failure was external. A very important aspect of his resurrection is simply that this kind of life cannot be squelched. Someone else will take it up. This kind of life is not subject to death. As long as there are human beings, it will be there. Even the death of the martyrs can become the seed for the faith, as we often say, because it can become the catalyst for others to act out of that same Common Sense.

CI: There's a line from Kierkegaard: "A tyrant dies and his reign ends. A martyr dies and his reign begins." You would say unequivocally that nonviolence makes the most Common Sense.

DS: Yes. But while I think that this is theoretically correct, I say it with great respect and awe for the people who heroically choose other paths. It is my luxury not to be under that pressure, and therefore I can talk about it with detachment. But if I were in the midst of it, I might not be able to see it so clearly.

CI: I'm interested in your personal views on death. I read your essay "Why a Man Becomes a Monk," in which you talked about the relationship that a monk has to death, and that it is a prerequisite—I'm paraphrasing here—to living one's life fully. What is your own relationship to death? Your feelings about death?

At this point in the interview the noon bell at the Zen center rang. Brother David suggested that I join him in one minute of silence for world peace.

CI: Do you do that everyday?

DS: Yes, and I have encouraged many people all over the world to do it. Thank you for doing that with me.

So you ask about death. When you say "feelings," what do you mean by that?

CI: Have you come to terms with your own death? Do you feel ready to die?

DS: Do I feel ready to die? Yes, I do. That isn't difficult to answer. Sometimes I would like to. [laughing]

CI: I know what you mean. [laughing]

DS: I've reached a stage in life where I can say, rather frequently actually, that if I were told now that I have only a very short time to live, I would be mostly sorry for those who have to clean up the mess I leave behind. This is really my main concern. I'm trying to straighten out my books and manuscripts so that there will not be much of a mess for other people. But as far as my feeling that I have unaccomplished, unfinished business, well, there will always be unfinished business. I have had a very, very rich and full life; I'm grateful for that and I can't ask for more.

But then I have other days where I see things that I could do and still be of service, so I'm very grateful to have some opportunity and some energy to do that.

CI: To be primarily concerned with leaving a mess behind is actually quite a refined place. It represents a kind of detachment that perhaps you have in your life as a monk—a greater detachment than a householder who would leave family behind. I wonder about this. You haven't married, your parents are gone, you haven't had children...

DS: I have lots of children, spiritual children.

CI: But in terms of those special bonds that one says yes to in a life—"Yes, I'll have a spouse. Yes, I'll have a family"—being willing to take on the kind of attachment which is a natural emotion when one has a family. Do you ever feel that was something you missed?

DS: No, I do not feel it as a loss, but I am very much aware and was always aware as long as I can remember that with everything you choose, you also choose not to take another path—the road not chosen.

CI: Yes, making a choice can also be seen as the death of options.

DS: And I was willing to do that—to let go of other options. Yet, my life is rich in so many ways that I cannot complain at all.

I also have this image—it's a real conviction—that our life is maturing toward death in every experience that we have. And we have experience not just because something happens to us—that's not yet an experience—but because we are mindful and we open ourselves. So in every moment in which we really respond to the world, there is a timeless element there. It's something that cannot be destroyed by time. Time comes and goes, but the "now" is not in time to begin with. In time, there is just this seam of "was" and "will be" without any remnant. Within the "now," we experience that which is not subject to time.

There's something in love and faithfulness, beauty and goodness, something that is not subject to time. For me, it is enormously consoling and reassuring that there is only a limited amount of time to work with, that sooner or later my time will be up. For when time is up, then all that has matured during my time remains. Only the aspect of time falls away. Only vanishing vanishes. And when vanishing vanishes, then "Is" remains.

CI: Suchness remains.

DS: Exactly. When time is up for me, then all that I ever had—all the relationships, all the friendships, all the beauty, all the goodness, is. From my present perspective I would say "will be" but that's not well expressed. And I then have the whole world through the window of my life which at that moment is completed.

Of course, as we look back on our life we also see shortcomings, many things that we wish we had done differently. And since that perpetuates itself in others, there will be a certain pain. When I see clearly how I have done ill to others, or maybe things that I thought were for the best but which had evil or life-denying effects, that is very painful. But I trust that in the overall view, it will all be meaningful or that we can somehow work that out. How one can work beyond time is a little difficult to explain and even a little difficult for me to understand, but we know that in some moments life seems to stand still for us, and in this experience, we do more, we work more, and more happens, than at other periods of even long, long stretches of time.

As T.S. Eliot put it, "What has been and what might have been point to one end which is always present." Somehow I trust that in "the now that doesn't pass away," all possibilities will be able to blossom forth.[7] Through people that I did know or through things that I did touch, I am connected with everything that ever was and everything that ever will be. Everything hangs together with everything. So when the limitations that time and space impose on me are removed because my time is up and my space is no longer there, then I will be in touch with all that ever was and ever will be. That's something to look forward to.

---

7 "The now that doesn't pass away" is St. Augustine's definition of "eternity."

Archbishop Desmond Tutu

Although Desmond Tutu had never met Stephen Biko, he was asked to give the funeral oration for the slain black activist who suffered a brutal death in 1977 while in the custody of the South African Security Police. A crowd of 30,000 attended the service, their mood volatile with sorrow and barely-contained anger. In Steve Biko they had lost not only a leader who had organized them, but one who had uplifted their spirits, given them pride in the color of their skin, and reminded them of their illustrious history.

Desmond Tutu spoke that day on forgiveness, as he had on many days before and has on many days since at funerals for martyrs and traitors alike. He exhorted the mourners to "pray for the rulers of this land, for the police—especially the security police and those in prison service—that they may realize that they are human beings too. I bid you pray for whites in South Africa."

In the tradition of Gandhi, Martin Luther King, Jr., and Stephen Biko, Desmond Tutu understands that "oppression dehumanizes the oppressor as well as the oppressed." He counsels his people to maintain their dignity, reminding them that no one can forcibly take that from them. And he continuously advocates nonviolent resolution of the freedom struggle for blacks in South Africa. For these efforts he was awarded the Nobel Peace Prize in 1984.

* * *

Near each urban area of South Africa is a segregated ghetto, called a township. Here blacks live separated from the whites of the nearby city or hamlet, dwelling in primitive conditions in ramshackle shelters deliberately designed to discourage even the *idea* of permanent settlement. The township's residents are not permitted to own the land or houses in which they reside. Many of the townships have no electricity, sewage system, or running water; large clouds of black smoke from burning stoves hang over the areas. An average of fourteen people live together in a four-room dwelling; disease and crime abound. In the squalor of these ghettos, many a precious flower fades before its bloom. It is a rare being who can rise out of such an existence, and when it happens one is reminded of the millions of others who never had the chance.

Born on October 7, 1931, in a gold-mining town in the Western Transvaal, Desmond Mpilo Tutu was raised in the black townships, the son of a schoolteacher and a domestic worker. An exceptionally bright student, Desmond grew up speaking several African languages and eventually English and Afrikaans, "the language of the oppressor." His childhood memories include not only the usual fondness for play and mischief, but also a growing sense of apartheid (lit. "apartness" in Afrikaans) at school and on the streets. He would bristle while watching his father's humiliation at being made to produce his passbook, the document which all non-whites are required to carry and show on demand. Nevertheless, the system was so pervasive that Desmond came to accept it as normal. He would later say that one of the greatest dangers of racial discrimination is, "You are brainwashed into an acquiescence in your oppression and exploitation."

His rise out of these circumstances began with an illness. When Desmond was fourteen years old he was diagnosed with tuberculosis and hospitalized for two years of treatments. During that time, a white Anglican priest, Father Trevor Huddleston, who served a large black parish, began to visit Desmond, delighting in the humor and intelligence of the young boy. Huddleston would become a leading force for change in South Africa and a major influence in the life of Desmond Tutu. Through Father Huddleston a religious devotion awakened in Desmond, and after he left the hospital he would often steal away from his playmates to pray alone at the township's church.

Meanwhile the system of apartheid tore deeper into the soul of South Africa. In 1948 the National Party won the General Election with a promise of apartheid to the all-white voting populace. Racial segregation, already in practice, was made law.

Desmond Tutu began to personally face the vicissitudes of apartheid as he entered the career world. He wanted to become a doctor but was too poor for medical school. He married Leah Nomalizo in 1955 and became a high school teacher. Although he loved teaching and was considered "a sensation" by students and colleagues alike, he resigned when the government implemented a system of inferior education for blacks. From there he turned to the Anglican church.

In 1962, as a newly ordained priest, Desmond Tutu left his country to study at the University of London. His wife and family soon followed. For the Tutus, it was a period of exhilaration. Although England was not a paragon of racial equality, it was a far cry from South Africa. For the first time the Tutus could move about freely, not worrying about obtaining permission or carrying their passbooks. They watched in amazement as mixed couples walked hand-in-hand in public.

After four years in England earning a Bachelors and a Masters Degree in Theology, it is small wonder that returning to South Africa prompted a painful contrast. Tutu wrote: "I don't want to sound melodramatic, but it is extremely difficult being back here, having to ask permission from various white officials to visit my parents!"

A social and political conscience began to stir in Desmond Tutu which would become an immutable force, deeply rooted in his religious beliefs. He began to speak about liberation theology, calling on ministries everywhere "to oppose oppression, injustice, corruption, and evil wherever these may be found. This could be a call to martyrdom, but if God is for us, who can be against us?" He could no longer believe that a separation existed between the spiritual and the political; indeed, he would call politics and religion "a seamless garment." He began to articulate the need for nonviolent resistance: "If laws conflict with the Gospel, then Christians not only have the right but the duty to agitate peacefully for their repeal." Tutu began to agitate. In numerous speeches and acts of civil disobedience, he drew the attention of the downtrodden masses as well as the white authorities to "the evil system of apartheid."

Tutu sometimes found himself in danger even among blacks. During a funeral of four youths, an angry crowd turned on a black onlooker they accused of being a spy. Tutu managed to drag the bleeding man into a car when a diversion was created by two other bishops. At another funeral, Tutu flung himself onto the body of a black policeman who was being stoned by a crowd. When the crowd had quieted, Tutu, covered in blood, returned to the podium. Tragically, the crowd later killed the policeman. Difficulties between Tutu and the white authorities mounted. They clamped down on him in every way they could, often revoking his passport, harassing his organizations, his friends, and sometimes, his family.

But it was not easy to silence Desmond Tutu. The church had power, and Tutu's rise within the church was meteoric. In 1975 he became the first black Dean of the Anglican Church in South Africa. He became Bishop of Lesotho in 1976, and returned to South Africa in 1978 as General Secretary of the South African Council of Churches. It was in his position as General Secretary that he began to feel the power of prophetic vision. He started to talk both at home and abroad about disinvestment in South Africa. He pleaded with white audiences to "throw off your lethargy and the apathy of affluence." He steadfastly maintained that whites could never be free unless blacks were also free. To blacks his rallying cry would be: "Nothing you do is insignificant. Everybody is a somebody."

Desmond Tutu was awarded the Nobel Peace Prize in 1984. He learned about the award on October 15 of that year while on a three-month teaching sabbatical in New York City. Tutu immediately flew home to share the award with his people. Greeted by hundreds of jubilant celebrants who defied orders to disperse, Tutu told them, "This award is for you mothers, who sit near railway stations trying to eke out an existence, selling potatoes, selling meali, selling pigs' trotters. This award is for you fathers, sitting in a single-sex hostel, separated from your children for eleven months of the year. This award is for you mothers, in the squatter camps, whose shelters are destroyed callously every day and who have to sit on soaking mattresses in the winter rain, holding whimpering babies and whose crime in this country is that you want to be with your husbands. This award is for you, three and a half million of our people who have been uprooted and dumped as if they were rubbish. The world says we recognize you, we recognize that you are people who love peace."

While the world rejoiced for the oppressed people of South Africa, the white authorities and media within the country did their best to ignore the award and to discredit Tutu's winning of it.

Shortly after learning of the prize, Desmond Tutu became Bishop of Johannesburg, the second most influential position in the Anglican Church of South Africa. He has since become Archbishop of Cape Town, the most important position within the Church. His stature in the world, his unflagging commitment to justice, his religious faith, and his oratorical skills have inspired comparisons to Martin Luther King, Jr. It has been said that Tutu, like King, could "hew a stone of hope from a mountain of despair." But beyond personal likenesses, Tutu is quick to point out one outstanding difference in the freedom struggles of the blacks of America and those of South Africa: in the United States, blacks fought for what was guaranteed in the U.S. Constitution; in South Africa, the law itself is against them.

Desmond Tutu fights his battles with remarkable wit and humor. He jokes about God looking despondent and lamenting that he has lost his copy of the Divine Plan, and about missionaries coming: "We had the land and they had the Bible. Then they said, 'Let us pray,' and we closed our eyes. When we opened them again, *they* had the land and *we* had the Bible. But maybe we got the better end of the deal."

His is a personal God, one who takes the side of justice—one who hears, sees, acts, and has a purpose for all things and creatures. Yet even in this faith, there is room for Desmond Tutu's wry wit, such as when he says, "All shall be well and all things in all manner shall be well. If not it will all have been a cosmic joke, and one in very bad taste."

In May 1989, Archbishop Tutu came to Washington, D.C. with colleagues Beyers Naude and Allen Boesak for a two-day whirlwind of speeches and meetings, including one with President Bush. I had worked on procuring an appointment with the Archbishop for more than a year, but at the last minute his schedule changed, and my time with him was cancelled. I was sitting in the coffee shop of Tutu's hotel feeling very disappointed and wondering what to do next when Tutu himself walked in, alone and dressed casually. The *maitre d'* seated him at the table right next to me, despite the numerous empty seats available in the restaurant. I introduced myself and told him of my efforts to see him. He agreed to do the interview right then and there as he waited for his daughter, who arrived just after our conversation began. We spoke for about twenty minutes, and as I took my leave, thanking him for his generosity in these unusual circumstances, he said with a hearty laugh, "My dear, how could I have said no? It was preordained."

Interview with Desmond Tutu

May 18, 1989 • Washington, D.C.

Catherine Ingram: You must feel a strong link with Mahatma Gandhi, given that South Africa was the site of his earliest battles against injustice. Do you see ways in which your life and his are interconnected?

Desmond Tutu: Well, I get very uncomfortable when I am compared with great people such as Gandhi, but, yes, most of us working in South Africa have of course been influenced by him and what he did there and in India. But I am not in Gandhi's league.

CI: Gandhi was successful in his struggle for independence. Is his success a factor in your commitment to nonviolence? If freedom does not come soon for South African blacks, can nonviolent strategies hold out?

DT: Well, of course, the fact that Gandhi was successful is very inspiring to us. But I have a theory that nonviolence requires that there is a minimum moral standard which is accepted by all the players, as it were, in the game. I think Gandhi himself said that if he had been operating in Nazi Germany, he is not quite certain that the method would have succeeded. Gandhi's way did succeed because the British were under a kind of moral imperative. I don't know whether this is a valid theory, but it is one that I have had.

Now with what has happened at home in South Africa, if we do not bring about an end to the violence of apartheid soon through the intervention of the international community, as some of us want, then obviously there will be an escalation of violence which will spill over from South Africa into other countries. That is why, when the United Nations says that apartheid is a threat to world peace, it is not just an empty slogan. Therefore the world is bound, in a sense, to be involved in apartheid, even if merely out of self interest.

CI: Watching from the outside there seems to be a growing disunity among the black community now, given this recent situation with Mrs. Mandela and her soccer team, or her bodyguards, or whoever they were.[1] I won-

---

[1] Winnie Mandela is the wife of Nelson Mandela, the imprisoned black nationalist leader in South Africa who is head of the banned African National Congress. Mrs. Mandela and several of her bodyguards, members of the Mandela United Football Club, are at the center of an

der if you are finding the walls of solidarity cracking inside the community.

DT: No, there is a remarkable level of consensus and agreement. When you look at organizations such as the United Democratic Front in South Africa, the level of consensus is quite considerable. Of course, when you look at political groupings anywhere in the world, you find that they are really coalitions. I mean, the Democratic Party here will say that it has a conservative wing to stretch from the radical left wing. The same is true for the Republicans. The leader is the one who is able to hold together these disparate parts in one group.

We've certainly been deeply distressed and affected by what happened with Mrs. Mandela, but I have said that it is important for people to realize that the remarkable thing is not that this happened, but that it took *so long* for someone placed under such very considerable pressure by the system not to have succumbed earlier. Now, one is not minimizing the seriousness of what happened when one suggests that people remember that Mrs. Mandela has been a tremendous symbol—twenty-five years without her husband, having married young, and having to look after the children all this time. And she's not the only one. Some people have other resources to handle this kind of pressure—internal resources—and maybe what we have to ask ourselves is how can we help to rehabilitate her. That is what I've been saying we need to do.

As to differences in the anti-apartheid movement in South Africa, by the nature of the case people are going to have different perspectives, different strategies. I, myself, am actually surprised that we can have as great a measure of agreement as we do. You know, when you look at the situation in places like Ulster, those who are

---

investigation involving three murders and a number of beatings of black South African youngsters. As a result, the two largest anti-government organizations representing blacks in South Africa have called on the black community to "distance" itself from Mrs. Mandela.

seen as traitors to the cause are given very short shrift.[2] The so-called black on black violence that is happening at home is not a phenomenon peculiar to us. We need to remember that the primary cause of all of this is the apartheid system, and until we remove the source and cause, we will be constantly dealing with the symptoms or the consequences of a very serious evil.

CI: I've read that you pray everyday for Pik Botha and his colleagues. Where do you find your source for forgiveness for those who are considered the oppressors of the black people of South Africa?

DT: Well, you can't pray for someone and also not be prepared to long for the best for them after awhile, because otherwise it affects your prayers and you get uptight. It is not a matter of personal achievement in this regard, it is just something which has to do with the dynamic of prayer. If you are praying to God, then you are in the paradigm of prayer, and we are told that God will forgive us only to the extent that we are willing to forgive others. It isn't easy. I mean, you can get very, very upset, especially when you see that the system of apartheid attacks not just you but your family.

I'll tell you, recently my wife was handcuffed and really sort of humiliated. Now whilst it is possible that this could happen to any of us, the minute they discovered that she was my wife...well, people would expect that they would have been apologetic and tried to redress, but they didn't. And it does get at you, which is what they want to happen. So when you think of things like that, you get angry.

CI: And of course, we can imagine what might have been her fate had she not been Mrs. Tutu.

---

[2] Ulster, in Northern Ireland, is a community well-known for violent clashes between Irish Catholics and British Protestants. Numerous murders of "traitors" within these communities have occurred over many years.

DT: That's right. And you know that happens all the time.

But, I belong in a community that prays for others. And I myself would not be able to survive without the intercession of other people. So the resources are not personal resources. I mean, there is from God and other people a very, very significant input into the kind of person I am. There is no personal glory. It is not a matter of personal achievement. It's that I have been influenced by many people, and I've also come to realize that I couldn't survive without prayer. After all, God is in charge of this world.

CI: What would you say is the lesson that South Africa offers to the world?

DT: I think that there is at least a twofold lesson. The first is that the methods of the South African government are not the way in which to solve problems. Their way relies basically on using force and refusing to realize that it is possible to sit down and actually discuss and sort out difficulties. The Rhodesia/Zimbabwe experience shows this.[3] They might have gotten to where they are now without the trauma of the many thousands of deaths that happened and all the tensions and alienation that have been part of the very high price paid for the liberation of Zimbabwe. We in South Africa ought to have learned from that. But don't the cynics say that we learn from history what we do not learn from history?

And the second thing is that despite what the government may be seeking to do, South Africa is going to demonstrate that it is possible for people of incredibly different cultural, racial, ethnic, and religious backgrounds to cohere as one people.

---

[3] A seven year civil war which took place in what was formerly Rhodesia brought down the white minority rule of Ian Smith in 1980. Rhodesia became the independent country of Zimbabwe. The civil war took 30,000 lives.

CI: You think that the whites and blacks will live happily together if blacks get their freedom?

DT: They're doing so already in Zimbabwe. And beautifully so, despite the way in which Zimbabwe got its independence. I mean, whites left Zimbabwe out of fear when it became independent, and they came to South Africa. Now they are returning in droves to Zimbabwe because they are saying that they don't want to go through that a second time. And in Zimbabwe they have discovered that actually very few things change, in a sense. Human beings can adjust to very many things. There are quite a few Rhodesians who probably were rabid racists who are now saying, "You know, our children died for nothing because we were trying to prevent a situation about which we were grossly misled based on the propaganda of a state-controlled communications and media system." As in South Africa. The perceptions of South African whites are being formed by a really evil and biased system, and they believe certain things about certain people which are totally at variance with the truth.

CI: Archbishop, we are facing a world in which there is tremendous despair and threat from environmental problems, violence, overpopulation, a taxing on all the world's resources, and so on. You talk and write a lot about hope. What hope do you offer for our world?

DT: The fact of the existence of human beings is the one wonderful sign, you know. I mean, when you can have an earthquake in Armenia, and all ideological, political, religious and other differences are forgotten as people are thrown together out of compassion and a desire to help; or when the tragedy of Ethiopia happened, you had concerts making people remember that We are the World. Yes, you can say that perhaps it's expensive if these are the only times people realize that we are human and therefore that we ought to be humane, but these are not the only times.

When you have young people committed to the struggle for world peace, and, as happened in England, you have young people who walked on a pilgrimage from Scotland to London in order to celebrate Nelson Mandela's birthday; when you have young people who are very comfortably off leave their homes and say they want to work in the Peace Corps in some of the most inaccessible parts of the world; when you have, such as in South Africa, white young people saying they refuse to serve in the South African Defense Force and this refusal is at great consequence to themselves—such as a young eighteen-year-old man sentenced to six years imprisonment for refusing the draft—you sit back and you say, Well yes, maybe God looks on the world and there are many, many times when he sees holocausts, genocides, and all kinds of extraordinary sufferings which have been done. You can imagine he might think, "I don't know what got into me to create that lot!" But, then he looks again, or she looks again, and sees all the compassion and caring and sacrifice and all the incredible things that people do, you know, and he must rub his hands in glee and satisfaction and say, "Aren't they neat? Aren't they a justification for what I did when I took the risk of making them?"

THE INSTITUTE OF NOETIC SCIENCES is a nonprofit public foundation and membership organization established in 1973 by Apollo 14 Astronaut Edgar D. Mitchell. The purposes of the Institute are to expand knowledge of the nature and potentials of the mind, body, and spirit, and to apply that knowledge to the advancement of health and well-being. Primary activities include scientific and scholarly research, education, and publishing. More than 20,000 members worldwide receive the quarterly *Noetic Sciences Review* as well as the *Noetic Sciences Bulletin* and other publications.

THE ALTRUISTIC SPIRIT PROGRAM was established in 1987 to help promote research and education on unselfish service motivated by love. The specific purposes of the program are to learn more about the nature, development, and expression of altruism, and to encourage its presence in our everyday lives. The Altruistic Spirit Program supports research grants, the preparation of scholarly papers, in-house research, network development, and communications projects. A grant from the Altruistic Spirit Program of the Institute of Noetic Sciences helped fund the publication of *In the Footsteps of Gandhi.*

For information about the Institute of Noetic Sciences or the Altruistic Spirit Program, contact:

Institute of Noetic Sciences
475 Gate 5 Road, Suite 300
Sausalito, California 94965
Telephone: 415/331-5650

PARALLAX PRESS

Parallax Press publishes books and tapes on universal responsibility and compassionate action—"making peace right in the moment we are alive." It is our hope that these books and tapes will help alleviate suffering and create a more peaceful world.

Some of our recent titles:

Being Peace, by Thich Nhat Hanh

The Path of Compassion: Writings on Socially Engaged Buddhism by the Dalai Lama, Gary Snyder, Maha Ghosananda, Joanna Macy, and many others

Dharma Gaia: A Harvest of Essays in Buddhism and Ecology, edited by Allan Hunt-Badiner

The Heart of Understanding, by Thich Nhat Hanh

Jai Bhim: Dispatches from a Peaceful Revolution in India, by Terry Pilchick

World as Lover, World as Self, by Joanna Macy

For a copy of our free catalog, please write to:

Parallax Press
P.O. Box 7355
Berkeley, California 94707